THE SPARTANS

A Story of Michigan State Football

THE SPARTANS

A Story of Michigan State Football

by

Fred W. Stabley

THE STRODE PUBLISHERS, INC.
HUNTSVILLE, ALABAMA 35802

To Fred, Jr., Nick, Lois, and the Spartan Sports Service gang for their help and to wife Alma for her love and patience.

George "Little Dynamite" Guerre explodes.

Contents

Photographs Courtesy Of The
Lansing State Journal and
Michigan State University

In The Beginning . . .

1896! William McKinley wins election as the 25th President of the United States. The radioactivity of uranium is discovered. Utah becomes the 45th state and an electric stove is invented. Discoveries are made in Alaska which lead to the Klondike Gold Rush of 1897. Trouble brews in Cuba, the Philippines, and elsewhere, which will result in the Spanish-American War.

Sarah Bernhart, Lillian Russell, and Diamond Jim Brady are celebrities of the day. Jim Corbett is heavyweight boxing champion of the world, and Cy Young moves toward his all-time record of 511 pitching victories. The modern Olympics begin in Athens, with John B. Connolly of the United States winning the hop, step, and jump and Yankee Tom Burk taking both the 100- and 400-meter dashes.

Intercollegiate sports, especially football, are very big in the Ivy League. The Intercollegiate Conference of Faculty Representatives, later to become popularly known as the Big Ten, is founded in Chicago. The hottest new offensive development in college football is the revolving tandem system as run by Princeton. The entire All-American team selected by Walter Camp comes from just four Ivy League schools—Harvard, Yale, Princeton, and Pennsylvania.

At Michigan Agricultural College, founded in 1855 and the prototype of the great land-grant college system of today, things are stirring. Jonathan LeMoyne Snyder becomes the school's seventh president. A course for women is introduced, which includes work in home economics, natural sciences, and the liberal arts. The long vacation is changed from the winter to summer months, opening the way to improved athletic programs. Organized football begins!

The first game in what is recognized as the first regular season of football at MAC caused few ripples and no waves. The *Lansing Republican* ignored it except for passing reference in an all-sports column that there had been played at Eltom Park the preceding Saturday, September 26, 1896, a game of football between MAC and Lansing High School. The score was not mentioned, which is a pity since it was 10-0 in favor of the Aggies and thus the only game won by the farmer's college that first season in which four games were played.

But the MAC *Record,* the new weekly newspaper published by the college, did carry a story of the game in its next issue. It was on page three along with an article by A. A. Crozier on "Trapping the Hessian Fly." The story was as follows:

"FOOTBALL.–MAC vs. LANSING HIGH SCHOOL.

"MAC and Lansing high school opened the football season at Eltom Park last Saturday afternoon. An element of uncertainty as to the outcome, from the fact that six of the MAC boys were new men, and that Cole, Judson, and Rork, three old MAC men, were to play with the high school team, gave interest to the game and brought out a good-sized crowd.

"Promptly at 4 o'clock the teams lined up as follows:

M.A.C.	Position	L.H.S.
Thompson	center	Wattling
Vanderstolpe	right guard	Childs
Becker	left guard	Hayden
Vanderhoef	right tackle	Hinchey
Price	left tackle	Graham
Bishop	right end	Rork, F. C.
Redfern	left end	Rork, C. E.
Miller	right half	Cole
Laitner	left half	Tompkins
Elliott	quarter	Judson
Wells	full back	French

"Wells kicked off for twenty yards, and Cole returned the ball ten yards. Cole went around the left end for ten yards more. In the next play Becker broke through and got the ball. MAC advanced the ball fifteen yards and then lost it on

10

Aggie team of 1884 played no games but organized to have pictures taken for yearbook.

downs.

"After Tompkins had gone around right end for seven yards, Lansing lost the ball on downs. MAC took the ball and Wells went through the center for ten yards. Successive gains through the line and around the ends by Miller, Laitner and Wells, put the ball over the line for a touchdown in 27 minutes. The goal was a difficult one and Wells failed on the kick. Score, 4 to 0.

"Cole kicked off and Becker fell on the ball at the fifteen yard line. MAC put the ball through the center for five yards, Miller took it around the end for ten yards, and successive rushes put the ball ten yards farther when time was called for the first half.

"In the second half Cole kicked to the 25-yard line and the ball went down there. MAC advanced the ball three yards, then Tompkins broke through and downed Wells with the ball five yards back of the line. MAC attempted to punt but fumbled and the ball went over.

"In the next play Tompkins fumbled and lost two yards. Third down, no gain, and French punted. Wells caught the ball and by a splendid run recovered all that had been lost. After gaining three yards, MAC again lost the ball on downs. Three plays advanced the ball 15 yards and then Lansing lost on downs. MAC gained five yards and then lost the ball on a poor throw. Lansing could not gain and punted again. Wells was again on hand and brought cheers from both high school and college students by his magnificent spurt, going down the right side of the field like a storm and turning Lansing's punt into a gain of five yards for MAC.

"Lansing did not again lay hands on the ball. MAC gained ·at every play, around the ends and through the center, until Wells was pushed over for the second touchdown. Time, 28 minutes. Wells kicked a goal and time was called. Score: MAC, 10; L.H.S., 0.

"The game seemed to demonstrate the fact that the class of '00 has some good football timber as well as base ball timber."

That account was quite detailed for a game story of the day. It was much better than the coverage accorded other contests involving MAC against college teams in that and other early seasons, possibly because of the home town angle of Lansing High School's involvement. For instance, later that fall MAC played Alma College, and in the October 27 issue of the *Record* this story appeared:

"FOOTBALL–MAC vs. Alma

"MAC and Alma played an interesting game of football at Eltom Park last Saturday. The teams were very evenly matched, so nearly that the game ended without either side scoring. The first half ended with the ball on MAC's 30-yard line, and the second with it on MAC's 15-yard line.

"MAC has improved considerably in her interference since last Saturday but still runs back occasionally. One of our best ground gainers has this fault. You're doing well, boys. Play faster and harder and go down to Kalamazoo for victory."

Kalamazoo, however, was just too much for the fledgling Aggies. Kalamazoo won 24-0 and later also beat MAC at Eltom Park 18-16.

That the one victory that season was not exactly a masterful triumph is indicated by the fact that later that fall Jackson High School beat Lansing High School 10-6, and Ionia smashed it 30-0.

A mysterious circumstance surrounding those early Aggie home games is that they were played at a site—Eltom Park—which has been lost in time. It was located somewhere in Lansing—that is certain. Both the *Lansing State Journal* and the *MAC Record* referred to it repeatedly. But it is not to be found in old maps and records, nor does the name ring bells with old-timers associated with sports in the Lansing area.

The 1896 team had no coach but a student named Scott Redfern, who also played left end, was the manager. Another student named Cass Laitner, who played left halfback, was the president of the MAC Athletic Association which coordinated all athletic programs at the college.

It was a humble beginning and a far cry from the glory days ahead. But it was a noteworthy achievement in that it was the culmination of years of effort, largely on the part of student-operated athletic associations and generally backed by college publications such as the *Holcad,* the *Speculum,* and the *MAC Record.*

The difficulty was that the college fathers—faculty and administration—traditionally frowned on all competitive sports as frivolous, of doubtful morality, and not to be compared to farm work as healthful exercise. This went double for football which was acquiring an unsavory reputation for many injuries and occasional fatalities. But the game was big in the East; the University of Michigan had been fielding teams since 1879; and even such church-affiliated colleges as Albion, Kalamazoo, and Alma had well-established football programs.

Finances were another problem because the administration would not contribute a dime toward buying baseballs or bats or gym equipment, let alone football paraphernalia.

Pressure must have had an effect, for at a meeting on April 8, 1895, the State Board finally legitimized what had been going on for years and must finally have seemed inevitable—athletic competition on an intercollegiate level for MAC students. The board passed a resolution allowing students to participate in field days and games of football and baseball. It established the first eligibility standard—regular attendance at college for at least one term preceding athletic competition—and set a minimum grade average "of eight on a scale of ten." The resolution also called for faculty supervision of field days and a written certification of eligibility for participants.

The die had been cast, but football particularly was far from being securely established. A faculty move to abolish it gathered some momentum.

Three men get major credit for spreading the sails and getting the Aggie athletic ship moving, albeit under fire.

The first was President Jonathan L. Snyder, who took office in 1896. He had been an outstanding college athlete at

Westminster College in Pennsylvania and remained an avid fan. He made his position quite plain when he declared to associates: "If we must have football, I want the kind that wins."

Abetting him in athletic issues was a young alumnus and State Board of Agriculture member named L. Whitney Watkins, who had been senior baseball manager and lightweight boxing champion of MAC. He was second to none as an enthusiastic fan and athletic advocate. Watkins carried the battle to the Board in 1899 to hire a real, honest-to-goodness coach like other schools had. The 1896 football team had had no coaching at all; the 1897 and 1898 teams had been coached after a fashion by an engineering student named Henry Keep, who also trained the track team.

The Board remained adamant until President Snyder proposed a compromise solution of hiring a minister, the Rev. Charles O. Bemies, to coach all sports and also assume leadership in chapel each morning prior to the students' 6 a.m. breakfast. This idea carried the day, and in 1899 Bemies became the first Professor of Physical Culture at MAC. He stayed in the position two years, and judging from the record of his football teams (2-4-1 in 1899 and 1-3 in 1900), he must have been stronger in the pulpit than he was on the sidelines.

But the major step to professional coaching had been taken, and the next big stride was made in 1900. Watkins proposed that the Board purchase for athletic purposes the 13 acres of land south of the Red Cedar River, now known as Old College Field. By 1902 it contained a quarter-mile cinder running track, a baseball diamond, grandstand, and MAC's first football field.

The third major figure in the toddler days in Aggie-land was Chester L. Brewer, who came on as Professor of Physical Culture and coach of all sports in 1903. The game which probably sent President Snyder scurrying after Brewer, then coach at Albion, was a 1902 disaster—when the Aggies played Michigan at Ann Arbor. That was the Aggie humiliation of which H. G. Salsinger, sports editor of the *Detroit News,* wrote years later:

"The late Fielding H. Yost (Michigan's coach) had his point-a-minute machine rolling at top speed and kept the gates of mercy securely locked. The Yost juggernaut crushed State 119-0, third highest score in Michigan's history."

It was the all-time record score rolled up on any MAC, MSC, or MSU team. It also was the game which provided the

President Snyder wanted the kind of football that won.

setting for one of the most revealing anecdotes in MAC athletic lore. Just before the end of the rout, Yost spotted an Aggie player passing behind the Michigan bench en route to the dressing room and inquired, "The game's not over yet, son. Where are you going?" The muddy, bloody, and weary Aggie smiled weakly at Yost and said, "Mr. Yost, they told us up home we were coming down here for experience, and me, I've had mine."

Although MAC's start in football was sputtering and discouraging before Brewer came in as coach in 1903, there still were some redeeming highlights which held promise for the

15

future.

There were two modest winning seasons under Keep, 4-2-1 in 1897 and 4-3 in 1898, and the emergence of the first heroes in the sport.

One hero, certainly, was William E. Russell, who lettered in 1897-98-99 and among whose accomplishments was scoring all of his team's points in an 11-6 upset Aggie victory over Ypsilanti—now Eastern Michigan—in 1898. Russell ran for two touchdowns, which in those days were worth five points, and kicked an extra point. The second TD was on a 40-yard run.

Walter Brainard, captain of the 1897 team, and Charles Tate were the big guns in a 38-4 victory over Alma in 1897. Each scored two touchdowns and Tate added five extra points.

Russell did it again to Ypsilanti in 1899 by running 70 yards for a touchdown and leading the interference as freshman prodigy "Big John" Alfson tore through tackle and ran 60 yards

Inter-class game on Old College Field.

Ellis Ranney captained 1898 and 1899 teams.

for a score. Russell also kicked the extra points.

It may have been in 1902—it could hardly have happened during Brewer's authoritarian regime—that President Snyder's love for competitive sports and its participants probably received its severest test.

At half time of a football game on Old College Field in those days, the home team retired to a small enclosure under the grandstand while the visitors simply sat down on the playing field to rest.

President Snyder on this occasion paid a visit to his student athletes, possibly to say a few words of encouragement toward greater efforts in the second half. He found the squad members (there would have been no more than perhaps 14 or 15 of them) sitting in a circle and passing around a bottle of a popular, powerful drink of the day—Duffy's Malt Liquor.

Can't you just picture the open-mouthed consternation of players and president alike? Pep talk forgotten, the prexy beat a hasty retreat and apparently did his best to forget what he had seen.

Miracle Brewer

Chester Brewer wrought an athletic miracle.

In 1903 he took over a bumbling Michigan Aggie football program, which in its entire history had compiled a 19-23-4 record through seven seasons, and immediately revolutionized it. His first team went 6-1-1, far and away the best campaign any Aggie team ever had enjoyed. He followed it with 8-1, 9-2, 7-2-2, 4-2-1, 6-0-2, 8-1, and 6-1 before going to Missouri to undertake new coaching challenges. In those eight falls his teams put together the fantastic record for the tiny farmer's college of 54 victories, 10 losses, and 6 ties.

His Aggies left the old natural rivals of the MIAA in the dust and even deigned to tie a Michigan colossus. Even more audacious, one Brewer club rudely smashed an otherwise undefeated Notre Dame team 17-0. His hypoed Aggies went undefeated in 44 games played on Old College Field.

Brewer completely won over a recalcitrant faculty, and not just because he won football games, either. Student support reached all-time highs. Financial problems abated.

Chester Brewer accomplished all these things because he had class. He looked it, lived it, exuded it. President Snyder spotted it in the skill and spirit shown by his Albion teams. His personal record at the University of Wisconsin—a bachelor of science degree and successful participation in four sports capped by All-Western football recognition according to the gospel of Walter Camp—demonstrated it.

Brewer was a vigorous, dynamic man with thick light brown hair, broad shoulders, and square jaw. He was born in Owosso, Michigan, the son of a farmer—exactly the right pedi-

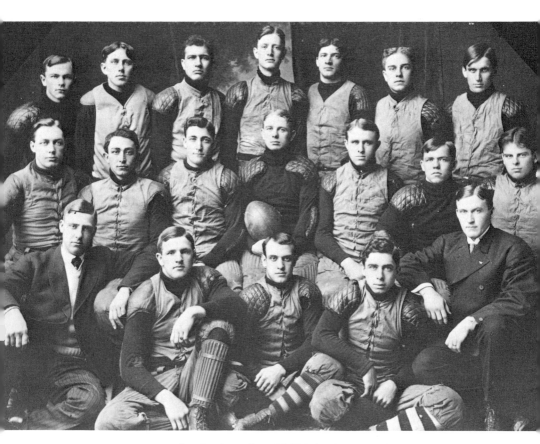

Brewer (right front) and MIAA champs of 1905.

gree for good faculty relations at MAC. His title of Professor of Physical Culture gave him solid academic respectability in a day when most collegiate coaches were hired seasonally like other transient laborers.

He worked at his job the year around, administering athletics and coaching successful teams in all sports, bringing rules and order to the one-time hurly-burly of class rushes, handling the traditional class barbecues, and introducing an athletic carnival. The carnival quickly grew to become the most popular student activity of the year and produced money for the athletic program. All this impressed faculty folks and excited the students.

His exacting standards of athletic performance and conduct were well exemplified in a speech he made at the student mass meeting prior to the 1909 Notre Dame game at South

Bend which his team lost 17-0.

"Boys, we're going to show them that we have a great team," he said. "That team of ours is going in to fight to the last ditch. We may lose, but win or lose let's show them that MAC has the cleanest, finest, and most gentlemanly bunch of sportsmen that they have ever played against."

"No one questioned Brewer's sincerity in that statement, which was unusual for its time," said Dr. Madison Kuhn in his *Michigan State—The First 100 Years.* "No man did more to persuade the faculty, the Board, and the older alumni that organized athletics could be compatible with higher education."

Not much was anticipated from Brewer's first team in 1903. Only four "old men," as the *Wolverine* put it, returned from the 1902 club, and "the new material" was mostly green and unknown.

But among the new men were such excellent athletes as Wilson Millar, who went on to become one of MAC's all-around star athletes, Edward McKenna, and Walter Small.

"It was by sheer pluck and work under skillful coaching of Professor Brewer, that the team reached the place it did," the *Wolverine* exulted. The team met all MIAA rivals, beat four of them handily, and tied Albion 6-6. MAC claimed the league title, but so did Albion, and a running argument was carried on in the student publications of the schools.

At this point MAC dropped out of the MIAA in order to schedule bigger and stronger teams. It continued to schedule its old natural rivals, however, especially when it proved to be difficult to come by those more glamorous schedules.

The really big accomplishment kept evading MAC until 1908, when Michigan was tied 0-0. This game was played on Old College Field before 6,000 fans. The MAC band played a new tune entitled "Rub It Into Michigan," composed by Carl Chapman, and, according to the *Lansing State Journal* account, the Farmer team almost did just that. Only the final whistle stopped surging MAC from winning, for it was on the move as the game ended. The paper also called the contest "the best game ever played in Michigan" and headlined it, "Farmers Hold Yost's Eleven."

Aggie heroes included Clyde (Octy) Moore, a roly-poly 212-pound center; team captain and end Bert Shedd; end Charles (Big) Burroughs, "who played a grand defensive game";

quarterback Ion Cortright; and halfbacks Leon Exelby and Roy Wheeler, "who pounded the Michigan line."

That is a lot of heroes for a 0-0 game, and there also was a "goat." Halfback Parnell McKenna, one of the finest Aggie players of the era, missed three dropkick tries, any one of which would have won the game and put MAC into national headlines.

"Brewer's men played rings around my boys in the early periods," admitted Michigan's Fielding Yost afterwards, "and had they played straight football instead of trying to make dropkicks, I believe they would have won."

Still, MAC adherents reacted to the tie as if it were a major achievement. At game's end, they "made the air black with hats and pennants," the *State Journal* reported. Players were carried from the field across the Red Cedar River on the wooden bridge to the locker room in the bath house, which stood where the Music Building now is located. Some 600 students later took streetcars to Lansing in their night shirts and snake-danced through the town. The windup was a big bonfire at Washington and Michigan avenues.

The following fall MAC achieved what might be called its first major victory—over Marquette, 10-0. The Hilltoppers, new to the schedule, were to become State's most cherished rival other than Michigan in the 1920s and 1930s.

But it was in 1910 that the Farmers (as they often were called and frequently designated themselves with pride) made their biggest thrust toward football's big time. They beat Notre Dame and Marquette back to back and had Michigan on the ropes before losing 6-3 amid considerable controversy.

The central figure in the Michigan game and controversy was Leon (Bubbles) Hill, outstanding MAC halfback and an excellent runner and kicker.

Here is what happened in the Michigan game, according to Hill in a recent tape of memoirs:

Hill kicked a field goal early to put the Aggies ahead 3-0. Later in the first half he ran back a Michigan punt about 70 yards for an apparent touchdown, but Yost took to the field and called attention of officials to what he claimed was a holding violation by MAC far downfield. The officials nullified the touchdown that would have clinched the game! Later, after the game, the Michigan player who allegedly had been fouled admitted he was not within fifteen yards of the place the foul was

Stars of Brewer's time (clockwise)—Walter Small, Ed McKenna, Stephen Doty.

supposed to have occurred.

But the climactic scene developed in the second half when Michigan made what Hill claimed was an illegal quarterback-to-fullback pass over the line of scrimmage.

"In those days the passer had to run out five yards, either right or left, before he could pass the ball," Hill relates. "But this time he tossed it right over the center of the line and Magnusson (the fullback) ran the ball to the four yard line where the MAC safety man stopped him.

"Our team pushed Michigan back to the seven or eight. But then the official called MAC offsides and put the ball back on our two or three yard line. Again we pushed them back to about the seven."

At this point Hill said he diagnosed correctly a fake field goal attempt and direct pass to fullback Magnusson. "I nailed this Magnusson on the two yard line and I had him boxed in there," Hill said. "He couldn't go one way or the other.

"Then this umpire came tearing over there, picked up the ball, and said, 'Touchdown for Michigan.'

"'What do you mean, touchdown?' I asked.

"'You pushed it back,' the umpire said, and I hauled off and kissed him one right on the chin. And I never got put out of

Action in controversial 1910 game won by Michigan 6-3.

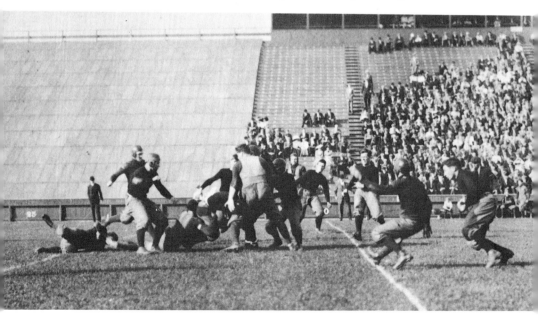

the game."

There also was a snafu over the conclusion of the game. The Michigan timekeeper said it was all over, and that word was followed by the officials. The MAC timekeeper who protested that there were seven more minutes left on his clock was ignored.

The *Lansing State Journal* ran a story about the controversy the next week, and feelings were ruffled for awhile. But one of the wonderful things about sports is that there is always another game with more action in which previous disappointments and bitterness tend to get lost.

So it was when MAC met Notre Dame just two weeks later on Old College Field and the Fighting Farmers crunched the Irish 17-0. It wrecked Notre Dame's undefeated season and sent Aggie elation soaring to unprecedented heights. It was easily the most important football victory MAC athletes had ever scored.

The event did not sneak up unnoticed. All seats were reserved for this one at such stiff prices as $.50, $.75, $1.00, and $1.50. The higher charges were for special box seats which had just been installed.

The Lansing, Detroit, and state papers were filled with pre-game stories which cited such facts as MAC had never even scored against the Irish and that the Irish were undefeated champions of the West the previous year and were unbeaten again in 1910. Word from around the state had it that large delegations of MAC alumni were coming to East Lansing to "help us cheer the boys to victory." Even the names of officials assigned to the game were worth special story treatment.

It was the Aggies' long-awaited day, and they completely dominated an excellent Irish team. Ben Pattison picked up an Irish fumble and pushed through the line for a touchdown in the first quarter. In the third period Bubbles Hill kicked a field goal to make it 8-0. In the fourth period quarterback Ion Cortright scored a TD and Hill added the point after to run the count to 14-0. Hill concluded scoring for the day with a fourth period field goal.

Notre Dame's coach, Shorty Longman, a product of the University of Michigan, lauded the Fighting Farmers that day. "We were simply outclassed," he said. "MAC is vastly underrated. There is no team in the West that can defeat the Farmers on their own field. We were licked, and the sting of defeat is allayed by the fact that we lost to such a sportsman-like bunch of men."

Notre Dame was paid $800 for the game, other expenditures were nearly $800, and the MAC Athletic Association cleared about $500.

Marquette's Coach Juneau and team captain Hanley scouted the MAC-Notre Dame game in preparation for their clash with the Aggies the following Saturday at Milwaukee, and reporters from the *Detroit Free Press* and *Detroit News Tribune* actually came in person to cover the game.

A demonstration was staged that evening, with several hundred students painting Lansing red. There was a massive bonfire near the Bijou theatre. Lansing businessmen and residents joined in the festivities. What a glorious day it was!

The exaltation was not to last. Coach Brewer put the kibosh on celebrating the following week by announcing he was leaving. Not even the subsequent 3-2 victory over previously undefeated Marquette helped allay the sick feelings over the impending loss. Brewer was simply the biggest thing that had ever happened to MAC.

Bubbles Hill's field goal from the 40 yard line in the second quarter against a bad wind stood up on a wet, disagreeable day in Milwaukee.

Concerning Bubbles (who died recently), he was one of the few left from those days over 60 years ago who could talk first hand about what happened and how things were. Some of Hill's reminiscences are worth hearing.

How did he decide on Michigan Agricultural College?

Germany Schultz, Michigan's great all-time All-American player, came to Benton Harbor to referee a high school game with Muskegon, Hill relates. Schultz was so impressed with Benton Harbor's team that when he returned to Ann Arbor, he asked Coach Yost why did he not recruit some of the Benton Harbor players. Yost allegedly replied: "There's never been a football player that came from Benton Harbor to Ann Arbor that was worth anything." This word got back to Benton Harbor and immediately decided several boys to attend MAC.

What about uniforms and equipment?

There was stuff like shoulder pads and helmets but Hill did not wear them because "I didn't like to be hampered with all that paraphernalia." He did admit to wearing knee pads, football pants, and cleated shoes.

How did he pay his way through MAC?

Aggies beat Notre Dame 17-0 in 1910.

"I got $20 when I left home, and I went through Michigan Agricultural College on those $20." He lived in the TKE house. President Snyder would not permit national fraternities, but the issue was skirted by literary societies which had "literary" meetings weekly. Two torn shirts started Hill in a business of laundry pickup and delivery which netted him about $15 a week.

How would Michigan State "Bears" or "Bruins" or perhaps "Cubs" sound to you? We will never know how close one of them came to being State's nickname, rather than "Spartans." "Brewer's Bruin" was a live and popular mascot for the football team of 1909.

He was a little brown bear cub who arrived by express in a box addressed to the MAC football team early that fall. He took up residence in a cage behind the Armory and made droves of friends. He was tagged "Montie" and was featured in drawings and many references in the student publication, the *Holcad*. There even was a full page picture of Brewer with the gentle little beast. Montie's captors and donors were graduate foresters and seniors from MAC working out in Montana during the summer. There was a cardboard tag attached to the box saying, "Not Ugly."

How could he miss becoming a permanent Aggie mascot? Somehow he did and disappeared finally without bestowing his name on the team.

A Big, Big Man

Jonathan L. Snyder and L. Whitney Watkins cranked the Aggies' football machine and started it running. Chester L. Brewer primed the motor. But John F. Macklin, Brewer's successor, threw it into high gear and drove it up the mountain to national prestige.

In a span of five seasons, 1911 through 1915, Macklin produced the school's best winning record in history with .853 on 29 victories in 34 games. He directed Aggie teams to their first conquests of such major foes as Michigan, Ohio State, Wisconsin, and Penn State. Michigan was undefeated in 1913 except for the Aggies' 12-7 victory at Ann Arbor; in 1915 it was undefeated and untied in four games before bowing to MAC 24-0 at Ann Arbor.

Such derring-do attracted attention to MAC like never before, and some Aggie players received unaccustomed recognition for excellence. Six of them—end Blake Miller, guard Faunt Lenardson, end Ralph Henning, tackle Chester Gifford, fullback Carp Julian, and tackle Gideon Smith—made All-Western in 1913. An even bigger surprise was the fact that Grantland Rice gave Lenardson a mention on his All-American. Two Aggies—fullback Carp Julian and end Blake Miller—made All-Western in 1914, and tackle Gideon Smith and fullback Jerry DaPrato followed suit in 1915. And in 1915, DaPrato and Miller became State's initial first team All-American choices, Jerry by the International News Service and *Detroit Times* and Miller by the *Atlanta Constitution.* The latter was a prestigious selection in those days, and the very fact that a paper so far down in Dixie even heard of a Michigan Aggie player was in itself a tribute to the emergence of MAC.

All this was done in the reign of John Macklin, but his biggest personal achievement probably was the thoroughness and ease with which he succeeded the beloved Chester Brewer and even won over faculty cynics.

Beal, in his *History Of Michigan Agricultural College (1915),* described Macklin's plight and his subsequent victory in these words:

"The circumstances under which Professor Macklin, or Coach as he prefers it, came to MAC could have been more favorable. There was a vague feeling that the man did not exist who could fill Brewer's shoes, either as a coach or as a personal friend. It was rumored that Eastern coaches were brutes, merciless drivers of men, without feeling and without sentiment. Macklin was received warmly enough, but there was a subtle sense of judgement reserved, waiting to witness results.

"Mr. Macklin proceeded at once to obtain results. No cruel system of driving appeared; he failed to play the brute; he studied the individual and acted accordingly. Without ostentation or display he took up Brewer's work where Brewer left off. There has been no halt, no slipping backward. Under his direction MAC has steadily risen in the Western athletic world, until she is just ready to take a place with the best.

"John Macklin must be given credit, not only for keeping the Green and White prominently on the athletic map, but for advancing its position to the very forefront. The judgement that was reserved is now given freely."

To do all that, a big man was required. And Macklin was a big, big man. Frim (Lyman Frimodig) remembered him as about 6-4 and 230, and "perhaps the biggest man the squad had ever seen."

An unidentified rhymster, setting the stage for the 1913 Michigan-Michigan Aggies game, wrote in the *Lansing State Journal:*

Where did we get our team?

Oh, what a husky eleven.

Who's the teacher of our team?

Macklin, six feet seven.

"I knew him from my freshman days until my graduation in the spring of 1916," said Merrill S. (Chief) Fuller, student manager of the 1915 team. "He stood about 6-5 tall and weighed about 240."

"John F. Macklin was a giant, the biggest man I had ever seen up to that time. He stood nearly seven feet tall and weighed around 275 pounds," recalled Charley Butler, who lettered in 1915 and 1916. "His shoulders seemed to be three feet wide and tapered at about 45 degrees up to his neck. By today's standards he would have made the most perfect defensive tackle for the pros ever."

Pictures confirm that he was indeed a tremendous hunk of masculinity. He towered over his players and undoubtedly acquired authority from his very presence.

The 1914 *Wolverine* described him as "handsome, haughty and heady." On the practice field he was immediately identifiable by two characteristics: he was the biggest man there, and he wore a cap on his balding noggin. Otherwise he looked like one of the gang in football jersey and khaki football pants.

He was an American of pure Irish stock, "the son of Robert Macklin of Ireland and Margaret (Wrey) of the same country," according to Beal's history of MSU.

He was educated at Worcester High School in Massachusetts; Exeter Academy of New Hampshire; St. Paul's School of Garden City, Long Island—all of which would indicate his family was not exactly indigent and the University of Pennsylvania.

By the time the finger was put on him to succeed Brewer at Michigan Agricultural College, he had become director of athletics and coach at Pawling Prep, Pawling, New York.

H. G. Salsinger, renowned for his scholarly accuracy and thoroughness as sports editor and columnist of the *Detroit News* for many years, said of him in an article written for *Spartan Gridiron News,* Michigan State's football game program, in 1953:

"Macklin had been an outstanding all-around athlete at the University of Pennsylvania. He captained Penn's freshman eleven and after that he played tackle and halfback for the varsity. He also played basketball for two seasons, hockey for one, baseball for two, engaged in track and field competition and rowed with the varsity crew on the days when he had no other engagement."

Macklin's coming to East Lansing is a tale of many tortuous twists and turns. He was, at the very least, the third man in the scramble for the Aggie job. From the many applications received, the State Board accepted one from Hugo Bezdek, a

Macklin in practice gear.

former star player under Amos Alonzo Stagg at Chicago. Bezdek came to East Lansing, accepted the job, and promptly disappeared. Sometime later he let MAC officials know he was declining the position. (Bezdek later became a highly successful coach at Penn State.)

Next in line was Jesse Harper, the Wabash College coach who had been making a big name for himself by emphasizing the new-fangled forward pass. He would come, he said, for $2,200 annual salary. That was more than Brewer had been earning, and the State Board of Agriculture nixed the deal. Two years later Harper (by then the head coach at Notre Dame) and his Irish team electrified the football world with a victory over Army at West Point via the forward pass as executed by Gus Dorais to Knute Rockne.

The situation now was becoming desperate. The 1911 season was at hand without a coach. Then President Snyder took charge. He hurried to his old Eastern haunts and consulted a friend named Mike Murphy. Murphy was the most famous athletic trainer of his day and was then employed by Penn after a period at Yale. He was perhaps even more famed as coach of the U.S. Olympic track and field teams of 1908, 1912, and 1916. Murphy recommended Macklin for the job. Snyder went to Pawling and signed Macklin for a salary of $2,000.

Some outstanding players from the 1910 team had graduated, such as Leon Exelby, Ernest Baldwin, Jim Campbell, Ben Pattison, and Ion Cortright (which fact possibly made easier Brewer's decision to move west). But Macklin picked up the reins and coached his first club to a creditable 5-1 record, marred, as in 1910, only by a loss to Michigan.

Veterans on whom Macklin built were captain Fred Stone, Leon (Bubbles) Hill, Jim McWilliams, William Riblett, and Ed Culver. A first-year man who played equally well at guard, tackle, and end was D. Ormond (Tuss) McLaughry. Soon after that one season McLaughry left MAC to finish his college career at Westminster College. He later achieved fame as a great coach at Brown and Dartmouth. Another freshman who was to leave an indelible mark on MAC sports before graduation was back George (Carp) Julian.

The Aggies put up a good scrap against Michigan. They battled Yost's usual powerhouse 0-0 in the first half. Each team scored a field goal in the third period, and Michigan burst through with two touchdowns in the final quarter to win 15-3.

32

The MAC crew's big hope was Bubbles Hill. A headline in the *Lansing State Journal* the week of the MAC-Michigan game said flatly, "Aggies Relying on Bubbles Hill." His kicking was expected to be a key factor in the game.

Bubbles lived up to expectations by booting a 40-yard field goal for MAC's only score and doing well otherwise.

The 1912 season was blighted by a 55-7 crushing under Yost's steamroller and redeemed by victories in the other six games, including a trophy specimen over Ohio State. The Buckeyes were first-year members of the Big Ten, although they did not start conference football play until the following season. But they were pretty good and brought a 6-2 record into the Thanksgiving Day game with MAC at Columbus.

A blocked kick and recovered fumble set up two early Ohio State touchdowns, and the game took on the aspects of an impending rout. But MAC's determined athletes pulled themselves together and got back into contention with a second period touchdown drive, which included a 45-yard fake punt and run by Carp Julian and a 30-yard pass from Bill Riblett to Blake Miller. The touchdown was scored by Larry Servis, who said of his effort years later that "for my part it was simply carrying the ball on a cross buck over the left side of their line through a hole wide enough to drive a truck." Earlier that fall Servis had clicked for five touchdowns in a 52-0 rout of Olivet.

Both teams scored again in the second quarter, MAC on a pass from drop-kick formation, by Riblett to Elmer (Chill) Gorenflo. So it was 20-14 for Ohio State at the half.

Buckeye fans really must have lost their Thanksgiving turkey appetites though, when the incredible spectacle of three unanswered Aggie touchdowns was paraded before them in the fourth period.

George Gauthier hit Miller with a short pass for one. Gauthier plunged for the second following a pass interception by Riblett and a 20-yard run by Julian. Riblett scored the finale after center Ralph Chamberlain covered an Ohio State fumble on its own 25. That wrapped up the neat victory package for MAC at 35-20. It was the first ever achieved over a Big Ten team.

"In spite of the handicap of inferior officiating," the *State Journal* reported, "MAC never became rattled or discouraged. Julian is the man who'll be remembered here the longest. He made the fullback position amount for something. There wasn't one point on the Ohio State line he didn't penetrate and he saved the center embarrassment by scooping up bad snaps several times."

The coach who got the MAC players ready for their success was, certainly, demanding.

"Macklin was a driver and would keep us at it far into the night and we would be too tired to eat even, which says something for a football player," said Herb Straight, a letter-winning lineman in 1914-15-16.

"He was quite a task master," Frim recalled. "Our practices were rough and bruising. After an afternoon workout we were usually called out again after dinner for signal practice. On the field he was *the* master, but off the field he was as nice a person as you ever wanted to meet."

"We have had any number of coaches who knew more football than Macklin did," Frim said. "Time and again he would come out with a play, and we as members of the squad would say, 'it won't work.'

"He wasn't the kind to say, 'I will determine.' He would always say, 'Let's try it.'"

Brownie Springer, who lettered under Macklin in 1915 and came back after a three-year absence to play again in 1919 and captain the team in 1920, echoed Frim's words, saying he thought Potsy Clark, whom he played for in 1920, was the best coach he had had at MAC.

But Macklin could motivate a team, coax it into doing its best, and work applied psychology to a refined degree. A favorite gambit was to bawl out one of his best players and later call his victim into his office and tell him to forget the riding, that he was really attempting to reach someone else.

One thing certain is that Macklin did a great public relations job. He had his players, faculty, students, and townspeople dancing happily to his tune. One of his good friends was C.P. Downey, of Downey's Hotel in downtown Lansing and a big wheel in the Lansing Automobile Club. Downey happened to own a large, isolated cottage in the middle of Pine Lake, now called Lake Lansing. By the fall of 1913 Macklin prevailed on him for the loan of this structure to the Aggie team for preseason training. Downey also threw in free the services of his chef and food for the team. There were only 15 men on the squad, so the cost was not prohibitive. Actual drills were conducted on a field on the mainland, just south of the amusement park, which was very big and active in those days. There was easy transportation available by means of the interurban railroad which ran from Owosso to Lansing. And there always was Macklin's own electric automobile, one of the first in the community.

Merrill Fuller, team manager in 1915, has a special memory of the training period that fall at Pine Lake. R. E. Olds, the wealthy auto pioneer, had a fashionable cottage on the north shore with a fine sailboat anchored at a dock. Since college kids were then what they are today, some of the players borrowed the boat for an extended cruise and failed to return it.

"Sunday morning we were all seated around on the wide sun porch that surrounded the cottage," Fuller recalls, "when a rowboat approached with Gladys Olds, daughter of the auto pioneer, in command. She wanted to know who had charge. I was manager so the guys all pointed to me.

"She stood up in the boat and delivered a splendid lecture about the difference between gentlemen and vandals. When she finished I proceeded in a hurry to get the boat back to where it belonged—and in good condition."

The pleasing successes of 1911 and 1912 proved to be the overture before the big show. It was in 1913 that the dreams of every Aggie who had ever seen his team disemboweled by a Michigan battering ram finally came true. MAC beat the Wolverines 12-7, the only loss of the season for the excellent

Carp Julian scores first Aggie touchdown in 1913 upset of Michigan.

Michigan team. Not only that, but the following week at Madison, Wisconsin, the Aggies upset undefeated Wisconsin, the defending Big Ten champion, by the same 12-7 score. And to complete the feast, the Macklinmen went 7-0-0 for the first perfect season in Spartan history.

The Aggies opened the action with 26-0 and 57-0 routs of Olivet and Alma.

Then, despite the 55-7 disaster his athletes had suffered at Ann Arbor the year before, Macklin must have sensed that now the time was at hand. He ordered week-long secret practices. He scrimmaged his club Tuesday, Wednesday, and Thursday. A score of uniformed ROTC members kept all outsiders north of the Red Cedar River. There were not enough daylight hours, so Macklin had 12 electric lights installed for work after dark. Players were excused one by one from practice, apparently when Macklin decided each had done his job well or was incapable of continuing.

Der Tag was October 18. The day was perfect, the weather fair and cool. Some 800 MAC students and about 200 faculty and staff members and fans jammed excursion trains to Ann Arbor that morning.

The game was a real bone-breaker, a crunching, physical battle. The Aggies suffered a great blow early in the game when ace sophomore end and sometime halfback, Blake Miller, was knocked cold and stayed under for several hours. Jim Totten's description of how it happened, in a carefully researched article for a Michigan State football program years later, gives a vivid picture of the ferocity of the action.

"After putting on a wonderful display of punting and line plunging, the 160-pound halfback (Miller) gained eight yards on a fake kick, was tackled, hit again while lying on the ground and carried unconscious from the field with a dislocated vertebra."

The following Monday the *Detroit Free Press* reported: "Blake Miller, MAC halfback, who was seriously injured and partially paralyzed in the game, woke up in Homeopathic Hospital here this afternoon, rational for the first time since he received the terrible blow on the head."

That his recovery eventually was 100 percent is demonstrated by the fact that, at this writing, Miller is very much alive at age 85 and still playing golf, at which game he spent some years as a professional. He fired a neat 45-45—90 on the very long and difficult Forest Akers west course the summer of 1974

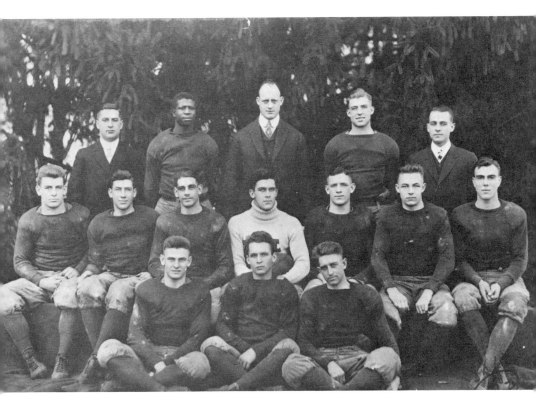

1913 MAC team, first to beat Michigan, first to go undefeated and untied.

while participating in a Ralph Young Scholarship Fund event.

MAC gave up 25 pounds per man on the line, but fought the Wolverines to a standstill. Aggie touchdowns were made by Carp Julian on a three-yard plunge and Hewitt Miller, Blake's brother, on a fumble recovery. Quarterback George Gauthier hit on seven of 19 passes for 100 yards, a phenomenal performance with the fat ball of those days. Newspaper accounts referred to MAC's "basketball tactics" and called the result, "a demonstration that Yost's men are unable to cope with a team that uses the forward pass as a primary offensive weapon."

Veteran Detroit newsman Eddie Batchelor said of the Aggie triumph many years later, "This must be ranked among the biggest upsets in all college football history." He credited the turnabout in part to some remarkable new sophomore talent, particularly Gideon Smith and Hugh Blacklock on the line and Blake and Hewitt Miller in the backfield. Smith and Black-

lock were called by Batchelor, "two of the best I ever saw playing on the same team at the same time."

"Smith had arms that seemed to be ten feet long," Batchelor said, "plus the agility of a cat. When a play came through
his position he folded up the whole side of the opposing line as
if he were playing an accordion. Blacklock was big and equally
active."

Starting as one end that day was O. R. (Dutch) Miller of
Saginaw, who was playing under the name of Schultz because
his parents were opposed to football.

MAC's ROTC Cadet Band paraded through Ann Arbor
afterwards playing "The Victors," because there was as yet no
fight song in Aggieland.

Other consequences included the inevitable bonfire and
snake dance in front of the state capitol building in Lansing,
free admission to the Bijou theatre for celebrants, and a day off
from classes on Monday. There also was a fire Sunday which
leveled the barn of Addison Makepeace Brown, secretary of the
State Board of Agriculture. It stood near the present Student
Union Building and was considered a very ugly, unacademic
structure by practically everyone.

The *Holcad* reported the fire had been due to defective
wiring. The *State Journal* said Brown's cow had been saved
because, by amazing good fortune, she had been led over to
meet the train full of students coming from Ann Arbor.

No one said so, but it appeared the fire was part of the
victory celebration. A few days later Edgar Guest wrote in his
Detroit Free Press column:

THE MAC GRAD
I met him on the street this morn;
His smile was good to see;
He walked about with chest puffed out
As proud as he could be.

All Aggiedom was in a state of ecstatic shock, sure enough,
and there were those who feared the consequences on the team
of such rampant joy and adulation. Another big game, with Wisconsin, was coming up the following Saturday that would be at
least as severe a test as the Michigan game had been. William
Chapman said in *Detroit Saturday Night* that many Aggie fans
felt their team was going to Madison with a "bad case of con-
ceit." The Big Ten champion Badgers were undefeated and
untied once again and now had the incentive of walloping the

team which had beaten Michigan.

If MAC went into the game fat-headed, it did not show. Wisconsin solved the Aggie passing game better than Michigan had, but the Badger line proved porous. Especially productive that day was the end sweep with captain Chester Gifford, Hugh Blacklock, and Carp Julian mowing people down ahead of Blake Miller. (Yes, Blake started the game despite his fearsome injury the week before and scored his team's first TD; in the second half he left the game with a sore back and bruised leg.) MAC's second score came late in the first half when Gifford blocked a Wisconsin punt—the ball rolled into the end zone, and end Ralph Henning fell on it. The second half was dominated by Wisconsin, but Macklin's men hung on to score their second major upset in as many weeks.

MAC closed out the 1913 season with victories over Akron 41-0, Mt. Union 13-7, and South Dakota 19-7 and was heralded as probably the best team in the Mid-West for the year.

The 1914 season was Macklin's poorest, the only one in his five at East Lansing in which his team lost more than one game. Only a victory in the season's finale at State College, Pennsylvania, over Penn State 6-3 distinguished the campaign. This vic-

Blake Miller breaks loose against Wisconsin in 1913 victory.

tory certainly rates as one of the most important of the Macklin era and is remembered by several veterans of that day. as, in some ways, the most satisfying of all their successes.

It was the first time MAC beat an important intersectional foe. The Lions were a power in the East, having stunned mighty Harvard, the 1913 national champion, with a 13-13 tie just a few weeks before. The Aggies had a presentable 4-2 record going into the game, but they were not taken seriously inasmuch as the victories were over Olivet, Alma, Akron, and Mt. Union and the losses to Michigan and Nebraska. The latter game, played at Lincoln, was MAC's first major intersectional and resulted in a 24-0 trouncing.

High winds may have been the strongest weapon MAC had against the Nittany Lions. The gusts hurt the Eastern team's vaunted passing game, although there were a number of long gains recorded, and played havoc with field goal tries and punts of both teams.

Old Aggies knew how to celebrate.

A rock-ribbed stand at its own one yard line was the back-breaker MAC applied to the Lions in the second quarter. Jerry DaPrato followed with a magnificent punt into the gale which carried from deep in his own end zone to Penn State's 45. On its next possession MAC mounted an 80-yard scoring drive on the ground to wrap up the decision. The big play in the series was a 55-yard canter around right end by Hewitt Miller, playing in the game as a substitute for injured star Blake Miller, his brother. The TD was scored by fullback Carp Julian from five yards. DaPrato missed the extra point. The second half was a scoreless joust between Penn State's desperate scoring tries and MAC's grim, sturdy defense.

The game was the highlight of a Pennsylvania Day celebration which had attracted a host of dignitaries, including the outgoing and incoming governors of the state. President Snyder headed a group representing MAC. The game was played on a Friday afternoon, an unusual circumstance which brought about a wholesale boycott of classes on the MAC campus. Many of the students gathered at the *Lansing State Journal* office in downtown Lansing to get the earliest possible telegraphic returns. They celebrated a little but withheld the main demonstration until the team arrived home on its special train the next day. Then came a massive torchlight parade up and down Washington Avenue in Lansing, a bonfire at the capitol, attempts to rush the Bijou vaudeville house, Roman candles, and finally an invasion of the movies.

The *Holcad* reported the following Monday that "Washington Avenue has never before seen such a maze of shooting stars and curling smoke and weaving figures."

The worst thing about 1914 was, of course, the outbreak of World War I. The best thing from the Michigan Agricultural College standpoint was the arrival on campus of Jack Heppinstall, a 23-year-old immigrant from England. He had been a carpenter in Lansing briefly until he heard that the athletic gang at MAC had need of someone with know-how in handling bumps and bruises. He knew plenty from his days as a professional soccer player in his homeland, went to see Macklin, and promptly became the school's first trainer. He stayed with the job through fair weather and foul; served perhaps 10,000 MAC, MSC, and MSU athletes; and retired in 1959, 45 years later, as one of the most beloved figures ever to work at the school in any capacity.

Jack once recalled that one of his first assignments from Macklin was to lay out a baseball diamond on Old College Field. Now Jack had never seen a baseball game and had no idea how to start. "Mr. Macklin," he said with a twinkle in his eye, "that isn't cricket."

Heppinstall went on to attain a national reputation as an athletic trainer and in 1948 had the honor of returning to his homeland as a trainer with the U.S. Olympic team.

Biggie Munn once described Jack as "the anchor for the ship of State."

The season of 1915, the final one in Macklin's term as MAC's head coach, was distinguished by one of the choicest victories ever scored over Michigan. It was the fourth game of the six-game slate and MAC had prepped for it with three wide-throttle romps over Olivet 34-0, Alma 77-12, and Carroll 56-0.

Practice the week of the game was a young war. "The

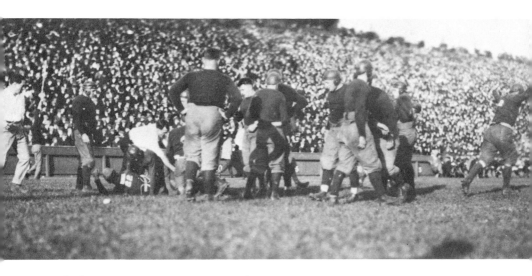

DaPrato scores first TD in 24-0 rout of Michigan in 1915. He made all MAC scores—three TDs, three PATS, and a field goal.

squad is being forced, driven and crowded in a way that will make the men like so many gladiators when they respond to the referee's whistle at Ferry Field," said the *Lansing State Journal*. During Wednesday's practice reserve back Al McClellan broke an ankle.

The team of Blake Miller, Jerry DaPrato, Hugh Blacklock, Gideon Smith, Charley Butler, Howard Beatty, Hewitt Miller, et al, was as primed and ready as a loaded cannon. Quarterback Bob Huebel worked with special intensity. He had been on Michigan's team in 1914 and had transferred.

An estimated 3,000 fans made the trip from the Lansing area to Ann Arbor. For those who could not be there, the *State Journal* gave a play-by-play report off the teletype machine to an estimated 2,000 people in the street in front of the newspaper office. They cheered with every Aggie foray, and there were many of them that day.

Michigan was no patsy. It had in action one of its all-time great backs, Johnny Maulbetsch, who was an All-American the year before. Yost's team had won four earlier games just as impressively as had MAC, and the game figured to be close and tough.

What happened was described in these words by reporter Eddie Batchelor in the *Detroit Times:*

MAC's Gideon Smith is believed to have been first black to play pro ball. Evidence is this picture of 1915 Canton Bulldogs with Smith far right second row. Player at center second row is Jim Thorpe. Ex-Aggie Carp Julian apparently is shown twice, far left second row from top and second left middle row.

44

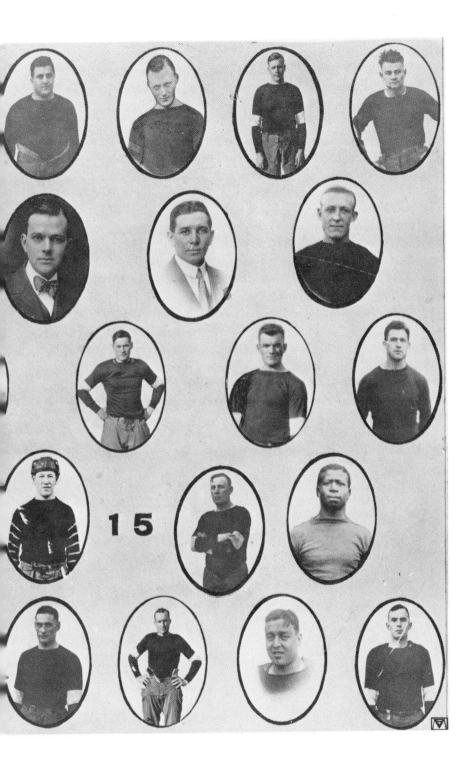

15

"What was the score? Just coming to that. It read 24 to 0 on the official blackboard and the men who possessed the two dozen points were the Aggies. Michigan claimed ownership of the zero and if there had been any numeral lower than that to hang up on the scoreboard they would have been forced to display it to indicate the Wolverines' accomplishments.

"Twenty-four to nothing sounds like a horrible beating, but it doesn't begin to express how completely the MAC team outplayed and outfought Michigan's. It wasn't merely a defeat for the Maize and Blue but a massacre, a rout, an annihilation. From the time the MAC Military Band came on the field until the same aggregation of virtuosos led a triumphal march profaning the streets of Ann Arbor, Michigan was beaten in everything. In music, cheering, fighting and playing football, the Aggies just naturally outclassed their foemen so badly that the Maize and Blue crowd could find no single straw at which to clutch as it drowned in a sea of tears.

"Three touchdowns and a field goal brought the MAC score to the enormous size it finally assumed. Every point was honestly earned by a team that so far outshone its rival that the affair hardly could be called a game. MAC was the winner from the first five minutes until the end, and there never was a bright spot in Michigan's gloom.

"When Michigan got the ball, which was seldom, the Aggies demonstrated that their defense is as good as their attack.

"Even the wonderful Maulbetsch couldn't pierce that adamant wall of Macklin's. It wasn't Maully's fault, though. He did everything that a human being could be expected to do, but no back can hope to advance any considerable distance toward the enemy's goal line when five or six men are sitting on his head. It cannot be done."

Fullback Jerry DaPrato was the superstar of the day. He scored all 24 of his team's points—three touchdowns, three points after, and a field goal. He gained 153 yards from scrimmage and had several other good gains called back for penalties. "He must have gained a mile of ground by one means or another in the course of the game," said one glowing account.

With assists from Blake Miller and Huebel, DaPrato did the scoring and the heavy work when action neared the goal line, but just about every Aggie seemed to get into the act. There were not only end-around plays, there were tackle-around plays,

Jerry DaPrato, first major MAC All-American.

with Gideon Smith and Hugh Blacklock carrying for good gains. Charley Butler, playing end, gained 24 yards on a split buck. He also was on the receiving end of a double-pass play.

"When it came to defense," a game account said, "Gideon Smith, the big MAC tackle, was far and away the best man in the game. This large person is a decided brunette as to complexion, but as a football player is pure gold all the way through." Gideon Smith repeatedly stopped Michigan charges dead, including some by the great Maulbetsch.

At game's end the sound of "The Victors" blasted forth, only it was the Aggies' gray-clad ROTC band playing it. MAC's "Fight Song" was being one-fingered on the Olympic House piano but had not been finished yet. The Aggie band had the innocent effrontery to play "The Victors" right back at the highly partisan and already disgruntled Michigan audience. As Frim observed years later: "It's a wonder they all weren't killed."

The joyous tumult following the biggest victory in Michigan Aggie history had subsided just a few decibels when the incredible happened, as it so often does in sports.

An unsung and apparently unscouted Oregon State team came to town the following Saturday and dumped the smug and happy Macklinmen flat. An unusual shift wrought havoc. Herb Straight recalls it as the most frustrating afternoon of his athletic career:

"We had never seen a shift of the entire line to a yard back of the line of scrimmage. Then with a well-timed 'hip!' and snap of the ball, they caught us off our feet all afternoon and nearly killed Gideon Smith.

"This shift was ruled out the next year. It was some time before we could find out what to do about it, which is to shift wider than they did and depend on the back field to stop the holes. But that is a long ways from stopping a well-trained line as they were that day."

Blake Miller recalls that Oregon State came in with the reputation of being a wonderful passing team, which may have thrown off defensive preparations. He also recalled that several players were hurt but played anyway, among them tackles Hugh Blacklock and Gideon Smith.

Anyway, down went the Aggies 20-0 to kill an excellent chance at an undefeated campaign. Marquette reaped the wild wind of the aroused Aggies the following week. MAC devastated the Hilltoppers 68-6 to end the year—and Macklin's career at State. It was the largest score any Aggie or Spartan team ever rolled up on the usually very difficult Milwaukee collegians.

The Awkward Years

After Macklin came seven years of turbulence, sometimes chaos. MAC's surge toward the collegiate football forefront met roadblocks that left it boxed in between the small church-affiliated schools of the MIAA plus a few minor independents—which it had outgrown—and the big powers—which it could not match.

Frank Sommers, a Penn graduate and Macklin's personal choice as his successor, lasted just the season of 1916 despite a modestly respectable record of 4-2-1.

The worst blows in 1916 for the proud and ambitious Aggie supporters were 9-0 and 14-0 losses to Michigan and Notre Dame, respectively, and a 3-3 tie with South Dakota. So much more had been expected since there were quite a few excellent men back from Macklin's splendid 1915 team, such as end and captain Ralph Henning, tackle Sherm Coryell, center Lyman Frimodig, quarterback Bob Huebel, and halfback and tackle Hugh Blacklock.

What a man that Blacklock must have been! George Alderton, who did a lot of digging into Aggie lore while sports editor of the *Lansing State Journal* and part-time MSC sports information director for many years, uncovered details of an incredible weekend of activity for Blacklock after his team's season finale against Notre Dame on Old College Field in 1916.

Blacklock went to Detroit and that night fought a ten-round boxing bout. He then went down into Ohio, probably to Dayton, and the next day played a pro football game. The following day he showed up on campus all battered and bruised and had Jack Heppinstall powder and paint him so he could have his picture taken with the squad without looking too terrible. Jack did a fine job. In the squad picture you cannot notice a thing.

The bottom really fell out of Aggie football fortunes in 1917 when the Aggies had the only perfect-in-reverse record in the school's gridiron history. Chester Brewer somehow had been enticed to come back from Missouri, where he had compiled another excellent record. But the Aggie team was stripped of talent by the draft calls of World War I, and there were no big training programs at East Lansing like those at Michigan and some other schools.

Another quickly evident point, when one checks the schedule for 1917, is that it was by all odds the toughest an MAC team ever had undertaken. The usual schedules had contained, at most, two or three major opponents. This one was loaded with seven toughies—Michigan, Detroit, Western State, Northwestern, Notre Dame, Syracuse, and Camp MacArthur, the latter loaded with ex-college stars.

Was football really rough in those days? This memoir involves a game (probably 1919) against Notre Dame at South Bend, as related by C. F. (Irish) Ramsay:

"We were having considerable success holding Notre Dame scoreless or almost so, but we could not mount any kind of an offense against them. Rockne must have given his team one of his famous between halves speeches because it came out roaring for the second half and played with a vengeance.

"I was never knocked down so many times in a football game. It did not matter whether the play was a wide end sweep to the other side of the field with me slowly catching my breath, walking back to the team, or some other play. I would find myself lying on the ground after being hit from behind by some Notre Dame player even though the play had stopped and I was far from the center of action. Rockne must have told his boys to knock everybody down regardless of whether they were involved in the action or not. I learned a good lesson that day— Never arise to return for the next play without first looking behind you. In those days there was no penalty for clipping."

Brewer moved on at the end of the season when selected by the U.S. War Department to serve as Director of Army Athletics, a remarkable tribute to the calibre of this man. His successor for 1918 was George Gauthier, one-time Aggie quarterback and, more recently, Aggie basketball and track coach.

50

The football team improved to a 4-3 record and also produced one of the most astounding upsets in Aggie history. It defeated Knute Rockne's first Notre Dame team, the star of which was sophomore back George Gipp, on Old College Field by a 13-7 count.

Here's how Bob Hoerner, sports editor of the *Lansing State Journal*, told about it in an article in the *Spartan Gridiron News* issue for the Notre Dame game of 1968:

"Heavy rains washed out a major share of Michigan State's double victory celebration planned for 50 years ago—November, 1918—that was when the German army capitulated to the Allies to end World War I.

"Officially, the war ended on Monday, November 11. Lansing, East Lansing, local military and state government officials planned an exciting 'victory party' for Saturday afternoon when Coach George Gauthier's Michigan State Aggies were to play their final home game of the season.

"It was Homecoming for Aggie Alumni.

"The Student Army Training Corps, a group of 1,100 soldiers at Michigan State, was to have a formal regimental review on the football field just before the game.

"At half time, there were to be boxing bouts between soldiers. Mass calisthenics and bayonet drills—with all the grunts that normally accompany them—also were planned as part of the half-time show.

"Gov. and Mrs. Albert Sleeper were to be at the game in a special box seat with many other government officials as their guests.

"The whole 'victory celebration' was to start with a huge pep rally on the campus on Friday night.

"Whenever you play Notre Dame in football, it's time for a party.

"A young coach who was in his first year as boss of the Irish was bringing in a pretty good team. It was undefeated. The coach's name was Knute Rockne.

"The first-year coach had a fine sophomore halfback prospect on his team. His name was George Gipp, a native of the Upper Peninsula.

"But it rained.

"It rained so hard that the regimental review and all of the other half-time attractions had to be canceled.

"But the football game was played.

51

"Accounts of the game in the next day's newspapers were far from complete. College football games just didn't receive publicity at that time as they do today.

"Coach Gauthier's Aggies saved the 'party' by scoring a decisive 13-7 victory over the Notre Damers. 'The game was played in a sea of mud, but Michigan State won without flukes or horseshoes,' the *State Journal* report of the game said.

"The Aggies—the name Spartans came several seasons later—scored the first time they had the ball with Edmund Young taking a 20-yard pass from quarterback Harry Graves. State fumbled the ball on the extra point attempt and led, 6-0.

"Gipp, who later became a legendary figure in Notre Dame football, scored a touchdown for the Irish to make the score, 7-6. 'Gipp, a promising sophomore backfielder, made several 15-yard gains against the Aggies,' the newspaper story said. The Aggies then went on to win it, but in no newspaper account is there a description of the winning score.

"It was Rockne's first defeat as a college coach and the only one he suffered in his first three seasons."

The Notre Dame rivalry in that day meant just as much to the Michigan Aggies as today's does to the Spartans.

I. John Snyder II tells this about his father Shorty Snyder, one of the Aggie halfbacks in the 1918 contest:

"That game meant so much to him that in later years as the Notre Dame-Michigan State rivalry increased, he used to throw his old square-cleated football shoes into the trunk of the car to take them along to the games that he attended just for good luck. Incidentally, I wore those shoes in playing grade school and my first couple of years of high school football also."

Shorty Snyder won eight letters at MAC, three each in football and baseball and two in basketball.

The season of 1919 started with war veterans pouring in to begin or continue their college education. Five Aggie captains were on the team: Del Vandervoort, captain-elect of the 1917 team before entering service; Sherm Coryell, who was named to fill Vandervoort's shoes, but who also wound up in France; Irish Ramsay, who finally captained the 1917 team; Larry Archer, captain of the 1918 team; and Harry (Siwash) Franson, captain-elect of the 1919 club.

The most propitious sign of all was that the great man himself, Chester Brewer, was returning to the helm. But enthusiasts

Early Aggie practice on Old College Field.

had overlooked the fact that other schools also were enjoying a great influx of war veterans, and the results of the season were typical of those awkward years. The Aggies beat Albion, Alma, South Dakota, and DePauw to absolutely no fanfare; lost to Western State, Michigan, Purdue, and Notre Dame; and closed out with a dull thud—7-7 against Wabash.

Then came 1920, new head coach Potsy Clark, and a 4-6 record. Once again MAC won no important games and was badly crunched by such as Wisconsin, Michigan, Nebraska, Notre Dame, and even Kalamazoo (21-2) and Marietta (23-7). Exit Clark.

It was following that season that MAC almost scored a coup with potential that staggers the imagination. MAC actually had Knute Rockne's name on the dotted line for a three-year contract as head football coach. The authority on this is Lyman Frimodig, whose veracity is challengeable by no man, and not only because he died in 1972 at age 80. Frim and other MAC oldsters recounted the story many times, but perhaps George

Yellmaster Lankey wrote Fight Song.

Van, long-time sportswriter for the *Detroit Times* and later the *Detroit News,* told it best in a column in the *Times* in 1957:

"Things might have been so different in football at Michigan State. As long ago as the early twenties they might have been known as the 'Fighting Farmers.'

"The tag would be a smothering thought to Spartan alumni today reveling as they justifiably should be in their school as Michigan State University.

"But there was a time back in 1921 when Knute Rockne signed a contract to coach State, then known as the Aggies.

"It's rather shocking to the Rockne tradition to learn that the ambitious young Norwegian was still shopping around for bigger dough during those first few years coaching at Notre

Dame.

"The Rock decided to stay at South Bend and the Fighting Irish legend was on its way.

"That contract is still in the drawer of Lyman L. Frimodig, State's veteran business manager. It's one of his treasures. It called for Rock to get $4,500 the first season of a three-year pact with a $500 boost each year.

"Frim came to East Lansing from Calumet and became a ten-letter man, the only athlete with that many numerals in the school's history. At Calumet High he played with George Gipp, later to become a Notre Dame football immortal."

When the Rockne deal fell through and he went on to the Four Horsemen and immortality, MAC took on as head coach in 1921 Albert M. Barron, a grad of Penn State. In Barron's two years as coach his teams beat the MIAA clubs as usual but lost to all the biggies. There were a couple of unfortunate exceptions. Albion beat MAC 24-7 in 1921 and tied it 7-7 in 1922.

The worst lacing a Barron team took was 63-0 at the hands of Michigan in 1922.

"In the 1921 game, two Michigan players were carried off the field on stretchers, one with a broken leg," according to a memoir from 1922 team captain William C. Johnson.

"One week before the 1922 game, six black hand letters were sent to our coach to be presented to six of our players, including myself. The letters were never given to us by our coach, but the contents of the letters were revealed to us after the game. We were accused of playing dirty football and charged with intent to cripple the university players so as to hinder their chances for a Big Ten championship. 'So please beware, because we are going to gang up on your fellows this year,' they said.

"Had the contents of those letters been revealed to us before the game, I feel that the score might not have been so one-sided, although we were up against a powerful team."

Johnson also remembers playing a Nebraska team at Lincoln in 1920 which boasted two huge tackles in a day when a 200-pounder was a rarity. The Cornhuskers won 35-7, thanks in large part to Wayne (Big) Munn, 265, and his brother—presumably "Little" Munn at only 235. Wayne went on after college to become heavyweight wrestling champion of the world and his nickname became attached to a young man in Minneapolis named Clarence Munn.

Aggie drops Chicago's Zorn in 1923 game.

The Nebraska "Biggie" had a strong competitive bent and some smarts, too.

"One time during the game out there when they had the ball and the quarterback was barking the signals, Wayne Munn said, 'Where's the fire?' and a couple of our linemen straightened up to see if there actually was a fire," Johnson relates. "At that moment the ballcarrier came through that spot for five or ten yards. When Munn talked his voice seemed to come from his shoe tops."

Several players of the in-between era of 1917-22 said they thought the best player of that period was fullback John Hammes, who lettered in 1917, 1919, and 1920.

Around 1920 it began to dawn on some loyal but frustrated MAC followers that perhaps one of the basic causes of the school's football malaise was the antiquated physical plant. Old College Field, with its 6,000 bleacher seats, was absolutely no lure either to stronger teams to come on the Aggies' schedule or for the better high school players to opt for East Lansing as their collegiate football home.

Once again it was the voice of L. Whitney Watkins, by now

a leading agriculturalist in the state and a highly influential veteran member of the State Board of Agriculture, which was loudest and most urgent.

"We may well wonder why we have not the four thousand or more students enrolled that we might reasonably expect," he said in the *Holcad*. "There may be various reasons, but I am convinced that the main one is that we have failed to make our institution as attractive as we should in recreational advantages.

"Nothing appeals so strongly to the boy or girl who is just finishing high school as a college furnishing high class athletic entertainment. In order to overcome this weakness, we must have a fine stadium."

Talk began about MAC one day becoming a member of the Western Conference, and there was general agreement that a prime prerequisite was a stadium which would compare favorably to those in the big league's schools.

Gov. A. J. Groesbeck joined the chorus with powerful voice. "It is absolutely necessary to provide a stadium on the campus," he said, "and I think a way can be found to make the general desire for one a real accomplishment within a comparatively short time."

Governor Groesbeck proposed that the state lend MAC the money to build a stadium, and the 1923 state legislature granted the school $160,000 for the purpose. The money was to be repaid from game receipts over a ten-year period.

The work was quickly undertaken and by the time the 1923 football season rolled around there was a fine 15,000-capacity concrete stadium south of the Red Cedar. It is still there and in use, the first stage in development of what now is the 76,000-capacity Spartan Stadium. The construction meant the demise of a campus golf course, which lay along the south side of the river in what today is occupied by the stadium, the Men's Intramural Building, the old ice arena, Jenison Gymnasium, and the open areas between those structures and the river.

While the stadium construction was well underway, a new head coach and athletic director arrived on the scene, the sixth since Macklin. This one came to stay awhile. His 31-year career at the school encompassed the period of the greatest growth and development of the total institution.

This growth and that of the athletic establishment were as one, and Ralph H. Young was an integral part of it all.

Young Spartans

Ralph Young was a lovable, roly-poly extrovert whose public relations talents overshadowed his coaching accomplishments and resulted in great things for MAC and Michigan State College (which it became in 1925 by act of the state legislature).

"I ate us into the Big Ten," he once said, proving once again the validity of the old saw that many a truth is uttered in jest.

Young had gargantuan appetites for food and people. His gastronomic exploits and staggering memory for names and details of long past meetings and incidents amazed and endeared him to people from coast to coast. Mama Leone of the famous restaurant in New York called him her favorite customer. His fabulous buffets at the Olds Hotel in connection with football games, track carnivals, or other major athletic affairs, were legendary. If he had any enemies, they were in the college's business office. His expense accounts must have had auditors climbing the walls. But it was not wasted money. Without Young and his exuberant public relations work, it is a safe bet that Michigan State would not be in the Big Ten today and would enjoy nowhere near the athletic prominence it came to know in his administration.

Young had excellent football credentials. He was one of the few men ever to play both for Fielding H. Yost of Michigan and Amos Alonzo Stagg of Chicago. He also played a couple of seasons at Washington and Jefferson College in Pennsylvania when it was in the big time. He was a tackle at Michigan in 1918 at 28 years of age while in army training during World War I.

58

Coach Young.

While at Chicago in 1910-12 and W. and J. in 1913-14, he had been a fireplug fullback at 5-8 and 210. He was an outstanding punter as well as a powerful line smasher.

In between collegiate years and sometimes mixed right in with them, Ralph Young also played professionally in Detroit and other mid-west cities. The story is that one Sunday morning in Ann Arbor an automobile pulled up to an interurban train stop. The driver, Fielding H. Yost in person, stared severely at the stocky fellow awaiting the train to Detroit.

"Ralph," Yost demanded, "where are you going?"

"Why, to Detroit for the day," Young responded.

"What's in that satchel?" Yost pursued.

It was a rhetorical question. Yost knew as well as Young did that it contained his football uniform and that he was en route to play a pro game in Detroit that afternoon.

"You're finished with football at Michigan," Yost concluded.

Only years later did Young receive a Michigan "M" blanket at a press party prior to a Michigan-MSU football game. It was a gesture which mightily pleased Young, then near the twilight of his career.

Lest readers think Young's professional play totally reprehensible, let it be noted that this was commonplace at that time. There were few collegiate rules and little enforcement. There was little or no scholarship aid to athletes such as there is today. Athletes often helped pay their way through college by pro activities on the side. They switched freely from school to school, giving rise to the expression "tramp athlete."

Brownie Springer, one of the outstanding Aggie players of the World War I period, wrote this revealing commentary on his era: "The only help I got from MAC was a job at the gym and meals at training table during baseball and football seasons. I believe I got $.40 an hour. Jack Heppinstall kept track of the hours I worked, and I must say he was quite generous.

"Many of the players played on Sundays on other teams to get extra money, I myself included. The Heralds at Detroit, the Fort Wayne Friars, and the team coached by Jimmy King, the former Harvard fullback. It was called the Pine Village Chargers. I played for them after the Purdue game. We played at Des Moines, Iowa. I got $150 and expenses. Later in 1920 I played for the Friars on Sunday.

"These teams were all composed of college players. Notre

Dame, Purdue, Indiana, Butler—many of whom we had played against the previous day."

Spring said he found out later that Coach Potsy Clark knew about it. "He also said they did the same thing while he was at Illinois," Springer added. "So you see why athletic scholarships came about, many of which far exceed what we got the hard way. I never could have finished school otherwise."

A favorite story often recounted by Wilfrid Smith, famed sports editor of the *Chicago Tribune,* concerned this freewheeling period in college athletics.

Smith, a giant of a man at about 6-6 and 275, played college football at DePauw University, Greencastle, Indiana, and professionally for the old Chicago Staleys, predecessor to the Bears. His head coach at DePauw was none other than Ralph Young.

Now, it so happened Smith also played pro ball on Sundays and once a horrible thing happened.

"As I ran out on the field for the start of the game I came face to face with Mr. Young," Smith related. "There he stood, the referee for the game. I never stopped running. I just turned a half circle and ran right back into the dressing room, changed clothes and got out of there."

From 1919 through 1922, Young coached at Kalamazoo College. His football teams ruled the MIAA. One of them walloped Potsy Clark's 1920 MAC club at East Lansing 21-2, which may have had quite a bit to do with Young's eventual appointment at MAC. It also may have been more than coincidental that Kalamazoo went off the Aggie schedule for six years.

Young led no resurgence in his five seasons as head football coach at MAC and MSC. His overall record was 18-22-1, and his only winning season was a modest 5-3 in 1924. But he brought stability to a program which needed it badly. He laid the foundations on which the school's athletic structure grew rapidly. For one thing he, Knute Rockne of Notre Dame, and Con Jennings of Marquette formed the Central Collegiate Conference in 1926. For many years this was a powerful collegiate association rivaling the Big Ten in all but football (which was never part of its program). The CCC was an important steppingstone in State's progress toward the Big Ten. It still exists but without the prominence it once enjoyed.

The closest things to major victories scored under Young

were triumphs in 1925 and 1926 over Centre College. That might sound ridiculous to today's young people who probably never even heard of Centre. But old-timers will remember the tiny Kentucky school which blazed across the collegiate football firmament in the 1920s, upsetting such giants as Harvard and West Virginia, utilizing a lock-step backfield maneuver called the "Sing Sing Shift," and boasting such All-America stars as quarterback Bo McMillin and center Red Weaver. McMillin later became an outstanding college coach at Indiana. State played Centre both times at East Lansing and it sneaked by (15-13) in 1925 and won big (42-14) in 1926.

Sophomore Paul Smith, one of State's all-time great field goal and extra point men, dropkicked a field goal from the 42 yard line late in the game to win the 1925 contest and quiet the alumni wolves. They had started to howl after successive losses to Michigan 39-0 and Lake Forest 6-0, just prior to the Centre College date.

"The main feature of the game is that it was won by a marvelously reorganized team," said a press report, "a team which the week before was playing listless football."

MAC's two TDs were scored in the first half. The first came on a 47-yard run off tackle in the first period by Jim McCosh. The second was cashed in the second quarter following a fumble recovery by Paul Hackett on the Praying Colonels' 24 yard line. Three plays later Rudy Boehringer passed to Dick Lyman for the six points.

The main grievance of fans who yearned for a return to the palmy days under Brewer and Macklin was, of course, the continuing losses to Michigan. It was not only the defeats, it was the devastating scores that hurt—37-0 in 1923, 39-0 in 1925, 55-3 in 1926, and 21-0 in 1927. In a string of 17 games, 1916 through 1932, Aggie and Spartan teams scored only one touchdown against the Wolverines. The frustrations were so intense that an 8-5 victory over the Wolverines in baseball in 1926 set off a wild demonstration.

Led by Skinny Skellenger, a cheerleader with madcap propensities, students set fire to the old center-field section of bleachers on Old College Field, which had been little used since football moved to Macklin Field. Groundskeeper Albert Amiss barely saved his beloved power lawnmower, the first ever owned by the school, from the little wooden shed in which it was stored.

1924 Stadium dedication scene.

Then the throng of students took off through Lansing, setting a number of small, harmless, but annoying fires as they went. Police were called in to handle the situation and finally had to contend with Skellenger who was up a telephone pole and armed with a basket of rotten eggs with which he bombarded would-be captors.

The one time in the Young football coaching era when the Aggies almost caught up with their Ann Arbor tormentors was on the most important occasion of all, the stadium dedication game of 1924. The team had started playing on the new site in 1923, but only a Michigan game would be a fitting occasion for the ceremonial anointing of the field. So the dedication was held off a year, and Michigan was coaxed into its first appearance in East Lansing since 1914—and its last until 1948.

It was in every respect a grand and glorious day. The weather was balmy, even a little too warm for football. More than 3,000 automobiles filled regular and newly prepared parking areas. Several special trains were on campus sidings. A souvenir program with color cover sold out its entire printing of 7,500 copies half an hour before game time. Governor Groesbeck spoke in pregame ceremonies as did Macklin, who was back on campus for the great day. Michigan's band played its "The Victors" and the Aggie band responded with its own "Fight Song," something it did not have the last time Michigan had been there. A record attendance for any MAC athletic event sat in on the proceedings—19,800 shirt-sleeved fans, every one of whom (save Groesbeck) was highly partisan for one team or the other. Groesbeck piously and politically announced his neutrality to the crowd.

A bronze tablet created by MAC lettermen in memory of three former athletes who had died in World War I was dedicated. It read: "In memory of MAC varsity athletes who gave their lives in the World War. Olen Hinkle. E. E. Peterson. F. I. Lankey." (Yes, that was the Lankey who had composed the "Fight Song," which rang out so gloriously that day.)

As to the game itself, it was a tension-packed deadlock between two strong defensive teams highly motivated for the confrontation. Both clubs had been well scouted. On the preceding Saturday when the Aggies had bombed Olivet 55-3,

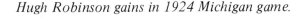

Hugh Robinson gains in 1924 Michigan game.

64

Coach Young and assistants John Kobs and Mike Casteel had watched Michigan crunch Miami of Ohio 55-0 at Ann Arbor.

"It was a nerve-wracking strain for any spectator who favored either side," the *MAC Record* reported. "It was such an exhibition as is given once in a lifetime and was declared by competent football critics one of the best contests ever played."

One crucial play, a 45-yard pass-and-run beauty from Freddy Parker to captain Herb Steger late in the fourth period, produced the lone score as Michigan won 7-0 and sank MAC hopes for a huge upset.

That touchdown lives in Michigan State legend for another reason. Sitting inside a telephone booth on top of the little wooden, open-fronted press box that day was Jimmy Hasselman, the college's extension editor and one-man-gang in handling public relations and publicity for the school. He watched the game through the glass in the phone booth door and spoke a play-by-play account into the mouthpiece. This was broadcast via WKAR to whatever radio audience there might have been in those days. Hasselman was a college sports broadcasting pioneer and very well could have been the first to broadcast full games in basketball and football anywhere in the country.

As the game-winning play developed, Hasselman told it like this: "The ball is snapped to Freddy Parker. It looks like it may be a pass. There's a man open down field. It's Herb Steger. Yes, it is a pass. It's going, going...Good God, it's a touchdown!"

The following week several letters were received at WKAR, Hasselman's office, and the president's office. One read: "Dear Lord: I didn't see you but I understand you were at the game Saturday. Your name was mentioned on the radio."

One reason Aggie records in the 1920s were not stronger was that the schedules were. There were fewer games with old MIAA foes and more with the likes of Chicago, Detroit, Northwestern, Wisconsin, North Carolina State, and Colgate.

The 1925 Colgate game at East Lansing, which State won 14-0, was the occasion for one of the weirdest incidents in the school's sports experience. It involved the visit of a notorious gang from Detroit and might have been developed into the scenario for a Mack Sennett comedy.

It seems assistant coach Tarz Taylor had become acquainted with some strange characters while on a summer job in Detroit. That fall he asked for and received eight tickets for some friends from the Motor City to come and see the Colgate game. Those friends turned out to be members of the Purple Gang, a powerful, murderous, prohibition era, liquor-smuggling mob of hoodlums.

"Somehow or other," Frim related, "the Michigan State Police got a tip that the gangsters were coming and immediately suspected they would hold up the gate. So preparations were made, and I was instructed to talk to my ticket salesmen and also to get the money up to our vault, which was then in the basement of the present women's gymnasium. Our sales in those days were greatest on the day of the game at the gate."

The gang members arrived in two big black limousines, just like in a James Cagney movie. They flashed no guns but did show their tickets and went to their seats.

School officials still were not sure they were there merely as fans, however, and at half time Frim stuffed all the money taken in that day into canvas bank bags, jumped into the side car of a police motorcycle, and sped off over the open field toward the gymnasium. Near the bridge over the river the motorcycle got stuck in a muddy spot, and Frim had to get out and push. In this process he dropped one of the bags, which was not discovered until they arrived at the gym. So back they went a-flying to locate the missing money. Meantime the Purple Gang members comported themselves well at the game. But they shook up the citizenry afterwards by drawing their gats and taking a few practice shots at the ducks on the Red Cedar River before heading back to their rum-running chores in Detroit.

The MSC gridders did not win too many big games in those days, but they did seem to have a lot of laughs. One involved burly lineman John Garver, one of the really outstanding Aggie players of the period who transferred in from Ohio State. The team was en route by train to play Penn State in 1925. Garver was roaming the aisles of the Pullman cars occupied by the team and official party when he came across an exceptionally fine-looking piece of luggage with the initials KLB on it. He could not identify the initials and finally, in typical brash, loud, Garver fashion, roared: "Who the hell is KLB around here?"

A drawing room door slowly opened and President Kenyon L. Butterfield stepped out. "I am, John," he said. "Can I help you?"

They say that for once John was left with his mouth hanging open and nothing to say.

John Garver, one of toughest young Spartans.

Allen Edmunds had vivid recollections of Coach Young on the day of a game. "Pedro (a nickname given Young by his players but never used to his face) always dressed his best for a game—tie, suit, hat, and so forth—and just before we went on the field, after our pregame warm-up, he would carefully put aside his new hat and go into a stirring and exciting pep talk. After he had built us up to a frenzy he would carefully adjust his tie, put on his hat, and walk out of the dressing room as if he had just left church."

Young turned over the football coaching reins in 1928 to Harry Kipke, a Lansing high school and Michigan star of recent vintage. He was received with great enthusiasm as the "home town boy who made good."

The season opener was against Kalamazoo College, back on the schedule again after the 1920 upset of Potsy Clark's team. The day was designated "Harry Kipke Day" and over 15,000 fans, largest opening game crowd in the school's history, showed up.

Harry and his lads gave the students and alumni a real show by rolling up 103 points on over 600 rushing yards and 34 first downs.

The surprise star of the game was a substitute halfback named Max Crall, who came in for starter Roger Grove when the avalanche score started to build up. Crall scored what probably was the all-time Spartan record up to that time of 29 points. He made four touchdowns, one on an 81-yard scamper, another from 60 yards away, and five of seven extra-point kicks.

George Alderton praised the Lansing lad highly the next day in the *Lansing State Journal:* "Crall kicked, ran and played defensive football in a pleasing manner." He also credited Crall with turning in "the two longest runs ever seen on the Michigan State gridiron."

Yet somehow Crall did not even win a letter that season, a campaign which went 3-4-1 and was graced only by additional victories over Chicago YMCA 37-0 and North Carolina State 7-0.

But the Spartans made a strong showing against Michigan in losing 7-0, and Kipke shuffled off to Ann Arbor where he succeeded Tad Wieman as head coach in 1929. In his nine years at the Wolverine helm he won several Big Ten and national titles, but also lost four games in a row (1934 through 1937) to Michigan State. This was a horrendous disaster for Michigan men and undoubtedly became a contributing factor to Kipke's move from coaching to great success as a Coca-Cola executive.

Spartan Horseman

Nothing in all the exciting lore of football possesses more charisma than the magic phrase: "The Four Horsemen of Notre Dame." One of that immortal foursome, Jim Crowley, succeeded Harry Kipke as Michigan State's head football coach in 1929. He brought with him all the glamour of his Notre Dame heritage and became the catalyst which transformed a mediocre win-one, lose-one gridiron nonentity into a nationally respected major power for the first time since Macklin.

Right away, in his initial season, he produced the first winner in five years at 5-3, the same mark which Ralph Young had accomplished in 1924. There were even two majors on the trophy list, North Carolina State which went down 40-6 and Mississippi State which surrendered 33-19.

This quick success suggests that there must have been some prior recruiting going on by Young, Kipke, and others. That was correct, but it was "Sleepy Jim" who had molded the squad into a winner, just as Munn was to do nearly two decades later with men brought together by Charley Bachman and his staff.

The Mississippi State victory was accomplished at Starkville, Mississippi, and was the first road win in six years for MSC. Captain Verne Dickeson scintillated for the Spartans with brilliant broken-field running that resulted in three touchdowns. The weather was just as hot as the Spartans.

That was the best which could be said about 1929, but 1930 was something else. Crowley's men went 5-1-2, with major wins over Cincinnati and Colgate and 0-0 ties with Michigan and Detroit. Michigan and Detroit were very strong that season. In fact, the 0-0 tie was the only blemish on the Wolverines' 8-0-1 slate that fall as it claimed a Big Ten co-championship with Northwestern.

A 0-0 tie might sound as dull as kissing your sister, as Duffy Daugherty said years later about tie games, but the 1930 tie with Michigan was not dull for Spartan adherents! State had suffered 14 straight lickings at the hands of Michigan. They had been humiliated by 392 points to nine in that span and had "cow college" ground into their very souls by the sporting gentlemen from the university. That 0-0 score was like manna from heaven, a gold strike, a "yes" from the girl in the rumble seat.

There are all kinds of gimmicks to inspire players to supreme efforts, but few to match the one Crowley came up with that day. Captain-elect and center Harold Smead had been seriously injured in a summer motorcycle accident in Massachusetts, so seriously that he was to miss the whole season of play. Up until the week of the game he was in a Boston hospital recuperating.

Crowley and some cooperative friends had Smead flown to Ann Arbor and moved in a wheel chair to the sidelines. As Spar-

Jim Crowley and pupils.

tan players went on the field, Captain Smead shook hands with each one of them and urged them to top effort. You think that did not fire up the Spartans to outdo themselves?

Alderton, never a timid Spartan advocate, inserted an editorial comment in his game story that he had noted through the years that whenever MSC gave Michigan a tussle it was because Michigan was lousy, never that MSC was good, and that he had heard the "Michigan is terrible" cry arise again from the press jury. Inasmuch as Michigan won all the rest of its games that season, he may have called the shot.

State's line was acclaimed for saving the tie, which was as good as a victory in the eyes of Spartan faithful. Guards Claude Streb and Milton Gross were lauded for continuous harassing of Michigan backs. Senior tackle Don Pridler was called "an immovable obstruction in the Michigan path." Three sophomores playing in their first major games were likened to "tried veterans." They were center Francis Meiers, tackle Ralph Brunette, and end Myrton (Red) Vandermeer.

Michigan substituted freely while State played just 12 men. George Handy substituted for Streb at guard near the end of the second and fourth quarters.

Where was State's offense? Roger Grove, MSC's seasoned senior quarterback, called a very conservative game because of the continuous poor field position his team held. Michigan, meantime, threw the works but could not capitalize.

MSC's other big victory that fall was over Colgate, an undefeated Eastern powerhouse coached by Andy Kerr which boasted an All-American fullback (Len Macaluso) and a great end (John Orsi).

A shivering crowd of about 10,000 Homecoming Day fans in Spartan Stadium was resigned to a 7-7 tie with Colgate. But with less than two minutes to go, a sophomore halfback named Bob Monnett, from Bucyrus, Ohio, brought it alive. He darted through a hole in the Red Raider line, stumbled and nearly fell over an extended enemy arm, regained balance, and weaved his way 62 yards for a game-winning TD. He then kicked the PAT.

"The surprising dash turned the stands into a madhouse of joy," the *State Journal* said in its game account. It was the first of many marvelous exploits by the gifted lad from Bucyrus.

State's first TD that day was on the sensational side, too. Roger Grove plucked an enemy fumble out of the air and ran it 37 yards for a score.

The big one that got away and ruined an undefeated season for State was Georgetown. The Spartans had victories over Alma, Cincinnati, Colgate, and Case already in their trophy room, along with the tie against Michigan. An undefeated season was in prospect. All that lay ahead was Georgetown at Washington and North Dakota State and Detroit at East Lansing. Crowley said openly that he wanted the goose egg in the loss column to remain there. If accomplished, it would mean the first unbeaten season since 1913 and only the third in the school's history.

Spartan fandom reacted predictably. It boiled over in enthusiasm. An 11-car special train was needed to take the team, ROTC band, students, and fans to Washington for State's first night game ever. A tour of the capital was arranged, including a visit to the White House and personal reception by President Herbert Hoover. Even the game site held a special glamour. It was Griffith Stadium, home of the Washington Senators—the place where Walter Johnson had pitched his way into the Hall of Fame; where some recent World Series had been staged; and where all the greats of baseball like Babe Ruth, Lefty Grove, and Lou Gehrig had played.

A noisy crowd of alumni and Michigan natives greeted the team at the railroad station after its all-night Pullman trip. Then came a near disaster, perhaps an omen of what was to develop in the game itself. When the party of 165 from East Lansing arrived at the Roosevelt Hotel (where Frim had made arrangements to stay), it was met by astonished, disbelieving stares. There were no reservations that anyone there knew about. The manager Frim had corresponded with had been fired the week before and, possibly to create embarrassment, had taken all reservations records and correspondence with him.

"The new manager had no information," Frim recalled. "But upon seeing my correspondence, including the guarantee, he got busy and with a little patience all was taken care of. Another crisis, one that could have cost me my job, was past."

The tour of Washington and Mt. Vernon came off in grand style, and the climax Friday morning was the reception on the White House lawn. Everyone shook hands with the President, and the band played the "Fight Song" like never before.

Later came the bad news. That night in Griffith Stadium it did not seem to be the Michigan State team playing. It fell behind 14-0 before it could get untracked. A little scatback

Fullback Eliowitz carries the mail.

named John Scalzi did the dirty work for Georgetown with two brilliant broken field runs. He scampered 58 yards for a TD near the end of the first half and took George Handy's opening kick-off in the second half 82 yards for another.

Finally State got rolling. Abe Eliowitz, Bobby Monnett, and Gerald Breen took turns carrying the ball on a long sustained drive. Eliowitz finally plunged home from the one yard line and Monnett added the point. That was it until with just five seconds remaining on the clock in the final period Jake Fase caught a pass for a touchdown. Monnett missed the try for the extra point so Georgetown won 14-13.

The second half comeback after a very flat beginning had been heartening, however. It led Crowley to say: "When we beat Michigan, I knew we had more than an ordinary team. When we beat Colgate, I was sure of it. But in that last quarter Friday night, I discovered that we had a great team and I'm proud of it."

Crowley's men came back the next week to beat North Dakota State 19-11 and then closed the campaign with a 0-0 tie with Detroit. This added up to a 5-1-2 season, the best since Macklin's time, and raised hopes of still better things to come.

Somehow it was not to be. The 1931 team possessed some talent—Monnett in his greatest season, Eliowitz at fullback, Art Buss at tackle, and others. But there was a quarterbacking problem. Roger Grove had left and Alton Kircher did not arrive until the following season. Some fine veteran players like Don Ridler and Claude Streb were missed. For whatever reason, the team slipped back into the old groove of the 1920s, beating the little · guys but losing to the big ones. A 6-0 revenge over Georgetown at East Lansing was a bright spot, but that game was so rough and took such an injury toll of the Spartans that it may have had something to do with a 15-10 loss to Syracuse at East Lansing the following Saturday. State played 11 men all the way against Georgetown, with Eliowitz scoring the lone TD of the game in the first quarter on a plunge.

The weatherman won the Michigan game; the official score was 0-0 again. A crowd of 51,000 fans was in Michigan Stadium, largest throng ever to see the intrastate classic. But it rained; how it rained. "The weatherman turned his sprinkling can bottom side up," was one newsman's description. "Either team might have won the game but neither had the ability to conquer the sodden gridiron and slippery ball," said another.

Both teams had scoring chances broken up by the elements. Monnett once broke in the open with an intercepted pass but slipped and fell. Eliowitz returned the second half kickoff to midfield and may have gone all the way, except he lost footing. Sophomore tackle Art Buss, destined to become one of State's great ones, fell on a Michigan fumble on Michigan's 38 for the Spartans' best field position of the game. But State fumbled the ball right back again. Statistically the game was very close. Michigan made five first downs and 131 net yards; State made 120 yards and four first downs.

Besides Syracuse, other winners over State that fall were Army (20-7) at West Point and pesky Detroit under Gus Dorais (20-13) in the Motor City.

While the 1931 season was mediocre, that word certainly does not apply to Monnett. The stubby halfback whose forte was zig-zag, stop-and-go running, saved the campaign for Spartan fandom by staging the greatest single-season, one-man scoring tour de force in the school's history. Statistics were not kept with thoroughness and precision in those days, so there exist no reliable records of his rushing yardage total that fall, but it very well could be the all-time tops at State.

74

Monnett, one of greatest all-time backs.

What is known with certainty is that he scored 127 points in just nine games. He rang up 16 touchdowns, 28 points after, and a field goal. In State's 100-0 rout of Ripon he amassed 32 points on four TDs and eight extra points while playing only half the game. Crowley substituted full "elevens'" by quarters in that game, and Monnett played just the first and third stanzas.

Comprehensive statistical records at State date back to 1945. These are the ones used by the sports information office to compile best performance lists and by newsmen to compare current efforts against past ones. But excluded because of their sketchy, fragmentary nature are such as Monnett's 1931 heroics, Paul Smith's kicking in the 1920s, Jerry DaPrato's scoring and rushing exploits in Macklin's days, and Bubbles Hill's achievements under Brewer. They are listed in a separate category of outstanding old-time marks which can be reasonably authenticated.

Monnett's 127 points tops the listed modern record of 110 in 1971 by Eric Allen, and his 32 points against Ripon beats the single-game record of 24 shared by three men: Clinton Jones, Bud Crane, and Eric Allen (twice). It would be interesting to know whether his yardage in any one game would have challenged Allen's all-time national mark of 350 against Purdue in 1971, but there is no way of checking it out.

Incidentally, Eliowitz also scored four touchdowns against Ripon, and Cliff Liberty, substituting for Monnett in the second and fourth quarters, scored three.

Then came the 1932 season. It was so good it would cost State its coaching staff. A 7-1 card topped by back-to-back victories over undefeated Fordham and perennial Eastern power Syracuse, earned for Crowley a call to the prestigious head coaching job at Fordham. He took with him line coach Judge Carberry and a young assistant line coach named Frank Leahy who had just come aboard that fall at MSC.

The only loss of the season was to Michigan 26-0, but that blow to Spartan pride was softened when Michigan went undefeated in eight games and was acclaimed the Big Ten and national champion. Since the Spartans had fought the Wolverines to two straight scoreless ties in 1930 and 1931, the game was rated a tossup. But a superb Michigan team with Harry Newman, Ivy Williamson, Ted Petoskey, Francis Wistert, and Chuck Bernard took care of that erroneous conception.

CASTEEL   CROWLEY   CARBERRY   LEAHY

Frank Leahy was Spartan aide one year.

Fordham was undefeated and had rolled up an average of 50 points against three foes going into the MSC game. News stories out of New York had it that the Rams were confident of winning the national championship. Major Frank Cavanaugh, the distinguished veteran coach of Fordham, had been quoted as saying he did not believe the so-called perfect plays of the Notre Dame system as employed by MSC would produce long runs against his team.

All that ammunition certainly loaded Crowley's psychological gun. He primed his team like never before for the collision with Ed Danowski, Johnny Dell Isola, and associates in New York's famed Polo Grounds—home of John McGraw and his New York Giants.

On the first play from scrimmage, Bobby Monnett sprang clear and zoomed for 80 yards and a touchdown. Later fullback Bernie McNutt rumbled 63 yards for a score, and Abe Eliowitz put the capstone on a terrific offensive performance by pound-

ing 75 yards for a score. So much for the myth that Fordham's defense was impervious to the big play. Sophomore quarterback Al Kircher had a brilliant day, particularly in play selection. He tricked the Rams repeatedly with unexpected calls.

State revealed a spectacular offense to the metropolitan press by employing single and double spinners, passes with laterals on the end and reverses and passes from fake punts. Russell Lay, Frank Butler, Art Buss, and Red Vandermeer were indomitable in the front line trenches. Yet another lineman, a reserve named Joe Ferrari, drew a comment from an assistant coach known for his restraint with the spoken word.

"Ferrari was a madman in there Saturday," said Frank Leahy to a newsman. "He certainly was climbing frames." It may be the only public pronouncement made by the taciturn Leahy in his one season at State.

State hit the national headlines like never before for its upset of Fordham and followed through beautifully the following Saturday at Syracuse. A cold driving rain marred the game and made Abe Eliowitz's brilliant punting a crucial plus for State. A spunky sophomore end named Ed Klewicki set up State's first score by blocking a punt. McNutt scored twice, Monnett and Eliowitz once each, as Crowley's men rolled up a

McNutt run beats Detroit in 1932.

27-13 count over the Orangemen.

The following week George Alderton wrote in a column in the *State Journal:* "The New York World Telegram carried a news story saying that Fordham was casting envious eyes at Michigan State's young coach, Jim Crowley."

Slip Madigan, of St. Mary's of California, was another popular choice for the post about to be vacated by Major Cavanaugh because of poor health, but Alderton's report of the developments in New York was to prove accurate.

The Spartans closed out the 1932 season by finally whipping a Detroit team coached by Gus Dorais (another Notre Dame hero) 7-0 in Spartan Stadium. McNutt scored the only touchdown of the contest, in the first period on a 34-yard run.

Crowley concluded one of the most colorful, albeit very short, coaching eras in State's history and went on to Fordham, the "Seven Blocks of Granite," and coaching immortality.

Crowley was beyond question a great coach. Tim Cohane, the noted author of many sports books and one time sports editor of *Look* magazine, knew him well. He was sports information director at Fordham during Crowley's tenure there. Of Crowley's talents, Cohane said in a recent book entitled *Great College Football Coaches Of The Twenties And Thirties:*

"Everything a great football coach needs, Crowley had in abundance. He was a natural leader, inspiring talker, assiduous recruiter, shrewd psychologist, sportsmanlike image, and manipulator of football's golden key: defense."

In a special piece written for a Michigan State football program in 1962, Cohane recalled the 1932 game with Fordham and Crowley's winning the Fordham post:

"Fordham was so impressed with the Michigan State team as coached by Crowley," he wrote, "that they invited him to succeed The Major. It was a remarkably wise choice. Crowley developed 'The Seven Blocks of Granite' which made the Rams, along with the Minnesota Gophers under Bernie Bierman, the most respected teams of the late thirties-forties."

One of those seven blocks was an intense young Italian-American named Vince Lombardi.

Spartans who played for Crowley have vivid, pungent memories of their coach. Bobby Monnett, perhaps Crowley's brightest star at State, performed three brilliant seasons for Crowley. How Monnett failed to make more than Honorable Mention All-America should be on the conscience of any of the old-time selectors still around.

"Coach Jim Crowley, as a guy, was very witty and liked to make puns at every opportunity," Monnett relates. "He was a great psychologist—able to inspire his teams for each game. He was quick to point out your mistakes in practice and in games. His constructive criticisms were well accepted by the team, and this was specially true with us backfield players. We all knew of his great record at Notre Dame as one of the Four Horsemen. He was good at demonstrating to his backfield men the proper way to run a play like, for example, a half spinner or a full spinner."

Ed Klewicki one summer had a head-to-head altercation with a huge clam shell bucket while working on a construction crew. It took many stitches to sew up his dome. He was lucky he was not killed. This was Crowley's sympathetic comment after the shaven-headed Klewicki made what was for him a poor play in early practice: "Listen, Klewicki, I wouldn't let a little bump on the head affect me."

Crowley came by his "Sleepy Jim" nickname honestly. It became attached to him at Notre Dame. One legend has it that he claimed he was the victim of insomnia and that he once told Rockne: "I sleep all right at night and in the morning, but in the afternoon I toss and turn something awful."

Spartan Max Crall recalls: "We all got a bang out of Jim Crowley. When on road trips he would stay in his berth all day long."

It was the tired-looking slouch that was his natural posture which brought on the "Sleepy" cognomen, according to Klewicki.

Jack Heppinstall remembered some practice scenes that illustrate the point, as reported in a *State Journal* column by Bob Hoerner:

"The football practice field was down near where the baseball diamond is now and there was an old shed there for the equipment. Crowley would stand in the doorway of the shed on cold days and work a yo-yo up and down, up and down. But at the same time he never missed a thing that was going on out there on the practice field. He never carried a play book either. He just stood at the sidelines in that 'sleepy' stance of his and could call out every mistake by every player on every play."

Scaling The Heights

Notre Dame men, either former players or assistant coaches, were eagerly courted for head coaching jobs in the 1930s, just as the "Made In East Lansing" label came to mean guaranteed quality coaching material in the 1950s.

At Michigan State, due to the invigorating consequences of Jim Crowley's regime, it was inevitable that another Notre Dame man would succeed him in 1933 if one could be found who was ready, willing, and able.

One such was located in Charley Bachman, then the head coach at Florida. His Notre Dame pedigree was impeccable, his coaching acumen proven by 16 years as head coach at three schools—Northwestern, Kansas State, and Florida.

Northwestern? Yes, Charley was the 24-year-old "boy coach" of the Wildcats for one season, 1919. He suffered through a loser before moving on to Kansas State and success at a school known as a "graveyard of coaches." His excellent 33-23-8 mark in eight campaigns at remote Manhattan got him the job at Florida. He carried on there in the same winning style, going 27-18-3 in five campaigns prior to answering Ralph Young's call to Michigan State. His 1928 Gator team charged to an 8-1 record, which still stands as that school's best single-season mark.

Bach's Irish heritage was pre-Rockne, but he knew the great man far better than any of his athletes could have. Bachman played tackle with Rockne under Coach Jesse Harper and was a pal of Rockne and Gus Dorais to the extent that they occasionally sneaked out of their dormitory together for a refreshing brew at a nearby pub. Later they became close confi-

Coach Bachman.

dants professionally, as well as family friends. They visited each other frequently and corresponded regularly. They filled many a table cloth with "x's" and "o's" and even lined up sea shells on a Florida beach a few weeks before Rock was killed in a plane crash. Rockne respected Bachman's football savvy and frequently sought his advice.

George Alderton, who moonlighted as sports information director from 1930 to 1944 while performing his regular job as sports editor of the *Lansing State Journal,* wrote this item in his *1938 MSC Football Facts Book* for the information media:

"Word sketch of Bachman: Tall, broad-shouldered, loose-limbed, baldish, grey-eyed, strong-featured, affable, kindly, keen and tireless. He lives football every minute he is awake although he enjoys other sports, particularly track. He wins friends among newspaper and radio people because he is easily interviewed and is sincere. Charley is a capable after-dinner speaker, ad libs exceptionally well over the air, has authored several books on football and is employed by a leading sporting goods manufacturer as a designer of football equipment. He is offense-minded, believing that you can't score touchdowns unless you have the ball. His attack is fundamentally the ortho-dox Notre Dame style although he is continually innovating."

As for the track interest George mentioned in his percep-tive thumbnail picture of the man, Bachman was an excellent field event performer and once briefly held the world record in the discus throw.

Tim Cohane said of Bachman in his *Great College Football Coaches Of The Twenties And Thirties* that "his strong, rugged face suggested a German U-boat commander's, and it was no facade. Charlie was a tough-fibered man, physically and men-tally."

Bachman inherited a good nucleus of players for the 1933 season, including Ed Klewicki, Art Buss, Al Kircher, Bernard McNutt, Charley Butler, and Russ Reynolds. There were some promising newcomers, too, especially a sophomore lineman from Lansing who sparkled in his very first collegiate game. It was against Grinnell of Iowa in Spartan Stadium that the *Lansing State Journal* said of Sid Wagner: "He was constantly in the middle of things, showing speed, a change of pace that let him spoil Grinnell plays in the making and his work at opening holes was as good as any on the field."

That may have been playing the home-town angle, an

excellent idea if one wants to sell newspapers, but Sid Wagner did go on to become State's first major first team All-American selection since DaPrato and Miller in 1915. Tackles Hugh Blacklock in 1916 and Art Buss in 1933 received honorable mentions from major selectors, but the first team designation was more elusive.

Fullback Jim McCrary, one of the rare blacks performing for State or any other major college team in those days, scored one touchdown against Grinnell, and halfback Gerry Jones accounted for a second in a 14-0 victory.

Michigan the following Saturday was something else. Kipke's team was en route to its second straight undefeated rec-

All-American guard Sid Wagner.

ord and another set of Big Ten and national championships. Herm Everhardus was the Wolverines' MVP that fall; center Chuck Bernard and tackle Francis Wistert made All-American. Languishing behind Bernard was a blonde junior center from Grand Rapids named Gerald Ford, at this writing the President of the United States.

Spartan sophomore Kurt Warmbein, another youngster with a great future at State, snared a short pass for his team's lone score in the 20-6 defeat. That in itself caused some elation where the Red Cedar flows. It was the first six-pointer MSC had registered on Michigan since 1916. The parade of zeroes in intervening years had been broken only by Paul Smith's field goal in 1926.

Bach regrouped his forces and the team went on to three straight victories over Illinois Wesleyan, Marquette, and Syracuse, a pair of 0-0 ties with Kansas State and Carnegie Tech, and a concluding 14-0 loss to very tough Detroit. That added up to a respectable 4-2-2 first-season mark under Bachman.

The Marquette game that season was one of the most unusual ever played by State or anyone else. A torrential rain abetted by high winds had pounded the Mid-West for two days. A car ferry plying from Muskegon to Milwaukee across Lake Michigan nearly was lost in the storm. It carried the Michigan State band. The anticipated game attendance had been 5,000, but about ten people were in the stands at the start. The Spartan team, wading in ankle-deep water on the sidelines, was joined by two hardy loyalists, Secretary to the Board John Hannah and State Police Commissioner Oscar Olander. Band director Leonard Falcone took one look at the field and signaled the return of the band busses to the hotel.

With the ball wet and slippery, State declined to play with it and opted to let Marquette do all the work. Hence State punted 20 times, often on first down. It made no first downs and put the ball in play (except by kickoff or punt) exactly six times. It recovered four Marquette fumbles.

The lone touchdown came in the first period when Ed Klewicki crunched a would-be Marquette punter who had fumbled the pass from center on his own ten. The punter recovered the ball just as Klewicki arrived but promptly fumbled again when steamrollered. Sophomore Lou Zarza recovered. On the next play fullback McNutt slid through left tackle on a reverse for the score.

A magnificent goal-line stand in which State held Marquette three times at the one yard line preserved the victory.

Playing end for Marquette was Jerry Liska, an amiable giant who went on to a distinguished career as an Associated Press sportswriter in Chicago. In his early AP days, he worked briefly in Lansing.

Featured in the 27-3 victory over Syracuse that season were Warmbein's 70-yard scoring run; Kircher's passing, including one to Klewicki for a score; and McCrary's fullback blasts, including a 14-yard smash to pay dirt.

1934! That was the memorable year Hitler became chancellor of Germany, the Dionne quintuplets were born, John Dillinger got his comeuppance outside the Biograph Theatre in Chicago, the Detroit Tigers won their first pennant in 25 years, and Michigan State whomped Michigan in football for the first time in 19 seasons.

The only sad part about that rousing 16-0 conquest of the Wolverines was that it nearly got lost in the World Series furor. This was the series matching the St. Louis Cardinals and their Gas House gang of Dizzy and Paul Dean, Pepper Martin, et al

Tough Ed Klewicki ploughs through tackle.

and the splendid Detroit club spearheaded by player-manager Mickey Cochrane, Hank Greenburg, Charley Gehringer, and Schoolboy Rowe. The series went seven games before St. Louis won it, and the Michigan papers were flooded daily with pages and pages of stories, columns, and pictures. The Michigan-MSC game was played at Ann Arbor while the fourth game of the series was on at Navin Field in Detroit. (Guess which received the big coverage!)

Warmbein led the Spartans as they completely snowed the Wolverines. He scored both State touchdowns, intercepted a pass which led to a score, and punted and passed brilliantly. On one series of plays he hit Klewicki on three straight passes, which were good for gains of 18, 10, and 20 yards. Steve Sebo, a peppy sophomore backfield prospect, kicked a field goal which made the score 16 for MSC.

State's defense was so tough Michigan moved into MSC's territory only twice in the game. The Wolverines netted 94 total yards to State's 268.

Everyone shared in the glory. State's line play excelled, with such as Klewicki, Zarza, Zindel, Wagner, and Dahlgren producing brilliant efforts. Zindel, who was called by Kipke the best player on the field for either team, also was the only sophomore starter for State. Among other things he made the tackles on Michigan's first two plays and covered punts so well that Kipke ordered fair catches in the second half rather than attempt runbacks. Perhaps his brilliant performance resulted from a visit he had from assistant coach Tom King just before the game.

"As we were waiting to go out on the field, fully dressed and raring to go," Zindel recalled, "Tom King took me to a secluded spot and began talking to me, calming me down. He said the Michigan team knew I was the only sophomore starter for State and that I would be in trouble all day unless I stopped them cold on the first couple of plays. Unless I wanted to be trampled all day, I had better be first off that line and into the backfield."

King's message obviously hit home.

The Michigan team captain that year was Tom Austin, and the most valuable player was first-string center Gerry Ford. Spartan team members were well aware of Ford. He showed in the scouting report as a good player.

Warmbein has a particularly acute recollection of Ford.

Michigan nemesis Howard Zindel.

"Gerry clipped me," Kurt recalls. "I walked up to him and said, 'if you ever clip me again I will kick your teeth in.'"

Another Spartan, center Archie Ross, had been a teammate of Ford's at Grand Rapids.

Inspired by the Michigan victory, fired up and confident, the Spartans rolled on to an 8-1 season, with important victories over Carnegie Tech, Manhattan, and Marquette in a row and Detroit, Kansas State, and Texas A&M.

The Carnegie Tech game in Spartan Stadium was broadcast on a national network by Graham McNamee with Bill Stern assisting. It probably was State's first national radio exposure.

All-America drums started to beat for Sid Wagner, the lineman from Lansing, after the Carnegie Tech game in which he had played superlatively. "That fellow could play anywhere on the football team," Bachman said of his junior guard. Voices were heard for Warmbein and Klewicki, also.

89

The Marquette team which fell to State 13-7 before a Homecoming crowd of 14,000 people boasted such performers as Ward Cuff, later a pro star with the New York Giants; Ray Buivid; and the Guepe twins, Art and Al. Scores were by Sebo, on a ten-yard scamper, and Klewicki, on the receiving end of a 33-yard pass play from Russ Reynolds.

Detroit—always a tough nut for State—capitulated 7-6 on a 20-yard TD run by Warmbein and the extra point by sophomore Art Brandstatter, who got his first starting chance when regular fullback McCrary was declared out for the season with injuries. Actually, Detroit dominated the game. It had four good touchdown opportunities and two missed field goals. State's lone touchdown resulted from Detroit's failure to down the ball on the opening kickoff. Wagner alertly fell on the ball and State had possession on Detroit's 25. Warmbein carried twice for the score.

A perfect 1934 season was ruined by a lapse at Syracuse against the undefeated and untied Orangemen. Syracuse had a strong team, which included such stars as All-America tackle Jim Steen and halfback Vannie Albanese. Even so, State was favored, but came up flat and expired 10-0.

Then State bashed Manhattan at New York 39-0, but the score was not indicative of the violence of the action. "I can always remember Kurt Warmbein coming off the field," wrote Al Baker, a letterman end on the 1934 team. "He had let his whiskers grow for a few days. He had injured or broken his nose, and blood had been flowing from his nose and had dried in his whiskers. He had also injured his shoulder and it was hanging. It proved one thing: the score doesn't indicate how difficult a game can be."

1935! Another eventful year in which Hitler rejected the Versailles Treaty and started arming Germany, Will Rogers and Wiley Post were killed in an Alaskan airplane accident, Mussolini's armies invaded Ethiopia, Congress passed the Social Security Act, the Detroit Tigers won another pennant (for crying out loud!) and played the World Series finale with Chicago—opposite the Michigan vs. Michigan State football game.

Once again the MSU-Michigan game got second billing around the state and nothing nationally, which was a pity from the Spartan standpoint because the game was a rout for State 25-6. The victory marked the first time in the long, one-sided series that MSC had won twice in a row.

State scored on the eighth play of the game after having kicked off to Michigan. Michigan had to punt and a 29-yard dash by Brandstatter, a Warmbein to Sebo pass for 22 yards, and finally a Brandstatter plunge for the score produced the six points. Dick Colina returned a Michigan punt 60 yards for a score to make it 13-6 at the half.

In the second half Warmbein threw to Colina for a touchdown, and sophomore "Agony" Al Agett cut outside Michigan's left tackle and sprinted 47 yards for the final score.

Plaudits were heaped on the Spartans. Brandstatter led in rushing with 57 yards on ten carries. Veteran guard Sid Wagner, on his way to All-America selection by United Press, *Liberty* magazine, International News Service, and others, fought a tremendous game up front, as did sophomore Jake Dahlgren and senior ends Lou Zarza and Bob Allman. Warmbein's triple threat play and Colina's quarterbacking were outstanding.

Howard Zindel was praised for a second straight great game at Ann Arbor. "He was in the Wolverine backfield so often that the Michigan blockers in the latter part of the game seemed to have given up trying to keep him out of the plays," said one press account.

State's other notable victory in its 6-2 season was against a powerful Temple team coached by the legendary Glenn (Pop) Warner. The Owls had a 15-game undefeated string going when Bachman's band showed up in Philadelphia with its 4-1 slate. Temple had won six straight in 1935 after having gone undefeated through a nine-game schedule in 1934.

Temple had a gimmick which undoubtedly had helped it on its way to such a record, along with some outstanding players like fullback Dave Smukler. The very articulate Frank Gaines, an end on that Spartan team and years later honored by *Sports Illustrated* on one of its Silver Anniversary All-America teams, tells of it this way:

"This was before football teams had to have numbers on both the front and back of their uniforms and helmets. Pop Warner used to take advantage of this situation by lining up his football team with the center over the ball, nine players in a line one yard behind the center, and one back, the fullback, about five yards behind this group. They all had their heads down and you couldn't tell a lineman from a backfield man. When they shifted into position, their line could be unbalanced to the right or the left and their backs would be already in the spot they

91

wanted them to be. In one second they could snap the ball before the defense had a chance to move to counter the formation.

"Charlie Bachman, to combat this, gave the two guards and two tackles on State's team a piece of black chalk. After the first play was over, all of a sudden four Temple men appeared with big black "X's" on the front of their jerseys as well as on their sleeves and it was then possible for us to identify that these were the backfield men.

"I can still see Sid Wagner walking up to one of their backs and turning him around and with this black chalk making a big black 'X' on his shirt with the man standing in complete amazement."

State's countermeasure did not seem to help too much at first. In fact, it might be conceived that it had backfired. Temple, thoroughly aroused, clearly outplayed State in the first half and went to the dressing room at intermission ahead 7-0.

Then Bachman threw another curve at the Owls. Despite being down by a touchdown, he started a team of reserves in the second half. This unit outplayed Temple in the third period but did not score. It may have done some real psychological damage to Temple, however, for when the Michigan State regulars came back at the start of the fourth period, they really went to town.

This shall always be remembered as the "Brandstatter period." Art Brandstatter took personal charge of things and produced what John Hannah years later called the greatest performance he had seen from a Spartan.

First came a 59-yard touchdown run of classic beauty. Art broke over his own right tackle and cut sharply left, reversing his field and spearing through the Temple secondary into open country. He outran everyone to pay dirt. But the extra point was missed and State still was down 7-6.

Later, with the ball on the Temple 18, Art acted again. He bolted over left tackle and headed straight for the corner. There was not much of a hole and he called on pure strength and resolve. Six would-be tacklers were strewn in his wake, one of them unconscious. All this impact had slowed his momentum considerably, and other Temple defenders flung themselves on him from behind. He carried several a few more yards and finally collapsed on the three. Moments later Zarza took the ball on State's greatly feared end-around play and carried into

Strong 1935 backfield of (left to right) Dick Colina, Art Brand-statter, Steve Sebo, and Kurt Warmbein.

the end zone for victory.

No wonder that for long thereafter, whenever Warner met anyone from MSC, he inquired, "Has that Brandstatter graduated yet?"

The Marquette game, Homecoming at State that fall, was another memorable affair for several reasons. The stadium officially was named for John Macklin, who returned for the day and participated in pregame ceremonies. The ostensible reason for this name change was to honor the old coach on the 20th anniversary of his final season at MAC and his greatest victory over Michigan. But cynical gossip mongers bruited it about that the college had an ulterior motive. Macklin had married the daughter of one of the big coal barons in Pennsylvania and had left coaching to become an executive in the company, reputedly worth some $60 million. The whisperers alleged that the stadium name change was made to buttress the hope that one day, perhaps in his will, Macklin would leave a hefty bequest to the old school. Be that as it may, the fact is that in 1957, not too long after Macklin's death and estate settlement with no gift for State, the football plant's name was changed back to Spartan Stadium, which it remains today.

The game itself ended in a 13-7 loss for MSU, but a Spar-

tan victory came very close to reality on a heart-stopping play in the final minute. The capacity crowd of 20,000, largest throng in Macklin Stadium since the 1924 dedication game with Michigan, saw this action as described by George Alderton in the *State Journal* the next day:

"In the last minute of play, Ward Cuff of Marquette fumbled the ball in a buck into the line. Lou Zarza, left end for State, caught the ball on the fly and headed for the goal line. His legs weary from play, he ran 20 yards and then decided that Ray Buivid, the only Hilltop player who had a chance at him, was going to tackle him. So Zarza tried a lateral that was fumbled by Brandstatter...."

In an adjoining column, George wrote: "Raw drama on parade,...glory beckoning to Lou Zarza in the last minute, and Lou, so very, very tired that his legs began to crumple beneath him...his desperate lateral pass...the best that Brandstatter could do was to throw up his hands and bat the ball."

Well, that play has become perhaps the most argued hot-stove-league subject in State's early gridiron history. Should Zarza have kept the ball or tossed it? Was Buivid really close enough to Zarza to tackle him? Did Brandstatter have a reason-

Agony Al Agett rambles against Kansas.

able chance to catch the ball? Or was it a bad flip that hit Art on the helmet? Did he get his hand on it at all?

Detroit papers blasted Zarza, particularly the *Free Press* in an article written by Eddie Edgar. The claim by many fans was that Zarza could have gone all the way and tied the game. Then an extra-point conversion would have won it.

This debate, alive even today among older alumni and fans, is a healthy indicator of the hold collegiate football has on its followers, the seriousness with which they analyze and argue. The game will be in trouble when such concern slackens or ceases.

The sad part in this particular instance is best expressed in Lou's own recent words: "Of all the football I played for Michigan State, people remember me specifically as the fellow who passed off a dumb lateral against Marquette." This is regrettable for Zarza was one of the finest players in one of the most brilliant eras of Michigan State football and later became a good pro player and excellent coach.

In 1936 Marquette wrecked an undefeated season for MSC with another 13-7 victory before the home folks in Macklin Stadium, but the rest of the campaign was just dandy. State added to its rapidly growing national reputation by whipping Michigan for the third straight time and taking into camp other such name teams as Carnegie Tech, Missouri, and Kansas. It also scored victories over clubs from Wayne State and Arizona and settled for ties with Boston College and Temple.

When a team has achieved the status that its victories are accepted without surprise or undue celebration and its losses are called upsets, then it is really big time. This had happened to State by 1936.

A 21-7 victory over Michigan a decade before would have been cause for burning down the entire state capitol, but more sophisticated Aggie students, alumni, and fans took it in stride, while Michigan men bemoaned their years of adversity and made Kipke's position in Ann Arbor an uncomfortable one.

Bachman even pulled one of his old daring gambits by

Running track eliminated, stadium seated 35,000 in 1930s.

starting a team of reserves in the second half, although the score was 7-7 at intermission. But what reserves! Long-legged sophomore John Pingel (in for Agett), sophomore fullback George Kovacich (in for Brandstatter), and veteran reserve quarterback Fred Ziegel led a third period touchdown charge. Pingel scored on a run from the Michigan 12.

All through the game Bachman substituted player after player, something approaching foolhardy heresy at the time.

Frank Gaines had started the victory ball rolling with a touchdown in the first period, after veteran tackle Julius Sleder set it up by recovering a fumble.

"I guess my biggest thrill in college," Frank relates, "was in scoring that first touchdown against Michigan in 1936 on an end-around play two minutes after the game had started. It was really a tribute to Art Brandstatter since Michigan's defenses were set up to try to stop his reverse play."

Another touchdown that day was an 82-yard romp by Agett, who had to beat only one Wolverine. Every other one who might have gotten close to Al was knocked off his feet by the great blocking that typified the game.

The top of the football mountain, which MSC had been scaling so assiduously under Crowley and Bachman, was reached in 1937. Every hope of every Spartan loyalist was fulfilled with a fourth straight victory over Michigan, a major All-America first team selection, and a splendid 8-1 campaign that resulted in the school's first bowl bid.

Every hope, that is, except one. For the fifth time in eight seasons a single stumble cost an undefeated record. As in most of the other instances, it was a frustrating loss to a team against which State had been favored.

But to the good news first. The Spartans triumphed 19-14 over the Wolverines in a game even more rugged and gut-wrenching than the bare score suggests. State made the scoreboard first, but twice Michigan forged ahead at 7-6 and 14-13. Each time MSC clawed back, finally to prevail. The 71,800 fans who bulged the Ann Arbor stands were alternately frenzied and limp from the electrifying action. It had to be one of the finest games ever played in the historic series.

Gene Ciolek thrilled the crowd with an 89-yard gallop to the "promised land." The extra point was missed.

Bachman had started his second team at the half as he had so often in the past, but the top eleven soon came back in. It put together a 74-yard scoring drive, the big effort of which was a 30-yard pass play (Pingel to Ole Nelson) for the score. This time the point was converted and it was 13-7 for State.

Moments later Pingel threaded the needle on a pass and hit Nelson's bushel-basket hands amid a swarm of defenders inside the Michigan 40. On the next play, the fourth after the kickoff, John faded to midfield, spotted Nelson deep in Michigan territory, and fired. Ole caught the ball with an heroic leap at about the 25 yard line and ran it home for the winning score.

Quarterback Halbert related that Nelson had gotten really mad for a change.

"Nelson, our left end, was a man who could not understand the enmity we could cook up for our foes in the short time we knew them," Halbert said. "However, on this day a Michigan man had purposely kicked Ole in the head as he lay on the ground, and for the first time Ole wanted to retaliate. He asked for button hook pass No. 79. He caught it and went down to the 25. Still mad, he said 'again' and went over for a TD."

Gaines summed it up well for all the Spartan seniors in that game and the seniors of the year before when he said: "Since then I have been able, because we beat Michigan in that game, to say for the rest of my life that I graduated from Michigan State after playing three years of football against Michigan and beating them every year; I have won a number of bets on this fact. Hardly anyone will believe me."

Such a splendid victory over a cherished foe can instill a winning momentum which makes a team almost impossible to stop. On the other hand, it sometimes can be followed by a colossal letdown and disaster. The Saturday after mastering the Wolverines, Bachman's men lost to a humpty-dumpty Manhattan team in New York 3-0.

"Michigan State College football moved mournfully through its annual depression period here Saturday afternoon," wrote Alderton somewhat bitterly in the *State Journal* the next day. George had seen it happen so often before—Marquette in 1936, Boston College in 1935, and Syracuse in 1934—for some examples of dire frustration. State kept coming so close to tremendous unbeaten seasons without bagging one.

But State finished the 1937 season well. Pingel had one of his greatest days in a 21-7 decision over Marquette. He scored all three Spartan TDs, including an 80-yard beauty in which his blockers wiped out Marquette completely and "Long John" streaked home alone ahead of a convoy of Gold and Black-clad Spartan athletes.

Then another able Temple team, unbeaten well into November, was edged 13-6. It took two fourth-period touchdowns to do it, too. The first was engineered by two first-year players, Helge Pearson and Tom McShannock. Pearson leaped to block a Temple punt, and McShannock fell on it in the Owls' end zone for the score. Then, with five minutes remaining and the score tied 6-6, "Old Reliable" Ole Nelson took a forward pass behind the line of scrimmage and swept down the left flank for 30 yards and the victory.

So once again the bowl breezes, which had been stilled by the Manhattan doldrums, started blowing. After climactic victories over Carnegie Tech and San Francisco, the breezes grew into high winds wafting the scent of oranges.

Sour Oranges

Coach Bachman was called off the train bringing his team home from the 1937 season finale with San Francisco. A telephone call was holding for him in the station master's office at Spokane, Washington. On the other end was an official of the Orange Bowl who extended an invitation for Michigan State to participate in the January 1, 1938, game.

Bach quickly polled team members and fired the word "yes" back to Miami, pending approval by college officials back home.

It did not take a lot of mulling over. This was the biggest honor that had ever been extended the college in athletics.

Bowls were just getting started. The Rose Bowl, the grand-pappy of them all, had been in business since 1902; but the Orange and Sugar Bowls debuted in 1935, the Sun Bowl in 1936, and Cotton Bowl in 1937. Because of the Big Ten ban on bowl games, only Michigan and Ohio State ever had been to postseason classics. Both had been in the Rose Bowl years before, Michigan in 1902 and Ohio State in 1921. So MSC had joined the bowl pioneers long before many bigger names became involved.

An excited student body and college community made ready to welcome the football team home from California. *State News* columnist George Maskin exulted that State finally had become a national football power. It was speculated, probably accurately, that Dick Richards, then owner of the Detroit Lions, and Harry Wismer, WJR sportscaster who had been a player for Bachman at Florida and came with him to Michigan State, had a hand in influencing the Orange Bowl decision in favor of the Spartans.

President Shaw announced all classes would be optional between 2:45 and 4:00 p.m. on December 2 to permit a proper welcome home to the team.

A police-escorted motorcade of about 1,000 people plus the cheerleaders, the ROTC band, and a portable speaker's platform moved from the Student Union Building to the Grand Trunk station in Lansing. Another thousand later joined the festivities at the big rally in the gym back on campus.

The bowl bid attracted more kudos than ever before. Pingel, still a year away from major All-America laurels, was named to the International News Service's third All-America team, the AP's second unit, and to honorable mention by the UP. Tackle Fred Schroeder made the NEA All-West team, and Pingel and Ole Nelson were second unit choices. Gene Ciolek received honorable mention on the Grantland Rice and *Newsweek* All-Americas.

Announcement that the Auburn Tigers, a 5-3-2 team, would be MSC's foe in the bowl came a few days later. This news was cheered by Spartan players, possibly under the impression the Tigers would not be as tough as some of the other teams that had been talked about, such as Texas Christian, North Carolina, and Fordham.

Coach Bachman attempted to put things back in focus by saying, "Auburn is the toughest eleven below the Mason-Dixon line. They couldn't have picked a harder opponent for us. Any team that can hold Villanova to a scoreless tie and beat Tennessee, Mississippi State, and Georgia Tech by big margins isn't to be considered a pushover. We wanted to play a good, strong football team and we're going to get that opportunity in this game."

Team travel plans were announced. The squad would leave East Lansing on Monday, December 20, and go by various trains via Jackson, Detroit, stops in Tennessee, and finally to a junction point in Florida called Waldo. There the team would jolt by bus to Bachman's old headquarters at the University of Florida at Gainesville, where it would practice for four days. Christmas Day would be spent there, and the trip to Miami would be made on the 26th.

A squad of 41 players, largest ever to travel to an out-of-state game, started work indoors on the tanbark of Demonstration Hall. Snow covered the campus and made any outdoor

State's Orange Bowl team.

drills impossible.

There was a negative aspect to the game which surfaced, but it never got an audience in the general enthusiastic din of preparations to go to Miami. It was that Auburn was not the happiest choice for State's opponent from the standpoint of staging a lively, exciting game. It so happened that the Auburn coach was Jack Meagher, another Notre Dame product playing the Irish system sanctified by Rockne. It was recalled that Crowley once had said, "There's little fun in going against your own stuff in a game. Each team knows exactly what the other is trying to do, and the defense is nearly perfect. A dull game results when two evenly matched teams meet."

The four days on the University of Florida campus were marked by excellent practices, perhaps too good.

"I always felt that the Spartans left their game back at Gainesville," Spartan oracle Alderton recalled years later. "They staged a final scrimmage there that shook the countryside. The divided squad took off in a bruising intrasquad game that left the natives, accustomed to more of the touch-and-pass brand of Southern football, agape. Those who were passed into the enclosure to witness the blood-letting went away shaking their heads."

"We play football down here—pretty good football, too—but nothing like that. That's mayhem," exclaimed one of the onlookers.

Then it was on to Miami to be met at the station by an official reception committee including Ted Husing, who was to broadcast the game on a national network. There was another interesting athletic event going on at the time, the Miami Open pro golf tournament. The same newspaper editions which carried stories of the Spartans' arrival in Miami also carried reports of Sam Snead winning the Miami Open and pocketing first prize money of $500. It raised his 1937 total earnings to a nifty $10,243.

Practices at Miami High School did not go well. The ground was dry and very hard. Players complained of sore feet. The heat was terrific. There was some fun, including sight-seeing and social events, such as an elegant luncheon thrown for the team and official party at the exclusive Surf Club by C. P. Bentley, of Owosso.

There also was time for a laugh or two. Fullback Usif Haney, a veritable powerhouse of a man, had hurt his leg late in the regular season, something teammates had believed impossible. They kidded him unmercifully about it, even alleging he was now so slow guards were catching him from behind.

At practice in Miami, Usif was noted staring skyward. "What," he said, "do you suppose that old buzzard is circling around up there for?" A tow-headed halfback named Jack Coolidge made the team-convulsing answer: "He probably has sighted that bum leg of yours."

The dopesters had their innings and favored Michigan State to win. State was made anywhere from a one to seven-point favorite. Said Hy Aronstam of the United Press: "It looks like the Yanks again in this annual North-South affair. Both teams are strong offensively and defensively, but form favors State. Johnny Pingel, Michigan State's triple-threat halfback, will bring victory."

A pregame story from the Associated Press noted that "Orange Bowl officials predicted Miami's new $360,000 stadium would be filled to its 23,000 capacity, but other observers were inclined to believe the attendance would fall slightly short of that figure. Sports fans were forced to decide between the game and a holiday racing program at Tropical Park."

The story also noted that the Spartans' potent passing combination of Pingel to Nelson appeared disrupted by an ankle injury to Nelson.

Later the story related that "the most colorful pageantry in Orange Bowl annals was planned for the intermission. Twelve bands and five drill teams were to parade with a color guard carrying the five flags that have figured in Florida history." So it was a big show, and the Spartans were lucky and happy to be there, but they lost.

Auburn won 6-0 and MSC's warriors fought a very lackadaisical battle. Those who prophesized the game would be dull were right. Those who picked Michigan State to win were wrong. Coach Bachman, when he said things were not going well in practice, knew what he was talking about.

All-American John Pingel and team captain Harry (Fire Chief) Speelman meet the Orange Bowl queen.

"Auburn's Plainsmen pushed the Michigan State football team all over the Orange Bowl today," the Associated Press's Larry Rollins wrote for his national audience, "but clicked with just one scoring thrust for a 6-0 victory, the first by a Southern squad in the four years the New Year's game has been played."

Auburn halfback Ralph O'Gwynne did State in with a one-yard second period plunge following a vital pass reception he made from George Kenmore.

Spartan advocate George Alderton said simply: "Auburn outplayed MSC all day." He added that a "big and fast-charging Auburn line bottled up Spartan running and stifled State's passing" and that "Eddie Pearce's 29-yard run on which he almost got away was State's lone chance to score."

Pingel's triple-threat brilliance was nullified by vicious Auburn tackling. Nelson's bad ankle was a factor.

Apparently Auburn had obtained wonderful scouting. State threw a new flanker attack at the Plainsmen, but the Auburn athletes never batted an eye over the threat. They seemed to know all about it.

One of the fine things for State that unhappy day was the work of the "S" line of captain Harry Speelman, Nelson Schrader, Fred Schroeder, and Howard Swartz. After all, Auburn only scored six points.

Perhaps the criticism which rankled most among Spartan fans was that leveled by Husing in his national broadcast. He really let State's team have whip lashes for a lack-lustre performance and State fans thought his criticism as described by Alderton in a back home column, "discourteous and definitely unsportsmanlike."

The disappointment was deep but not too long-lasting. Wiser, cooler heads finally prevailed in their judgment that the important thing was not the winning or losing but having gotten there. In that respect both Auburn and Michigan State were winners. The game itself in that context was an exhibition between two fine teams being honored for outstanding seasons.

Slide Down And Wartime Blues

The fine 1937 season and Orange Bowl participation was . one of the glowing achievements in Spartan football annals. It was the culmination of a nine-year building effort begun with four Crowley teams and finished with five Bachman ensembles.

Many Spartan supporters may have felt that the crest which had been achieved would be a plateau on which they and their favorite athletes would loll indefinitely, feasting happily on the bounteous produce of a rich land. But the crest turned out to be a peak, with an up side and a down side. In one step State's football fortunes went over the top and slid some distance down.

Much was expected of the 1938 team. John Pingel, Ole Nelson, Dave Diehl, Eddie Pearce, Usif Haney, Lyle Rockenbach, Les Bruckner, Al Diebold, George Kovacich, and Mike Kinek were all back. And there were some promising rookies on the scene, fellows like Paul Griffeth, Jack Amon, Ed Abdo, and Bruce Blackburn. Another great record seemed all but assured.

But there is a verity in football, as in most aspects of life, which says that nothing remains constant. When something or someone stops improving, deterioration begins. The slide down can be a lot faster than the climb up. That may have had some bearing on State's case. Another relevant factor may have been the arrival in Ann Arbor of a vigorous new regime headed by Fritz Crisler, which quickly cut into Spartan recruiting successes. People like Tom Harmon, Forest Evashevski, Bob Westfall, and Ralph Heikkinen were going to Michigan. Increasingly difficult schedules also may have played a part, and basically, it may have been a simple matter of the cycle turning against

State for awhile.

However one explains it, the fact remains that after 1937, the season records began to contain three or more losses for the first time under Bachman. From 1938 through 1942, it was 6-3, 4-4-1, 3-4-1, 5-3-1 and 4-3-2. In 1943, intercollegiate football was abandoned for a year because of the war.

None of these years was really disastrous; the wolves did little howling. It always seemed as if State had just barely missed and that next year would surely be different. There were frequent thrilling victories and outstanding players were numerous.

The 1938 season started as if the Spartan juggernaut was still in high gear. It rolled over Wayne State 34-6 in the opener before an all-time record throng of 22,000 in Macklin Field. Bachman alternated three teams. Gene Ciolek scored two touchdowns.

But next week was different. Michigan won 14-0 at Ann Arbor, snapping the four-game Spartan string and starting one of its own which was not to end until a Biggie Munn team broke through in 1950.

Then three straight victories brought the glow back to Spartan cheeks and revived hopes for a big killing which might bring another bowl bid.

The most storied one was a 26-0 smashing of strong West Virginia at Morgantown. Dave Diehl had one of his finest days as a Spartan end with two touchdowns and tremendous defensive play which repeatedly snarled Engineer running efforts. Sophomore guard Paul Griffeth did the heavy work on the first Diehl score by blocking a kick in the West Virginia end zone. The ball flew high in the air, and Dansville Dave snared it like an outfielder for the TD. Later he picked off an errant pass and ran it home for a counter. The scoring was rounded out by Pingel on a plunge and a beauty of a 66-yard pass interception return by little Eddie Pearce.

Quarterback Don Rossi recalls an off-beat incident from the game.

"We had just scored," Rossi says, "when a West Virginia player held up the game by running up into the stands and beating the hell out of a guy who was booing his team and sitting with the player's girl. He hurried right back for the kickoff."

Football trips were taken mostly by train and were leisurely, fun-filled affairs. Eating in the plush dining cars was very educational for some of the youngsters. Rossi recalls sitting at dinner on the West Virginia trip with tackle Helge Pearson from Norway, Michigan. After studying the menu for awhile, Pearson announced that he was not going to have that filet mignon because he did not care much for fish. Another Spartan on that trip astonished one of the waiters by ordering pie a la mode with ice cream.

It was on another train trip that Rossi claims a first.

"I had a berth above Dr. John Hannah, who at the time was secretary of the college," Rossi relates. "After the first night on the train I jumped out of my berth naked as a jay bird to get dressed just as two lovely ladies walked by. There wasn't anything I could do but keep getting dressed. This was the start of streaking in railroad trains back in the late '30s. I thought Dr. Hannah was going to have a fit laughing."

Johnny Pingel, the backfield ace, who made All-American and later the Hall of Fame, was identified by veteran trainer Jack Heppinstall as the finest all-around football player he had seen at State. Pingel could do everything a modern day back is required to do; in addition he was the master of a lost art— quick kicking. The kick was a part of the offensive repertoire of State and other teams in those days. That helps account for Pingel's 99 punts, many of them quick kicks, during the 1938 season. That total plus his kicking yardage (4,138) are the oldest marks in the NCAA records book.

"Johnny Pingel," said Bachman, "was the best quick kicker I ever coached. His kicks naturally went low, and many of them went 70 yards. Many rolled over the goal line. Usually there was no return by the safety. We always opened up a hole over center in order for a low kick to go through or the kicker to convert the play into a run if the ball was mishandled."

After 1938, State suffered severe personnel losses, including Pingel. The result was a 4-4-1 campaign in 1939 that could boast only two major victories, 14-3 over Syracuse and 18-7 over Temple. The Spartans' back was broken early when, after an easy opening victory over Wayne, they lost to Michigan, Marquette, and Purdue in a row.

Harmon, nearing the peak of his powers, had a hand in all four TDs scored by the Wolverines in a 26-13 victory. He passed for two and set up the other two with brilliant runs in which, according to one writer, "he raced like a wild steer." State center Bill Batchelor achieved a lineman's dream by intercepting a Michigan pass and running it in for a score. State's other six-pointer was engineered on a pass and run play from sophomore halfback Bill Kennedy to Wyman Davis that carried 65 yards to pay dirt.

It is often debated whether players really hear crowd sounds and public address announcements or whether they are so wrapped up in the game that they are oblivious to anything else. Kennedy has a memoir from the Michigan game which throws some light on the subject.

"Michigan was on our four yard line in the second quarter when the field announcer said that Joe DiMaggio had just hit a home run in the World Series," Kennedy relates. "Tony Arena, who was backing up the left side of the line, hollered 'The wop has hit another one.' Just then Michigan started a play which sent Harmon right over Arena for a score." Kennedy goes on to say he thought Tony was the best Spartan player of his time.

The 1940 team brought the first losing record to East Lansing in 12 years. It was 3-4-1, the same as Kipke's card in 1929. But the team managed to triumph over three major clubs (Purdue, Kansas State, and West Virginia) and put up a remarkable battle against one of Crisler's finest Michigan teams before bowing 21-14. That outfit had Evashevski and Harmon as seniors and Bob Westfall, Davey Nelson, Ed Frutig, and Al Wistert among others.

Michigan scored first and stayed ahead throughout, thanks to the Harmon magic. He scored all 21 points for the Wolverines, the touchdowns coming on runs of 13, 10, and 2 yards. State nearly matched him with a sophomore surprise star of its own, a 5-8, 157-pound scatback named Walt Pawlowski. His stock in trade was quick starting, fair speed, gymnastic jumping, and suction cup hands. He made two circus pass catches near the goal line for touchdowns and wrote his name indelibly on the list of the series' greats.

A prized victory was recorded over Purdue, the first ever over a Big Ten team at East Lansing. The score was 20-7, the same score as the year before at Lafayette, Indiana, when the Boilermakers won. State's first two touchdowns came on passes from Mike Schelb to Pawlowski and Wyman Davis to Lew Smiley. The final one was produced on a run by a sophomore halfback named Chuck Carey, who had twin brothers at home in Charlevoix who one day would make blazing headlines for

State. Co-captain and fullback Jack Amon was praised for the best game of his career.

Victories over Marquette, Temple, and West Virginia spiced the 5-3-1 record in 1941.

The unpleasant surprise of the campaign had to be Missouri, which beat MSC 19-0 with the split-T invented by its coach Don Faurot. Three great backs, Bob Steuber, Red Wade, and Harry Ice, did the damage that day on Macklin Field.

A 46-0 conquest of Temple was the positive surprise of the campaign. The Owls had been beaten only once and had such terrific players as All-American Andy Tomasic at halfback, Francis (Killer) Kilroy at tackle, and Al Drulis at quarterback.

Mike Schelb scored two touchdowns on consecutive punt runbacks. End Bob Friedlund took a pass from Dick Kieppe for 24 yards and a score. Lansing's Bob Sherman jammed home two and Wyman Davis and Walt (The Champ) Pawlowski, one each. It was a rout, the worst lacing ever absorbed by a Temple team.

But the last game, a 14-12 victory over West Virginia at Morgantown, was the classic of that fall. Memoirs from players indicate it to be a bruising brawl with numerous injuries to both clubs.

Bill Kennedy, who later played with the Detroit Lions, El Toro Marines, and the Boston Yanks, says that "in all my football career I have never played in a game that was as tough, aggressive, and hard-hitting as that one." Bill, whose son Marty joined the Spartan football ranks as a freshman guard in 1974, also called it the most satisfying victory of his college days.

Bob Friedlund, a senior that season, recalls a moment after the West Virginia game: "I stood on the field realizing that I would never again play college football. I am not ashamed to say I wept."

He could have been weeping for all of us. The season ended on November 29. Just eight days later the holocaust of war was to engulf the country when the Japanese struck Pearl Harbor.

State still had some pretty good football talent returning in 1942. College students generally were receiving educational deferments, and many of the athletes were advanced ROTC students. On the other hand, State had missed out on navy and air force recruiting programs, the kind that brought so many fine athletes into Michigan and other schools. MSC did have several army programs, but the army had established a wartime prohibition on inter-base athletic competition. The navy and air force encouraged it, which is why North Carolina Pre-Flight, Randolph Field, Great Lakes Naval Training Station, Bainbridge Navy, El Toro Marines, and others built football empires. Fortunate colleges and universities such as Michigan and Missouri also cashed in, but Michigan State was among those that suffered.

But in 1942 the full impact of the war had not yet been felt. State capped a 4-3-2 season against very strong competition with a stunning upset of a Great Lakes Naval Training Station team which was loaded with such ex-college and pro stars as Bruce Smith, Bob Schweiger, Pete Kmetovic, Rudy Mucha, and Carl Mulleneaux. Their starting line averaged 218 pounds per man, enormous for those days.

Practically no one gave the Spartans a chance, not even the coach. Bachman told the Lansing Rotary Club on Friday before the game that if his team won, he would wade across the Red Cedar River at high noon Sunday.

The Spartans overcame the sailors' muscle with speed and agility. A crowd of 12,000 fans whooped with delight in Macklin Field as Lansing's Dick Kieppe played one of his finest games to lead the Spartans to the 14-0 triumph. The Spartan touchdowns were scored by Walt Pawlowski, flanker and prime target for Kieppe passes, and Russ Gilpin, a sophomore quarterback. State's line, led by co-captain Dick Mangrum, George Radulescu, Ken Balge, and Bob Fischer, played a stellar game.

Promptly at noon the next day a car pulled up to the river near the bridge by the women's gymnasium, and a smiling Bachman got out. He acknowledged the cheers of the several hundred fans gathered on both banks, stepped into the water—pants, shoes, and all—and waded through the waist-deep stream.

A nine-game schedule was arranged for 1943, but it was never played. Competition was cancelled because 134 of 135 varsity and freshmen football players expected to be in school that fall were called into active service. However, 3,500 army trainees sent to MSC provided the manpower for a five-team campus league that fall. The squads practiced 50 minutes each day as part of their regular army schedule and played doubleheaders in Macklin Field each Saturday. Michigan State was the only college known to have sponsored campus leagues for army trainees.

Bachman did not let the year go to waste. He coached at Camp Grant and developed the flying-Z offense which he

Army units had 1943 campus league.

installed at Michigan State the following fall. Michigan State reinstated varsity football the next year because it felt football was necessary for student morale. A schedule was arranged compatible with the personnel—all 17-year-olds or 4-F's.

Bachman's flying-Z, a controversial system of play which Bach defends vigorously to this day, was born in 1942 when Edo Mencotti ran the wrong way on a spinner play in a practice scrimmage.

Bachman tells it this way:

"It was a half spinner play designed as an end run for halfback Dick Kieppe. I was standing behind the defensive team, and the first time Mencotti made his mistake, I momentarily lost sight of the ball.

"When the play was repeated, I noted that Mencotti, instead of running behind Kieppe and feinting to receive the ball, was in front of him feinting a fullback buck to the weak side.

"Rehearsal showed that the ball had been screened, and there started the idea of building an offense with the threat of the fullback hitting the line on each play."

Bach worked with the theory until it blossomed into a book published in 1969 entitled *The Modern Notre Dame Formation.*

In a letter to the writer dated September 4, 1974, Bach wrote:

112

"My book has been slow in catching on, but it will have its day. Michigan State gave to football in the early 1940s what has today been called play-action football—that is, that every play starts as a threat into the line. Strangely enough, our formation is the only one that has been able to run the so-called triple option play with good success. With us the play is a single option on the defensive end."

State flashed the new flying-Z formation in the 1944 opener against Scranton and won 40-12. Big plays included an 84-yard return of the opening kickoff of the second half by new fullback Jack Breslin for an apparent touchdown; however, it was called back for a holding penalty. A short time later Breslin cashed one on a plunge from the four yard line. Bob Bruegger, an impressive freshman, ran 67 yards for a score. Then Breslin scored another one on a plunge. Fred Aronson passed to Don Grondzak for another.

Wayne State was demolished 32-0 with Breslin accounting for 102 of his team's 138 yards rushing in the first half. He scored two touchdowns on smashes of 18 and 13 yards.

Maryland was a double victim that fall as State played a rare home-and-home pair with the Terps. The first one, played at College Park, Maryland, on a rainy Friday night in October, has special meaning for the writer. He covered that game for the Associated Press out of Baltimore, Maryland, and suffered through the hardest downpour and muddiest mess of a football contest in his experience. There was no glass front to the press box and the rain swept in, in drenching sheets that disintegrated the paper in his typewriter.

After the first play or two, all numbers on players' jerseys were obliterated by the ooze that covered the field. George Alderton, who was reporting the game for the *Lansing State Journal*, called out the names of Michigan State players he could identify through the curtain of rain and body stockings of mud. We took his word for it that Breslin scored the lone touchdown of the game on a 12-yard plunge in the second period and that he also punted an incredible 78 yards in the fourth period to set up a safety. The final score was State 8, Maryland 0.

One story said Breslin "used the Australian crawl to score his touchdown." Another referred very inadequately to "the most miserable weather conditions any teams have played under in years."

The Spartans did it again to Maryland 33-0 in the season

finale and Homecoming at East Lansing. This time Breslin scored three touchdowns and ran for 127 of State's 253 yards.

Missouri had wrecked State's hopes of going undefeated the preceding Saturday at Columbia by a 13-7 count, but the season ended with a cheering 6-1 record. It was the best record posted by State since 1937 and drew acclaim from many quarters.

"Breslin and Pete Dendrinos, it was generally conceded, could have played on any of the teams State has developed in the past dozen years," Alderton wrote.

"If fullback Jack Breslin is the only player Coach Charley Bachman gets back next fall," wrote Lew Walter in the *Detroit Times* at season's end, "Michigan State will still have a whopping football team."

Breslin deserved all the praise he got. He personally outscored all seven of State's opponents 55-31. In rushing yardage he was 521 to the opponents' combined 711. His seven successful passes picked up 274 yards to the opponents' total of 189. His 27 punts averaged over 40 yards. He was named "most valuable player" by his teammates and received the Governor of Michigan Award.

Because of a wartime rule waiver, Breslin was allowed to play in the 1945 East-West Shrine game even though he had a senior season left at State. End Frank Brogger also represented State in that game.

Francis Powers, renowned sportswriter for the *Chicago Daily News,* wrote: "Bachman's top player and key to his 'Z' formation is Jack Breslin, 185-pound fullback who can run, pass and kick to the highest standards prescribed for grade 'A' triple threats. Breslin demonstrated his skills in the East-West game and drew many press box plaudits."

There was no agreement in those days with the professionals that they keep hands off college players until their class had completed college play, and Breslin received several offers to turn pro before his senior campaign. One was for $2,500 a season plus another $1,500 if the team made the playoffs. But Jack stayed in school.

A huge new athletic symbol, the Spartan statue, greeted football fans in the fall of 1945. The creation of Prof. Leonard Jungwirth of the MSC art department, it was dedicated at ceremonies on June 9, 1945, and was believed to be the largest freestanding ceramic figure in the world. The statue quickly

Sparty unveiled in 1945.

acquired the nickname "Sparty" and has come to hold a special place in the hearts of the Spartan sports faithful. However, no one has suffered more indignities in the Spartan cause; Sparty has been doused with more coats of paints—mainly maize and blue—than a Paris street walker.

The season itself just missed being an outstanding one. The final tally was 5-3-1 and was against, perhaps, the strongest opposition a Spartan team had faced. There were victories over Kentucky, Pittsburgh, Wayne State, Missouri, and Penn State; a bitter tie with Marquette; and losses to Michigan, Great Lakes Navy, and Miami of Florida.

Kentucky had a splendid team with George Blanda at quarterback. State finally won the rugged defensive battle on Macklin Field 7-6 when new Spartan backfield star Russ Reader ran 13 yards for a touchdown and Bob Malaga kicked the extra point.

The 12-7 conquest of Pittsburgh in Pitt Stadium was a national shocker. Clark Shaughnessy's Pitt team was loaded as usual and had top stars in All-America end Joe Skladany and a freshman backfield flash named Jimmy Joe Robinson.

A 60-yard quick kick by Breslin set the stage for the first Spartan score. Pitt had to punt after failing to gain. Three Reader passes moved the ball inside the Pitt 10, and halfback Steve Contos scored for MSC on a burst inside tackle. Breslin intercepted a pass to get State moving towards its other score. This one he made himself on a three-yard sweep around left end, which, he says, is possibly the most satisfying score he ever made.

"They had done a good job scouting us," Breslin recalls. "They were pinching our center in the certain knowledge that I never ran wide. So we did and fooled them completely. I got a big charge out of running outside for a change."

State had been expected to lose by three or four touchdowns. Poets in the press box wrote odes to the Spartans the next day. "The Spartans of Michigan State College registered one of the nation's major gridiron upsets Saturday when they completely outplayed the Pitt Panthers to win 12-7," wrote Eddie Edgar in the *Detroit Free Press.* "Pitt's Panthers unex-

Crack 1945 backfield of Glenn Johnson, Steve Contos, Jack Breslin, and Russ Reader.

Pitt defender wants Breslin's head and ball.

pectedly stepped on a live wire at the stadium yesterday and got the shock of their young lives—a 12-7 defeat by a Michigan State eleven that had dropped into town with no great reputation behind it," said Chet Smith in the *Pittsburgh Press.*

Pitt Coach Shaughnessy said afterwards: "Breslin is the best college back I've seen in five years."

Despite the surprise performance of Russ Reader as a passer and runner, Breslin was the mainspring of the 1945 team, as he had been in 1944, and was once again chosen for the East-West Shrine game. Had State been the big name gridiron power it was to become a few years later under Biggie Munn, there is no doubt he would have been a sure first team All-America selection. As it was, he only made honorable mention.

The Chicago Bears, Boston Yankees, Washington Redskins, and Los Angeles Dons bid for his professional football services.

But Jack turned them all down to take a position with Chrysler Corporation. After several years he returned to his alma mater, served it in various capacities, and rose to executive vice-president, a position he now holds.

Finally the great war was over, and in the fall of 1946, thousands of veterans poured into the nation's colleges. Michigan State football received a potent injection of fresh talent, including a marvelous group of 20 to 25-year-old freshmen. Their presence stirred expectations of immediate success, but when they could produce only a 5-5 record on a quite difficult slate of games, the general disappointment undoubtedly had quite a bit to do with Coach Bachman deciding to call it a day.

Two freshmen, center Pete Fusi and right halfback Lynn Chadnois, became starters right off the bat. By midseason three other newcomers—center Bob McCurry, left halfback George Guerre, and fullback Frank Waters—had moved into starting roles. Major victories were registered over Penn State (19-16), Marquette (20-0), Maryland (26-14), and Washington State (26-20). But huge losses to Kentucky (39-14) and Michigan (55-7) more than offset them. Reports were rife that Bach simply could not handle the tougher, more experienced, older ex-servicemen on the club.

Little George Guerre had his first great day against Penn State. He recovered a Lion fumble on the Spartan 48 and on the first play from scrimmage ran 52 yards for the score. He also sparked the second touchdown drive and led Pennsylvania sportswriters to refer to him in the English translation of his family name, "Mr. War."

At the team banquet after the season's end, Bachman announced his retirement from the head coaching job.

"You haven't seen this fine team at its best," he told a subdued audience. "It could be another 'Four Horsemen' team. We were just beginning to realize its strength and possibilities in the late games of the season. I predict great things of it in years to come. I believe someone else can do a better job under the circumstances."

Thus ended a thirteen year coaching career, longest in State's history to that point. Bachman left a record of solid accomplishment which has come to be more appreciated as passage of time increases objectivity.

Biggie Boom Begins

Michigan State was not a football wasteland when Biggie Munn came to East Lansing. He found a school ripe and ready for athletic greatness, particularly in football. It was bursting its seams in size and improving rapidly in academic variety and quality. It boasted an administration as eager for gridiron success as he was. At its head was a president (John Hannah) who was personally caught up in the sport to the extent that he had not missed a home or away game for many years and frequently got involved in the recruiting of choice high school players. He paid almost daily visits to practices and came to know coaches and athletes intimately. An enlarged stadium and Big Ten membership was coveted, and a successful team was a prime requisite for fulfillment of both ambitions.

There was no extensive rebuilding job to be done. Munn inherited a squad which included 26 lettermen. The program roster for the 1947 home opener against Mississippi State listed 54 men, including 39 sophomores, many of whom had won letters as freshmen.

Among that potent assemblage of second-year men were Lynn Chandnois, Frank Waters, Ed Bagdon, George Smith, Hal Vogler, Pete Fusi, John Gilman, Horace Smith, Gene Glick, Jim Blenkhorn, Bud Crane, John Poloncak, and Ralph Wenger. They were the very heart of Biggie's first three teams.

Munn's main chores were to assess the playing personnel and install his own offensive system, which had the team line up in the T and either go from there or shift first into a single wing. He and his talented staff accomplished this and had a smoothly functioning machine ready by fall. Key assistants were Forest

119

Biggie and first staff. From left, Kip Taylor, Forest Evashevski, and Duffy Daugherty.

Evashevski, Kip Taylor, and Duffy Daugherty, who came with him from Syracuse. John Kobs, Al Kircher, and Lou Zarza also aided.

Biggie met his Michigan State squad at a dinner in the student union building the evening of his arrival from Syracuse. As he moved through the players, one extended his hand and said: "I see you followed us here, coach." Biggie laughed and shook hands. It was Gene Stroia, an end and one of several players who had been on wartime Michigan squads when Biggie was line coach under Crisler. Others in that category were Guerre, Bob Fischer, and Bill Baldwin. Another who followed Biggie, but from Syracuse, was Don Mason.

Biggie's selection was a popular one at the college and around the state. Press comment was laudatory of his career as a two-time All-American football player and shotput and discus star at Minnesota and his subsequent coaching career, particularly his eight years as Michigan line coach. About the only person who did not seem to think much of his coming to MSC was Fritz Crisler, Biggie's old mentor at Minnesota and head coach at Michigan during Biggie's years there. At a public athletic affair where they met for the first time following Biggie's return to State, Fritz fixed his old protégé with an icy stare and demanded: "And what are you doing back in the state of Michigan?"

Scheduling in those days was not the long range affair it is now. When Biggie arrived, the schedule for the 1947 season—due to open in about seven months—had not been completely set. Most uncertain was whether there would be a Michigan-Michigan State game that fall, and if so, when and where. It was finally worked out that there would be a game between the intra-state rivals at Ann Arbor on Saturday, September 27.

Crisler underscored his rhetorical question about Biggie's return to this state by hurling the stars of one of his finest teams at State for a full 60 minutes and destroying Biggie's debut 55-0. It seemed to some that he was trying to destroy the man.

There was little that was funny about that game, but Russ Gilpin, once a quarterback but in this season playing guard, suffered a special embarrassment which was not without its humor.

"After Michigan scored its first touchdown," he relates, "I tried to block the kick by jumping over the line on the anticipated fourth count. I landed on Whitey Wistert's back and scratched it pretty badly. The only bad thing was that they snapped the ball on the sixth count, and there I was standing in the backfield next to the kicker. Have you ever heard 100,000 people laugh?"

The 55-0 disaster might have crushed lesser men but not Biggie. If there was one thing he had been all his life, it was a fighter. Born on the wrong side of the tracks in Minneapolis, he knew the use of adversity: you turned it to your advantage. For the rest of his coaching career he used the memory of that embarrassment at Ann Arbor to fire himself to a frenzy as each Michigan game approached and to goad his athletes into stupendous effort toward revenge.

Lyall Smith, then sports editor of the *Detroit Free Press,* wrote in his "As of Today" column that he believed Biggie became a great coach that very day. "Biggie was downcast and he was sick as he slowly trudged from the MSC bench up through the dark tunnel which led to the Spartans' locker room deep beneath the stands.

"'I didn't even want to show up,'" Smith quoted Biggie as saying. "'I didn't know what to tell those kids. I felt that I had let them down some way. I was low, I was discouraged.

"'And then, just as I reached the door I got mad...at myself. What right did I have to feel so low? How about those players of mine? How were they feeling? How could I cheer them up? What could I do to help them forget?'"

One thing he could do was to come out swinging, to go on the offensive. So he railed about the conditions of the stadium dressing room assigned State. Something had gone wrong with the plumbing—Biggie would always believe it happened on purpose—and water and overflow from toilets were inches deep all over the floor.

"Biggie was so mad, tears came to his eyes, and he vowed at that time to get even with Michigan," Lynn Conway recalled. "It took him years to do it, but he did."

Another Spartan there that day also spoke of Biggie's anger.

"Biggie surprised everyone," Howard Adams recalled. "He was so mad the tears streaked down out of his eyes, and his face was beet red as he raged about Kris Kringle (Fritz Crisler) unleashing the sewage into our dressing room at half time."

Biggie turned that team around, and the following Saturday it licked a good Mississippi State team. Then it beat Washington State at Pullman, despite severe air sickness suffered by most of the squad on a very rough flight west, and Iowa State at home.

Next came Kentucky at East Lansing. Paul (Bear) Bryant was head coach, and he had such splendid players as George Blanda at quarterback; Wash Serini as a tackle; and Dopey Phelps, the nation's leading kickoff and punt returner in 1946, in the backfield. The Spartans gave the potent Wildcats, who came in with a 4-1 record, a dilly of a battle before bowing 7-6. Biggie said afterwards that the line "from end to end functioned on defense the best of any line I have seen."

The game loss was the least of it, however. The Spartans also lost their No. 1 offensive ace, George (Little Dynamite) Guerre for the remainder of the season with a broken leg. Ironically, it happened on the play in which Guerre scored State's touchdown. That was the fifth game of a nine-game slate, but Guerre still wound up as the Spartans' leading rusher that fall with 354 yards on 47 carries, which figures out to 7.5 yards per carry.

At the end of the season Guerre attended a prep banquet in his home town of Flint and was asked, "What kind of a coach is Biggie Munn?"

"He's the kind of a coach a fellow would be glad to break a leg for," Guerre replied promptly.

After the Kentucky loss, State went all the way over Marquette, Santa Clara, Temple, and Hawaii, to end the season with an excellent 7-2 record.

The Hawaii game at Honolulu (a 58-19 victory) established important friendships. Munn and his coaching cohorts met Tommy Kaulukukui, then head coach of the Hawaii team, and the outcome was a pipeline to the island, through which poured the succession of brilliant Hawaiian players who starred at Michigan State. Kaulukukui himself came to Michigan State a couple of years later to take an advanced degree. He worked as a graduate assistant coach and drew ever closer to the Spartan coaches, particularly Munn and his youthful line coach, Duffy Daugherty. When Tommy went home and moved out of active coaching, the imports to the mainland began to include almost as many football players ticketed for East Lansing as pineapples. Spartan fans can thank Tommy for such as Billy Kaae, Bob Apisa, Dick Kenney, Charley Wedemeyer, Charley Ane, Larry Cundiff, Roger Lopes, Jim Nicholson, and Arnold Morgado.

The season was rated a singular success. Recruiting went very well, and before the final home game, work had begun to convert Macklin Field into a bowl. Engineers and construction workers were busy behind the east stands as the team prepared to meet Santa Clara in the home finale.

The 1948 curtain raiser again was with Michigan, this time in East Lansing. It was the dedication game for State's newly enlarged Macklin Stadium, and a crowd of 51,526—double the biggest throng that had ever seen a home game before—filled the new reinforced concrete stands. A new press box, perched on the western rim of the stadium, also was jammed.

Before the start of the game a program was held on the field. President Hannah presided, and with him were honored guests President Alexander Ruthven of Michigan, John Macklin,

Spartan Stadium was enlarged to 51,000 in 1948.

Harry Kipke, Chester Brewer, and Charley Bachman. Most significant of all was the presence of Kenneth L. (Tug) Wilson, Big Ten commissioner, and three faculty representatives from Minnesota, Ohio State, and Michigan. It was clearly part of State's pitch for Big Ten membership.

Leonard Falcone's MSC Marching Band did a routine in which a big "M" (for Michigan, of course) advanced to crush a little "s". The "s" suddenly changed into a firecracker that exploded the big "M". The routine was very nearly prophetic.

After that 55-0 crusher the year before, what happened was a miraculous turnabout and an omen of things to come. The Spartans fended off several dangerous Wolverine thrusts in the first half, giving up just one touchdown. Then in the third quarter they had the effrontery to score a touchdown of their

124

own against the self-styled "Champions of the West," kick the extra point, and tie the score. The Spartan TD was set up when MSC end Warren Huey intercepted a lateral flipped by Wolverine quarterback Tom Peterson on the Michigan 15. He might have gone in for the score but stumbled and fell. Little Dynamite Guerre went around end for three, and Chandnois, faking the run, tossed a pass into the end zone to end Hank Minarik, and State was on the board. George Smith converted.

It mattered little that Michigan came on to win with a fourth period touchdown. The central truth was that State had closed a vast gap in just one year's time and was ready to play Michigan or anyone else. State out-rushed Michigan 158 yards to 106, with Guerre and his backup man, sophomore Jesse Thomas of Flint, each contributing 61 yards. Guerre's was compiled on 12 carries and was no big surprise after his many great performances. But Thomas was playing in his first college game and carried the ball just four times.

Michigan went 9-0 that year and was rated No. 1 nationally. No other team came so close to dumping the Wolverines.

Awesome offensive power began to develop, as indicated in such scores as 68-21 over Hawaii at East Lansing, 61-7 over Arizona, 46-21 over Oregon State, 47-0 over onetime toughie Marquette, 48-7 over Iowa State, and 40-0 over Washington State.

The 1948 season ended on a sour note when an underdog Santa Clara club, albeit coming into the game with a 7-2 record and several bowl feelers in hand, rose up and tied the Spartans 21-21 in Kezar Stadium in San Francisco. Munn heaped praise on the Broncos and never once mentioned an important fact about his team: many of his players had contracted some type of Montezuma's Revenge during a brief training stay at Sonoma Mission near San Francisco. Some could scarcely answer the starting whistle; others got sick on the field and had to be sidelined.

Another disappointment came in the Penn State game. It ended in a tie after a 105-yard run with an intercepted pass for an apparent touchdown by Guerre was nullified by a questionable clipping call well behind the action. Starting from midway in the end zone, Little Dynamite—always a Penn State nemesis—must have covered 150 yards on the play. He darted hither and yon, stopping dead, sprinting off on a new tack, stopping again, whirling off anew. It was a seven-alarm crowd rouser that ended with Guerre sitting exhausted in the Penn State end zone and a handkerchief lying downfield.

Biggie reported later that a study of the films showed there were six Spartan blocks on that play. "If any of them was clipping, then every block in the game was," Munn said.

Graduation losses were not heavy in numbers, but they were in quality. Two all-time greats wore the "green and white" for the last time, Bob McCurry and George Guerre. McCurry, probably the only three-time captain of a major college football team in history, is now a high-ranking executive with Chrysler Corporation. Guerre, a thrilling runner as well as the last outstanding Spartan quick kicker, has become a prominent insurance executive in Lansing. Both played in the 1949 All-Star football game in Chicago.

Guerre was not particularly fast afoot, but he had an amazing talent for varying speed and changing direction to confound would-be tacklers. And he had the power in that 5-7, 165-pound body to break tackles and plow for an extra couple of yards when hit.

Little Dynamite's running technique was partly God-given and partly developed. "I had a drill I used in summer training at

Biggie and three-time captain Bob McCurry.

our family cottage," George says. "I would go out into the woods with a football and run through the trees, twisting and turning to avoid them like they were real tacklers. I think you can see how one can develop a fast change of pace and direction when you see a tree coming up on you."

Between the 1948 and 1949 seasons the fondest hope of Michigan State officials, faculty, and alumni was realized— membership in the Big Ten. What had once seemed a forlorn dream was brought to reality by the efforts of several men in various spheres of action and influence. President Hannah probably was the most powerful single force. He obtained support of school presidents around the league. Ralph Young did a beautiful public relations job. Dean Ralph C. Emmons, a scholarly and dignified faculty representative for athletics, presented State's application for membership in meetings with conference officials and representatives of the other nine schools. He did a very able job and won over several fence-sitters. Also, Biggie was a highly regarded product of the Big Ten and obviously had a strong football program building at East Lansing. This impressed conference people, too.

At a meeting on December 12, 1948, Michigan State was accepted into membership on the condition that a committee of faculty representatives determine, "that rules and regulations and other requirements of the conference are completely in force at that institution." This determination was made by the next spring, and on May 20, 1949, Michigan State joined the league, succeeding the University of Chicago, which had dropped out in 1946.

It is no exaggeration to say becoming a member of the Big Ten was the most significant event in the history of the school. Its ramifications have extended far beyond athletics and have helped move the Michigan State University of today into elite university company nationally.

One disappointment was that, while all other Spartan athletic activity in the Big Ten was to begin in the 1950-51 school year, football had to wait until 1953 because of advance scheduling practices in that sport.

The 1949 season began with another Michigan game. Once again the Maize and Blue triumphed, this time by a 7-3 count, the narrowest margin since State's last victory in 1937. In Biggie's three seasons at the helm, the margin of Michigan superiority had been reduced from 55 points to four.

Senior quarterback and place-kicking ace George Smith put State ahead with a 28-yard field goal early in the first period. Early in the second period Michigan scored its lone touchdown on a pass from Bill Putich to Irwin Wisniewski. Both scores were set up by fumbles. For the rest it was a defensive scrap with both teams failing on several scoring chances.

Lynn Chandnois was State's leading rusher with 54 yards on 14 carries; Michigan's Don Dufek accumulated 56 on 15 tries. The Wolverines' Chuck Ortmann made 86 yards passing to 85 by State's Gene Glick. And it was as close a game as these figures indicate.

The major Spartan stars in the game were three linemen, guards Ed Bagdon and Don Mason and tackle Don Coleman. Fritz Crisler called Bagdon and Mason "the best pair of guards ever to play in Michigan Stadium." They were seniors that fall, smart, tough, experienced and headed for All-America honors.

Mason and Bagdon, the "finest pair of guards to play in Michigan Stadium."

Coleman came as a stunning surprise to the sports world, however. Here was a sophomore in his first game, a rookie weighing less than 180 pounds and deigning to play tackle in the Big Ten. And how he played! One exploit above all others stamped him as a super star in the making.

State had jumped off to its 3-0 lead, but a fumble in the closing seconds of the first period gave the Wolverines possession of the ball deep in Spartan territory. After several rushing attempts failed to gain much yardage, and with the ball resting on the Spartan 11, the Wolverines decided to go to the air. Quarterback Bill Bartlett handed off to right halfback Leo Koceski, who ran wide to his left as if he intended to skirt the end. Bartlett, meanwhile, flared and then sped toward the end zone for the pass from Koceski.

Coleman was lined up across from Michigan's weak side away from the flow of the play. After contacting Michigan tackle Al Wahl and maintaining position for a second, he diagnosed the intended play perfectly and sprinted approximately 40 yards cross field and into the coffin corner. He arrived in time to deflect the apparently sure TD pass to Bartlett with a headlong leap. Michigan scored on the next play on another pass to win the game, but it took nothing away from Coleman's deed.

"It was the finest sophomore performance I have ever seen in my 25 years of football," Biggie said afterwards.

Other Spartans cited for excellence against Michigan included tackle Pete Fusi, the rotund fireplug from Flint; center and linebacker Ralph Wenger, possibly State's most underrated player; and fullback LeRoy Crane, a master of the spinner.

After this near miss against Michigan, State went on a spectacular five-game winning streak, all before the home fans.

Marquette went down 48-7 as the Spartans went pass crazy and rolled up 332 aerial yards, a record still on State's books. Quarterback Gene Glick did the heavy work with seven completions in eight tosses for 231 yards.

Maryland was made of sterner stuff but finally succumbed 14-7.

William and Mary, a powerhouse team in that period, was trampled 42-13. Chandnois paced the offense with three touchdowns, and Bob Carey, Horace Smith, and Frank Waters got one each. Little Johnny Poloncak, as gutty a back as ever wore the "green and white"—all 145 pounds of him—intercepted three passes. This ties him with several other Spartans for the single game record.

Coleman had one of his finest days in that game. His man all day was Lou Creekmur, a giant tackle who went on to stardom as a pro with the Detroit Lions. What Coleman did to Creekmur sent MSC coaches back to the game film for years to show other athletes how the job should be done. Repeatedly Don popped big Lou twice before the latter could react, often dropping him flat on his back. With the first pop he straightened him up; with the second he decked him.

"Coleman was the toughest lineman I ever faced," Creekmur said in later years. "He made a fool of me."

Don's spectacular blocking ability led to an important modification of the Michigan State multiple offense, which in the early 1950s was the rage of the country.

"We have Coleman to thank for what is known as the Michigan State offense," said then line coach Duffy Daugherty. "On straight-ahead blocking or downfield blocking he did so many improbable things that we adopted plays never before attempted. When these plays got established in our system, we got the habit of looking for a lineman who could play what we call the 'Coleman tackle,' because he played it as it had never been played before. That led us to experiment with light, quick men in other line positions.

"I'd estimate that Coleman got the key blocks on about 80 percent of our plays. It was nothing unusual for him to take out two or three men on a play."

Small wonder that in 1975, Coleman was voted into the National Football Foundation's Hall of Fame, the second Michigan State player thus honored. John Pingel was first.

Michigan State then played Penn State and won 24-0 in a game dominated by Lynn Chandnois, who was heading toward All-America recognition at season's end. The lean flyer from Flint went 60 yards for a touchdown to open the scoring in the second quarter. He rolled up 107 yards rushing and made two pass interceptions.

Temple, coached by Al Kawal (former Spartan assistant and a great favorite in East Lansing), was obliterated 62-14 despite coming in with an impressive 4-1 record, which matched State's own.

State's versatile offense was never more brilliant. It rolled up 694 net yards from scrimmage, a figure which stood as the

Lynn Chandnois steams against Michigan.

all-time team record until 1971, when a rout of Purdue moved
the figure to 698.

State had worked up a fearsome head of steam when
Frank Leahy and one of his all-time super Notre Dame clubs
moved in next Saturday. The Irish prevailed 34-21 with people
like Leon Hart, Jim Martin, and "Six-Yard" Emil Sitko pacing
a powerhouse attack. But State's three touchdowns were
impressive. One came after a fumble recovery by Coleman and
was scored on a short plunge by Grandelius. Glick passed to
Chandnois for 83 yards to set up another. He was run out of
bounds on the Irish 11. From there Bob Carey scored on the
next play, taking a pass from Glick.

The final Spartan tally resulted from two pass plays, the
first for 39 yards from Glick to Bob Carey and the next from
Glick to Dorne Dibble for six and the score.

It was the best showing any team made against Notre Dame that season and clearly forecast the Spartan successes of the 1950s against the Irish. Leahy called Coleman "the toughest tackle we have seen all season," and Don was named to his first of an unprecedented three Notre Dame all-opponent teams.

However, the loss to Notre Dame took its toll. Biggie could not get his men keyed up again for a game at Portland's rickety wooden Multnomah Stadium against Kip Taylor's first Oregon State team. The Beavers were a pretty good club, boasting stars like Ken Carpenter and Stan McGuire, and they pulled off a 25-20 upset.

Unprecedented honors were heaped on the team at the 1949 season's end. Three men, Chandnois, Bagdon, and Mason, received first team All-American ratings. Bagdon won the prestigious Outland Award as the interior lineman of the year. The three All-Americans played in the East-West Shrine game, in which Chandnois performed so brilliantly he was named to the game's all-time, all-star team.

Football fever hit a new high at Michigan State. The team successes, the enlarged stadium with its fine facilities, the Big Ten membership, the pioneering spirit which enveloped the whole institution as it burgeoned in size and quality in that early postwar era—all played roles. But there were some fears that the end of the football victory splurge might be in sight. Graduation losses were huge, and even tougher schedules containing such Big Tenners as Minnesota, Indiana, Ohio State, and Purdue were in the immediate offing.

Kip Taylor had left after the 1948 season for a coaching job at Oregon State, reportedly after Forest Evashevski had turned the job down but recommended him. Then, after the 1949 campaign, Evashevski himself pulled out for a seemingly less inviting job at Washington State. He took Spartan assistants Al Kircher and Bob Flora with him, and that led to campus gossip that Evy saw the handwriting on the wall and was escaping ahead of a football decline.

If that was the case, it was a bad guess. Biggie rebuilt his staff with Red Dawson, Steve Sebo, Hal Vogler, and Dan Devine. Earle Edwards had come on for the 1949 season to replace Taylor. They quickly knitted into an excellent coaching corps, found plenty of fine football players in school, and immediately embarked on four tremendous seasons which brought Munn's coaching career to a roaring climax.

132

Biggie's assistants went on to considerable success of their own after their Michigan State careers. Edwards became head coach at North Carolina State, and Dawson moved to Pittsburgh as head coach. Sebo became head coach at Pennsylvania, later general manager of the original New York Titans under owner Harry Wismer, and now athletic director at Virginia. Devine moved on to a very successful career at Arizona State, Missouri, the Green Bay Packers, and finally Notre Dame.

In Biggie's final season of coaching, almost as if to prove he had not lost his touch, he came up with another high school coach. This one was a veteran of fourteen seasons of teaching and coaching in Michigan prep ranks and had an outstanding record—52-9 in seven seasons at his last stop before State. The fellow had about given up coaching, figuring school administration might be the better bet for a guy in his late 30's, when Biggie beckoned. That man was Bob Devaney who, after a four-year stint at East Lansing, moved along to coaching niches at Wyoming and Nebraska and into football immortality.

Twenty-Eight Big Ones

Preliminaries out of the way, Biggie and company got the main event underway in a hurry.

The 1950 club won eight and lost one and finished in the top ten in national wire service ratings for the first time in history. The AP rated the Spartans 8th; the UP, 9th. Important breakthrough victories were scored over Michigan and Notre Dame, natural rivals who had dominated State for years.

State opened with a satisfying revenge walloping of Oregon State 38-13 at East Lansing. Grandelius began his All-America charge with 184 yards rushing, and Carey entered his claim for consideration by accumulating six pass receptions and kicking five straight extra points and a field goal.

Grandelius led the way again the following Saturday by scoring both touchdowns when the Spartans burst past Michigan 14-7 at Ann Arbor, the first time in 14 years the Green and White came out on top. One touchdown came on a 68-yard run; the other, on one of his three pass receptions. Coleman, too, had an incredible day and was named Mid-west lineman of the week by the UP.

Carl Johnson, who was assistant student manager, recalls an incident which may have had something to do with the win over Michigan.

At a squad meeting the night before the game, backfield coach Red Dawson took the floor.

"He told the players he was going to touch the player who would win the game the next day," Johnson said. "He went down the aisle and rubbed Jesse Thomas's head. Jesse ran a punt back the next day to set up the touchdown that allowed us to beat Michigan for the first time in years. I felt his action had no small effect on Jesse's performance and the outcome of the game."

Then came one of the all-time shockers. Maryland, a team which State had beaten four straight times in the recent past without much trouble, came to town and blasted the Munn men 34-7. The reason was the split-T system the Terrapins used, especially the new-fangled option play. On this, a magician quarterback named Jack Scarbath ran laterally behind the line of scrimmage with a trailing back, usually Bob Shemonski, and either kept the ball or flipped it out to his teammate. It completely bamboozled the Spartans.

"Biggie always referred to this game as the 'Maryland fiasco,'" Don Coleman recalled. "The option play was the newest innovative idea of the year, and Maryland had beaten Navy soundly with it prior to our game. We practiced very hard to stop it in practice, and definite assignments were given to our defense to take either the quarterback or the pitch man. Indecision and failure to follow our coaches' instructions killed us on defense.

"As for our offense, we failed miserably to seal gaps on passing situations and neglected to fire out at the defense. We were pitiful that day, a day I can't erase from my memory. We played terribly."

Al Dorow, who quarterbacked State that fall, said simply: "That day we couldn't do anything right, and everything they did was right."

At least one person knew the Spartans would lose before the game was played. On Thursday night the writer ran into a visiting coach in a restaurant in Lansing. The fellow had been imported for the express purpose of coaching the Spartans in defending against the split-T. He had been on campus about ten days, and the whole deal was very hush-hush.

I asked him how things were coming, and he startled me with a bitter response.

"Terrible. Things are terrible," he blurted. "They brought me here to show them what to do against the split-T, and they won't do a thing I say. You're going to get your heads knocked off Saturday."

Then there was the radio interview Dave Froh did on WILS on the eve of the game with Morrie Siegel, a well-known sportswriter for the *Washington Star* who had come in with the Mary-

135

land team.

"Well, Morrie, how do you see the game tomorrow?" was Dave's innocuous opening query.

"You're going to get whipped 100 to 0," Morrie fairly screamed. "They'll butcher you."

Many players recall this game as the most disappointing of their careers. For the sophomores of that season it was the only one they would lose during their varsity careers.

Maryland coach Jim Tatum pulled out all the psychological stops he could find to help his team win. In the dressing room he waved a game program in his players' faces. The cover showed a cartoon of a Spartan making terrapin stew out of an unhappy-looking Maryland player.

"There, that's what they think of you!" he roared.

Then he pulled out a game ticket and proclaimed that State charged $.50 less for that ducat than it had in other games (which was true enough). He said that showed what a low regard State had for his team's abilities (which was not true at all). The extra $.50 was charged for games against Notre Dame and two Big Ten teams on the home card that fall. The others all were priced at the Maryland rate.

After the Maryland game Biggie showed his ability to rally a team. On successive weeks his revived club beat William and Mary 33-14, Marquette 34-6, Notre Dame 36-33, Indiana 35-0, Minnesota 27-0, and Pittsburgh 19-0 to close out the schedule. Those six victories started the Spartans on their fabulous 28-game winning streak.

The William and Mary game which started the long victory string was highlighted by a 90-yard punt return for a touchdown by Jesse Thomas, at that time the longest such play in Spartan history.

In the next game, against Marquette, Dorne Dibble and Dick Panin each scored two touchdowns. Grandelius scored one and rushed for 122 yards.

Then came the Notre Dame game. Biggie called it the greatest offensive duel he ever saw or heard of.

It was the first season of the NCAA "Game of the Week" presentations on television and the Spartans' first appearance on the tube—no better setting for an all-out offensive. State led 20-13 at the half with Spartan scores registered by Vince Pisano, Sonny Grandelius, and Doug Weaver. Doug had set up Grandelius' touchdown with an intercepted pass and scored his

136

own by recovering a blocked kick in the Notre Dame end zone. Spartan end Jim King did the blocking.

Second half scores were on touchdowns by Grandelius and Don McAuliffe and a field goal by Bob Carey. That field goal was the winning difference.

Dick Panin, a sophomore whose greatest moment was to come a year later against Notre Dame, already had learned something about what makes football players tough.

"I remember being awakened one morning in the dormitory by loud, hideous noises," Panin related. "Standing toe to toe throwing tremendous body punches at each other were my roommates, halfback Vince Pisano and tackle Bill Horrell. I tried to separate them until Bill hollered at me: 'Cut it out. We're just doing this to stay in shape.'"

In the Indiana game Grandelius put on a big show. He had 177 yards rushing and scored three touchdowns. The following week he scored one TD and passed to Dorow for another in the Minnesota romp. The Minnesota game was the one in which Dorow and a Minnesota linebacker convulsed the Macklin Field crowd. Just as the ball was snapped, the play was blown dead by the referee. Dorow ran it out anyway toward the end and suddenly realized he was being run down by a burly Gopher who apparently had not heard the whistle.

"We were the only two players in the stadium playing out the play," Dorow recalls. "He chased me what seemed like a minute all over our backfield area with the officials tooting

Vince Pisano scores for State in wild 1950 Notre Dame game. Other Spartans are Frank Kapral (58) and Bob Carey (88).

their whistles and the fans laughing. He finally tackled me, too. It was the only way to get him stopped."

In the windup at Pitt, Grandelius clinched All-America honors by gaining another 73 yards and boosting his season total to 1,023. He thus became only the 17th man in college football history to rush more than 1,000 yards in a season.

The writer was keeping account of Sonny's progress. When Sonny went over the 1,000 mark, he stood up and called the information to the writers in the Pitt press box. Just then another Spartan play went off, and Sonny was thrown for a five-yard loss. Thus his total slid below the 1,000 level, and the sports misinformation man was treated to a volley of jeers and boos.

Spartan tacklers threw Pitt runners or would-be passers for 110 yards in losses, which helped produce minus eleven yards offense for the day. Grandelius failed to score for the only time that season. Dorow passed for two TD's, one to Hank Minarik and the other to Bob Carey.

Thus 1950 ended with 8-1 and the winning streak at six. Two other Spartans besides Grandelius made All-American that year: ends Dorne Dibble and Bob Carey.

State's 1952 team was to achieve No. 1 national rating on both wire service polls, while the 1951 club ended up ranked No. 2 in both. But Biggie is known to have felt the 1951 team was the stronger one, and there was no sense arguing with Biggie on that count. Who would know better?

However, the 1951 club almost blew the whole winning streak in the opening game against Oregon State. It won 6-0 at East Lansing but needed a fluke play to do it.

On the last play of the first half, State had the ball on the Beavers' one foot line. A direct snap from center struck fullback Dick Panin on the chest and bounded into the air. Quarterback Al Dorow fielded it, spotted Don McAuliffe open, flung a lateral to him on the ten, and he wheeled in for the score. It was close, but it counted as a victory and also made it four straight shutouts, largely engineered by a magnificent defensive line called Duffy's Toughies. The surprise star of the contest was a new sophomore defensive back named Jim Ellis, from Saginaw, who intercepted three passes.

Michigan went down with a gratifying thud 25-0. The Wolverines were held to minus six total offensive yards. State produced a devastating offense, particularly pitchout plays which

Sonny Grandelius was first Spartan to run 1,000 yards in season.

went for big yardage. But the major spectacular was Ellis' 78-yard return of the opening kickoff of the second half. He was knocked out of bounds on the Michigan 14. Dorow, McAuliffe, Pisano, and a promising freshman named LeRoy Bolden, from Flint, scored the TDs. From that stupendous defensive unit, linebacker Bill Hughes, tackle Dick Kuh, and a sophomore end from Ann Arbor named Don Dohoney received especially loud press plaudits.

An unpredictable free spirit of that time was Al Dorow. Few fans were neutral on the talented, daring quarterback from Imlay City. To watch him was to love him or hate him.

Something that even discerning fans could not have known, but which was a blood pressure exploder to his coaches, occurred in the Michigan game.

"I decided because we were well ahead," Dorow related years later, "to employ a spread like the one I had seen Southern Methodist use on TV the week before. In the huddle I told the players where to line up. You can imagine what Biggie and the coaching staff thought when we broke out of the huddle in that new formation. We went from our own 22 to the Michigan 14 on seven straight pass completions before I had a pass intercepted on the ten. Well, when I arrived on the sidelines Biggie had a few well chosen words for me that I never forgot."

Perhaps this is why so many coaches insist in calling all the plays today. Dorow did not lose his job, though.

Next week came Ohio State at Columbus. It was Woody Hayes' first season, but he had a strong team which included All-America back Vic Janowicz. It also was the "transcontinental pass" game.

Paul Chandler's lead in the *Detroit News* the following day captured the significance and the dynamic tensions of this all-time classic.

"By every test conceivable to the mind of football man," he wrote, "Michigan State qualified today as the grandest team in the land.

"Desperately trapped, their spirit staggered by some terrible luck, Coach Biggie Munn's Spartans clawed their way out while the clock raced and arrived in time to win perhaps the most thrilling victory in the school's history, 24-20, over mighty Ohio State."

The Spartans were down ten points, 20-10, with ten minutes left in the final quarter. A Dorow-to Dekker TD pass from three yards out narrowed the score to 20-17 with 5:46 left to play. Ohio State, of course, would play ball control, which it did so expertly. But a few plays later Buckeye Bob Keopnick fumbled, and Spartan defensive end Ed Luke covered the ball on the OSU 45 with four minutes to go.

In came the "pony backfield" or "light brigade backfield," as it would be known a year later. Sophomore Billy Wells, who later got the tag "Menominee Meteor," moved the ball to the 28 on two runs. Then sophomore Tom Yewcic came in with a "Thursday Special," a play installed for the first time on the final day of serious drills, for psychological as well as strategic purposes.

It was a play from the old buck lateral series, which some people say was invented by Minnesota's Bernie Bierman. It was fourth down, now or never.

Fullback Evan Slonac took a direct pass from center. He

faked a line buck and slipped the ball to quarterback Dorow, who had turned his back to the enemy and waited for Slonac to pass by. Most of the Buckeyes did not know what was going on. At the snap of the ball Yewcic had moved to his right, and Dorow flipped the ball to him. Yewcic kept on running for an apparent end sweep. Ohio's defense reacted accordingly. Dorow took off to the far left of the field as soon as he got rid of the ball. He was almost all by himself, but a couple of Buckeye backs tagged along medium close just to keep things honest. Suddenly Yewcic stopped dead, turned, and flung a long flat pass—the Trans-Continental—almost from one side-line stripe to the other. Dorow took it on the enemy 12, skillfully dodged the two would-be tacklers (one of whom was Janowicz), and glided into the end zone.

After that fans must have wondered what one does for an encore?

The answer came next Saturday. The Spartans had let down after a herculean effort at Columbus and found themselves behind Marquette 14-6 in the last quarter. So they scored two touchdowns to pull it out as fans went wild.

Biggie loved to tell a story about the first of these game-saving scores.

"I felt a sudden tap on my shoulder and turned to find an excited fan," he recounted. "Apparently he had stepped out of the stands to visit with me.

"'Wise up, Biggie,' he said. 'You need a quick touchdown, and the way to get it is for Dorow to throw a long pass to Wells.'

"Before I could reply, a couple of uniformed officers closed in and escorted him back into the stands.

"As luck would have it, for I didn't send in the play, a few moments later Dorow did fade back and toss a long one which Wells took for a touchdown.

"My friend was back at once. 'That's the boy, Biggie,' he said. 'But you're on your own now. I'm due on the swing shift down at Oldsmobile.'"

An away game with Penn State the following Saturday was another special one in which the Spartans came from behind to win 32-21. The most spectacular play was a 57-yard punt return by Jim Ellis for a score. The AP game story said that on that play, "Ellis operated so fast that some of the would-be tacklers were still running in the opposite direction when he crossed the goal line."

Other Spartans also had an outstanding day. Bolden made the final score on a 66-yard romp down the sidelines. Bill Hughes corralled three Penn State fumbles. Coleman had the partition torn out of his nose by an enemy finger late in the first half but had it sewn up and played the rest of the game. He also made every tackle on every Spartan kickoff or punt in the entire afternoon.

After that, things certainly had to quiet down a little, only they did not. The following Saturday State found itself down 20-19 to Pittsburgh at intermission so threw the offense into overdrive and roared on to win 53-26. State's statistics were incredible. Fullback Dick Panin carried the ball just eight times for 147 yards. Dorow completed 11 of 16 passes for 117 yards and two touchdowns.

Next Saturday marked the first time in five games the Spartans did not have to come from way back to win. This time they went ahead of their victim, a good Notre Dame team, the first time they got the ball. Spartan fullback Dick Panin barreled through the middle on a trap play and ran 88 yards for a touchdown before many patrons reached their seats. Five radio networks and national television covered the game in which the final count was 35-0, the worst lacing ever handed a team coached by Leahy.

Heavy snow had fallen on the Thursday prior to the game, and fans drove through snow-banked roads to get to East Lansing. But when they walked into the stadium, they found it bone dry. The field was emerald green and solid; their seats and the aisles, completely cleared. Student volunteers by the hundreds had worked over Thursday night and Friday to clear the snow via chutes down the stands and onto trucks. The field itself had been covered with a tarpaulin, and it was relatively easy to remove that snow and have the field in perfect shape.

State was supreme. In the words of AP sports editor Ted Smits, in from New York to cover the game, a"pulverizing line" was headed by Don Coleman. Panin ran for 150 yards on eight carries. Dorow hit 11 passes of 17 for 112 yards and two TDs.

Could there be more to come? There was. The next Saturday at Bloomington, Indiana, State was completely flat and had to fight for its life before squeezing out a 30-26 victory over inspired Indiana. The score was tied 14-14 at the half. All-America-to-be Dick Tamburo had engineered an early 14-0

Spartan lead by falling on an Indiana fumble in its end zone for one touchdown and recovering another on the Hoosier 25 to set up a second TD. An 83-yard TD run by Billy Wells was the big Spartan blow that broke the half-time tie and put State ahead to stay.

However, the following day Tommy Devine, a colorful writer known for his emotional outbursts, wrote this lead for the *Detroit Free Press:* "Champions one week, stumblebums the next!"

The word "stumblebums" clapped on a bunch of college kids repelled fans. The *Free Press* sports office was deluged with letters and telegrams protesting Devine's harsh judgment of a team which, though suffering a letdown, pulled out its 14th straight victory, the second longest unbroken string current in the country. The heat became so intense that the *Free Press* pulled Devine from the Michigan State beat. Tommy did not show in East Lansing again for some time.

State concluded its campaign the following week with a 45-7 romp over Colorado of the Big Eight.

Honors for the Spartans rolled in. Four made All-American. Don Coleman was a unanimous choice. Anyone who did not pick him would have been declared an enemy alien. Bob Carey

Four All-Americans make this play go in 1951 Michigan game. Don McAuliffe (40) carries ball as Don Coleman (78) and Al Dorow (low and driving) block. Looking on in background is center Dick Tamburo.

missed out on one or two but was a consensus selection. Al Dorow and Jim Ellis attained one major first team each. There were others who deserved high honors, too, but there is a limit on how much will be extended to any one team.

The season record was a perfect 9-0, and the victory string had reached 15. State now was at center stage nationally and was rated among the top college teams from the beginning of their 1952 campaign.

Munn and company did not disappoint the fans. They opened the action with a third straight conquest of Michigan at Ann Arbor by a 27-13 count. However, the victory was not as easy as it sounds. Michigan stunned the Spartans by rolling to a 13-0 lead in the first ten minutes of play. Pointing up the importance of mental attitude, writer Paul Chandler said in the *Detroit News* the next day that Michigan players "started with the fury of wild animals."

The startling surge provided all the stimulus State needed to snap out of its typical early-game lethargy and get going. On the first play from scrimmage following the kickoff after Michigan's second score, team captain Don McAuliffe went 70 yards for a touchdown that said clearly to the 97,239 fans that "the Spartans are back." Fullback Evan Slonac was credited with the key block.

Guard Gordie Serr had a worm's eye view of McAuliffe's sprint. "I remember very well that we were in an unbalanced line with me at left guard," Gordie recalled recently. "It was my job to pull and lead McAuliffe. I threw a block on someone and was lying flat on my back with him on the ground when here comes Don hurdling over us. The roar of the crowd told me the rest."

After McAuliffe's score, Bolden scored from the three, Wells went in from the ten, and State led at half time 20-13. Bolden made the only TD of the final half from four yards out on a pass from Tom Yewcic. Yewcic, playing his first full game at quarterback, struck on seven of 14 passes for 171 yards.

Charles Clapp, sports editor of the *Grand Rapids Herald,* wrote: "Magnificent Michigan State, the Rocky Marciano of football, got up off the floor twice this beautiful afternoon and clearly proved its right to be considered the nation's No. 1 team."

Next Saturday State played Oregon State in Portland again and squeaked through with a 17-14 victory, thanks to a second

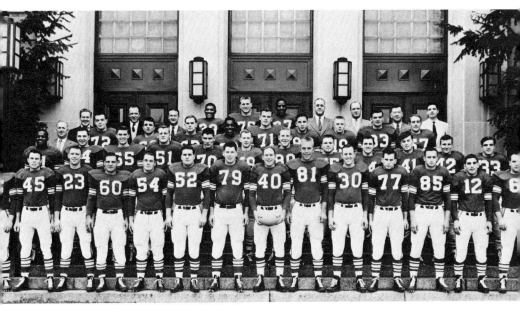

1952 national championship team.

chance field goal by Gene Lekenta. Two passes for touchdowns,
Yewcic to Paul Dekker and Yewcic to Ellis, gave State a 14-0
lead, but the Beavers came back to tie. It was left up to Lekenta
to ice the game. Gene missed the first try from the 12 yard line
with only a couple of seconds left on the clock, but Oregon
State was declared offside. Lekenta tried again and hit it with
no time left, to run State's victory string to 17.

Bert Zagers, a fine Spartan backfield man, recalls that in
the dressing room after the game a news photographer asked
Biggie to kiss Lekenta's foot. Biggie's explosive refusal rates as
the funniest thing Bert recalls from his football days.

State made No. 1 on wire service polls the next week when
it massacred a good Texas A&M team 48-6, in the first game of
the season at Macklin Field. The Spartans' ascendancy was
helped by the fact that on the same day Penn ended a 24-game
Princeton winning streak.

Using 44 players, State rolled up 592 yards on offense.
Yewcic had another big day at quarterback, completing seven of
13 passes for 292 yards and two touchdowns. Both TD passes
were to Duckett, one for 81 yards, the other for 46. Willie
Thrower, an octopus-fingered senior, relieved Yewcic and connected on seven of nine throws for 107 yards and two more

145

scores. Thrower's two were to Bert Zagers from 19 yards out and Bernie Raterink from 24.

Thrower came from the western Pennsylvania town of New Kensington, which had phenomenal prep football for a small community. With him on State's 1952 team from New Kensington were All-America linebacker Dick Tamburo, his brother Harry, star halfback Vince Pisano, and first string tackle Joe Klein. Another top-drawer tackle from the town was Bill Horrell, who finished his play in 1951. Thrower never made it big on the Spartan team, but he had such a powerful throwing arm that he was used in punt return practice. Simulating the punter, he would throw the ball 65 or 70 yards to the exact spot Biggie wanted it in order to work out the proper return.

Syracuse (3-1) went down 48-7, and Penn State (4-0-1 and rated in the top 20 nationally) succumbed 34-7. Stars of the Syracuse rout were Bolden, with two touchdowns, and Jim Ellis with a 59-yard punt return for a score. Against Penn State, quarterback Yewcic flung three orbital passes for touchdowns: 61 yards to McAuliffe, 56 to Duckett, and 45 to Doug Bobo. Ed Luke and Don Dohoney had great days at defensive ends, and All-Americas Dick Tamburo and Frank Kush and should-have-been All-America Hank Bullough were awesome in the middle.

Purdue was very tough at Lafayette but finally yielded 14-7. The Boilermakers had a rugged team with such as Dale Samuels, at quarterback, and Froncie Gutman, Tom Bettis, Bernie Flowers, and Fred Preziosio. Spartan linebacker Doug Weaver, from Goshen, Indiana, saved the game by intercepting a Samuels pass on State's four with less than three minutes to go. Kush and Luke helped the cause greatly by recovering fumbles.

Billy Wells did it again the following week against Indiana. In 1951 he had been the Spartan ace in the squeaker against the Hoosiers, and this time he barreled for 135 yards and two touchdowns. McAuliffe also scored twice, once on a 57-yard play involving a pass from Thrower.

At East Lansing the following week Notre Dame coughed up the football seven times to help State to a 21-3 decision. Tamburo smothered three of them. McAuliffe scored twice on short plunges, and Bolden registered on a 24-yard scamper. The Irish came in with a 5-1-1 record and had such stars as Heisman Trophy winner John Lattner, Ralph Guglielmi, and Neil Worden. Lattner was held to 65 yards rushing and it was the first

All-American guard Frank Kush.

time any team whipped a Frank Leahy-coached club three times in a row. A potent defensive weapon was Yewcic's punting. He booted nine for a 45-yard average.

A quartet of Spartans who played brilliantly in that game—McAuliffe, Tamburo, Kush, and Gordie Serr—had yet another reason for never forgetting the occasion. They were roommates, very close friends, and poor as the proverbial church mice. The game was a sellout well in advance, and tickets were at such a premium that reports had it that as much as $50 might be paid for a good ducat. McAuliffe had a telephone call from a man making such an offer.

"So Kush gave him his four tickets, I gave him mine, and so did Tamburo," Serr recalls. "As team captain, McAuliffe got eight, so that made 20 he had to sell. He was to meet this fellow in an apartment building downtown. He goes down there and meets the guy right in the lobby.

"'Do you have the tickets?' the fellow asks.

"'Yeah,' says McAuliffe, and hands over the tickets.

"Instead of handing him the money, the guy pulls a gun and sticks it in Don's face.

"He says, 'You wait five minutes before you go out the front door,' and exits through the side door.

"Well, McAuliffe comes back and tells us this story. At first we didn't believe it, but he finally convinced us.

"Now, McAuliffe was a boxer at State. So I asked him, 'Mac, why didn't you hit the guy? Why didn't you pop him?'

"'You know,' he said, 'that damn pistol was a pretty good equalizer.'"

Serr was named "Spartan of the Week" for his play against the Irish which included making the tackles on a couple of punts and recovering a couple of fumbles. His particular thrills were nailing Lattner on a punt return deep in Irish territory and meeting Coach Leahy after the game in the Irish dressing room.

"The following week," Gordie recalls, "I received a note from Coach Leahy saying how he appreciated my coming over and saying hello to him and telling him that I always wanted to meet him. Imagine that! I still have that letter."

State's victory gave Munn a career edge over Leahy of three victories to two, a rare achievement. The two teams did not play in 1953, and Biggie took his margin over Leahy into retirement.

The 1952 finale with Marquette was a Spartan romp. The

score was 62-13, and all 60 MSC players in uniform saw action. A massive 601 yards total offense was recorded. Big plays included a 59-yard Yewcic-to-Slonac pass play and a 43-yard run by Bolden. Slonac scored two touchdowns and eight straight extra points. Five pass interceptions played a big role. Two were by Rex Corless, of Coldwater. All this was accomplished on a slippery, muddy Macklin Field which had been deluged with rain up until game time.

State's winning streak had hit 24, and the season record was another perfect 9-0. A king's ransom of honors was heaped on Biggie, his team, and individual players. Biggie was named "Coach of the Year" nationally. His team was acclaimed No. 1 on everybody's poll. Six Spartans were named on one or more first team All-Americans. Three attained consensus All-American—guard Frank Kush, halfback Don McAuliffe, and linebacker and center Dick Tamburo. The other men making All-Americans were end Ellis Duckett, quarterback Tom Yewcic, and defensive back Jim Ellis for the second straight year.

Biggie coached the East team in the East-West Shrine All-Star game and used Spartan players Paul Dekker, McAuliffe, and Tamburo in the game. Kush, McAuliffe, and Tamburo participated in the Senior Bowl game, and Dekker, Kush, and McAuliffe were in the All-Star game in Chicago the following summer.

John Wilson, a slender, ascetic-looking defensive back from Lapeer, was named to the inaugural Academic All-America football team. This young man, the first of three brothers to play varsity ball for State, also won a Rhodes Scholarship, making him the first major college football player to do so since Whizzer White of Colorado. Whizzer White is better known these days as Supreme Court Justice Byron White, and John Wilson is vice president of Virginia Tech.

In the 1950, 1951, and 1952 campaigns State had won nine straight games over league foes without a loss and now stood squarely on the apex of the collegiate football world. National magazines gave it a parade of treatments. The Spartan nickname began to appear in punch lines of cartoons and jokes with the Irish of Notre Dame and the Trojans of Southern California. Press assemblages at home and away games were increasingly huge, and the major national writers and columnists were being attracted to East Lansing for the first time. It was not

149

unusual to have several national radio networks plus national television on major games. The glamour boys of the electronic media–Red Barber, Bill Stern, Ted Husing, Van Patrick, Harry Wismer, Lindsey Nelson, et al–frequently worked Spartan games. The press box also was graced by national press writers such as Red Smith, Fred Russell, Wilfrid Smith, H. G. Salsinger, Stanley Woodward, Tim Cohane, Iggy McVay, Bert McGrane, Dick Cullum, Leo Fischer, Jimmy Breslin, and Ted Smits.

Such success often begets suspicion and investigations. It happened to State, and in February of 1953, the school was put on probation by the Big Ten for activities of an organization known as the Spartan Foundation of Lansing. It was accused of soliciting funds for assistance of Michigan State athletes and administering this aid outside regular college channels. The NCAA followed suit, and something of a blight fell on State. The college's protests that it felt no responsibility for any such alleged activities by an outside organization over which it had absolutely no control fell on deaf ears.

State opened its first regular Big Ten football season at Iowa against Forest Evashevski's second Hawkeye team. The historic date was Saturday, September 26, 1953.

With State's big power backs–Don McAuliffe, Vince Pisano, Wayne Benson, and Dick Panin–all gone, the incredible Light Brigade backfield of Tom Yewcic (5-11 and 172), LeRoy Bolden (5-7½ and 157), Billy Wells (5-9 and 175), and Evan Slonac (5-8 and 170) came into its own. These little men electrified the collegiate football world with their giant play, starting with the opener.

There had been serious doubts about their ability to get the job done. It was not because of their offensive talents. These had been well established in the two preceding seasons. But now these veritable midgets were going to have to play defense too. The days of free substitution (and hence, platoon play) had just been ended by order of the powerful NCAA football rules committee.

Some coaches were for the rule change, but not Munn. He added one more thought which some folks were not so sure about: "As to its effect on our team, I don't think the new rule will hurt us any more than anyone else."

Biggie knew the talent and heart possessed by those big little men, and game results soon convinced every doubting Thomas.

150

At Iowa, Yewcic hit on nine of 13 passes for 109 yards, including a 43-yard picture play for the final tally, with Wells on the receiving end. Earlier, Wells had plunged home from the three, and Diamond Jim Ellis, heretofore a brilliant defensive specialist, had gone in from the two. Four fumble recoveries helped State. So did two pass interceptions by sophomore Jerry Planutis (later to make his main mark as a tough fullback on the 1956 Rose Bowl team). The final score was Michigan State 21, Iowa 7.

Dale Hollern, a sophomore guard making his first college team trip, had a special reason never to forget that trip to Iowa. "I recall the excitement of being named to the traveling squad for that Iowa game," the then 5-11, 185-pounder said recently. "But I had a worry. My wardrobe was very bad. I had nothing to wear. Somehow Duffy knew it and in his own way—without embarrassment to me—gave me one of his own sports jackets to wear and keep. I'll always be grateful to him for that and many other things."

The next week Biggie took his Spartans to Minneapolis, where the information media, the university family, and the twin cities accorded him a royal homecoming. It was the first time Munn, one of the Gophers' proudest products, had brought a team back to play his alma mater. An incident which Biggie did not think was very funny at the time, but which he came to laugh about later, occurred as his team left the busses to enter the stadium dressing room. The players made it all right, but Biggie was stopped by guards who demanded to see his ticket. He did not have one and had a hard time convincing them he really was the coach, name of Biggie Munn.

The Gophers did their best to blight Biggie's visit home, holding the Spartans to a 0-0 tie in the first half. But then that fantastic little dynamo LeRoy Bolden took personal charge and scored three touchdowns on runs of 69, 9, and 11 yards—all within a space of 22 minutes.

Tom Yewcic had been hurt at Iowa, so a green sophomore named Earl Morrall, from Muskegon, got his initial starting shot at quarterback. He showed some promise by engineering State's first two TDs and connecting on seven of nine passes. Minnesota's ace All-American, Paul Giel, was well contained by the Spartans. He carried the ball 20 times for a net of 23 yards.

Bolden suffered an embarrassing moment when the Gopher defenders literally tore his uniform from his body while

trying to stop him in the heavy third period action. The rest of the team gathered in a tight circle around him while the remnants of his jersey and pants were removed, and a new outfit was donned.

State's winning string reached 26 with the Minnesota win.

The team opened at home the following weekend against Texas Christian, and fans were treated to a cliff-hanger.

Abe Martin's Horned Frogs acted like they had never heard of Biggie's magnificent gridiron machine. They gave up an initial touchdown to the Spartans and then took charge. By the end of the third quarter they had scored three touchdowns on a scintillating passing attack which would have done alumnus Slingin' Sammy Baugh proud. They were going for another one—which surely would have put the game beyond reach—when they were finally headed off.

State had been guilty of all kinds of goofups—fumbles, penalties, defensive lapses. The score was 19-7 against State entering the fourth period. But as writers noted in their stories in the Sunday papers, State never lost its poise. It had been behind many times before and knew how to come back. The Big Green went 69 yards on ten plays for a score, with Bolden carrying the ball across the final stripe.

TCU cooperated with a fumble on the second play following the ensuing kickoff, and big, mean, alert Bill Quinlan fell on the ball on the enemy 27. Yewcic called a screen pass, set it up perfectly, and hit Slonac. Little Evan zigzagged it home for the score. He also booted the extra point to put State ahead 20-19 and send fans into a state of delirium. TCU began desperation passing, and Slonac picked off one of the errant aerials. A 65-yard drive followed, with Yewcic passing to Ellis for the final score. No one asked for his money back in that game!

The streak reached 27.

Shaken by this near disaster, the Spartans disintegrated Indiana the following Saturday 47-18 at East Lansing. Big plays included a 67-yard TD pass from Morrall to Duckett. Wells intercepted two passes and ran one 58 yards for a score. Yewcic found another budding sophomore named John (Big Thunder) Lewis for a 34-yard TD romp.

State had seldom looked sharper, and its winning streak reached 28.

Biggie and LeRoy Bolden.

153

The stage was set for certain rout of a Purdue team which was in deep doldrums. Purdue had lost four straight games, it was beset by multiple injuries, and the press and alumni were howling for the scalp of Coach Stu Holcomb. Almost no one gave the Boilermakers a prayer of winning.

On Friday morning, in Lafayette, the writer chanced upon a young man named Danny Pobojewski, who was just emerging from a dry cleaning establishment with a freshly pressed suit. Danny was from Grand Rapids, played a little football at Michigan State without lettering, and then transferred to Purdue. He was a reserve fullback who had done nothing of note for the Boilermakers either.

We chatted a few minutes and then parted with these final words from the misguided publicist: "Good luck tomorrow, Danny. Hope you get into the game."

He got into the game, all right. He carried the ball half a dozen times for negligible yardage, but he plunged for the game's only touchdown. It stood up for a 6-0 upset, and it shattered State's 28-game winning streak, a marvelous skein which even today rates among the highest modern victory strings.

The Spartans almost pulled it out. On the kickoff after Pobojewski's score, Bolden received and ran it back 95 yards for an apparent touchdown, but a clipping penalty was called far behind the flow of the play. Five pass interceptions certainly contributed to State's demise.

The loss was not without its compensations. The winning streak had grown oppressive. State had been faltering. It was playing defensive football instead of the all-out, hell-for-leather game of which it was capable, and even mediocre clubs were giving it fits. This loss shocked it awake, and Munn's men swept through the remaining four opponents to a Big Ten conference tie with Illinois and subsequently the Rose Bowl bid.

Oregon State caught the full brunt of State's resurgence the following Saturday at East Lansing, going down 34-6. Diamond Jim Ellis made the game's big play with a 76-yard runback of a punt for a score.

The next week at Ohio State, Bolden put on a one-man tour de force with 126 yards rushing and three touchdowns. He ploughed through Buckeye tacklers like they were straw men as State won 28-13. The man who marveled most was Woody Hayes.

"We knew what he could do," Woody told the press afterwards. "He did it to us two years ago, and we were ready for him this time. But he did it again. He's a great back."

Michigan at East Lansing was next on the agenda. The Spartan avalanche was moving with implacable force. State won with Bolden and Slonac leading the way offensively, Bert Zagers intercepting two passes on defense, and the team holding the Wolverines to 81 yards rushing. The score was 14-6.

The season finale was against Marquette, a club with a 6-2-1 record and bowl feelers already in hand. All the relevant Big Ten action had been completed, and the Spartans just could not get up for the Hilltoppers. They finally fended off the Milwaukee collegians 21-15, but the poor performance raised concern that they might have blown the Rose Bowl bid, which would be determined by a vote of the conference athletic directors.

The aftermath of this splendid rookie season in the nation's toughest collegiate football conference was to include the Rose Bowl bid for State and high honors for numerous Spartan players. Team captain and end Don Dohoney achieved consensus All-American. LeRoy Bolden and tackle Larry Fowler were named to one first team each. Dohoney and Bolden became the first All-Big Ten first team selections. Dohoney, for attainment beyond the stadium confines, was named to the Academic All-American, as was tackle Carl Diener.

A final happy development was that on December 10, 1953, Big Ten commissioner Tug Wilson announced that MSC had set its house in order and was removed from probation.

First Smell Of Roses

"SPARTANS WIN 28-20" screamed the *Los Angeles Times* in 48-point type across the top of the front page. "WELLS SPARKS ROSE BOWL WIN" exulted the *Lansing State Journal* in giant green type atop page one. Such headlines were repeated in papers all over the land!

And the stories....

"They've got bigger things in crackerjack boxes than what Michigan State put on the field yesterday. But never was anything crammed with more heart and hustle than those little green-shirted guys from East Lansing, the newest dot on the Big Ten map. They were battered and beaten, physically and numerically, in the first half, then gamely rebounded in the second to soundly thrash UCLA and earn a 28-20 victory in the Rose Bowl game, the 40th in a long line of lustered events."—Bob Hunter in the *Los Angeles Times.*

"Somewhere in the 20-minute intermission between the first and second halves, Coach Biggie Munn of Michigan State found himself a football team and a tremendous Rose Bowl victory."—Leo Fischer in the *Chicago American.*

Millions of words in print and off the tongues of radio and TV broadcasters heralded the most glorious achievement in Michigan State athletic history. But there was so much more to the Rose Bowl experience than the game itself.

It all began with a telephone call received by the writer on Sunday evening, November 22, 1953, at his East Lansing home. The call was from Big Ten commissioner Tug Wilson in Chicago and was intended for MSC faculty representative Ed Harden. But Harden had wearied of the long vigil and gone home, leaving the smoke-filled, camera, tape recorder, and typewriter-littered house to the 40 or so newspaper, radio, and TV people who had been awaiting the news since mid-afternoon.

"Well," Wilson began. "The athletic directors have voted to send Michigan State...."

The writer clapped his hand over the mouthpiece, turned to his rapt audience, and said, "We're in!"

It was like flipping a lighted match into a bucket of gasoline. The media people exploded from the house to make quick phone calls to their offices and track down Biggie at a party across town. Wilson's further words were lost in the confusion, but no more were necessary.

The student body, band, football team, alumni, faculty, and everyone even remotely connected with Michigan State were caught up in a whirlwind of activity. Some 15,000 of the faithful traveled by special trains, chartered planes, and a nearly unbroken caravan of automobiles to the West. The *Lansing State Journal* ran Seth Whitmore's stories of motorcades all along route 66. Some business places on the way made a big deal out of bannering free coffee and doughnuts to Michigan travelers. It was reportedly the largest invasion of midwesterners in the bowl's history.

Long before the opening whistle sounded on New Year's Day, Michigan State had scored a notable public relations victory which was important to itself, the Big Ten, and the entire Rose Bowl promotion. Ever since the start of the Big Ten pact with the Rose Bowl people in 1947 there had been seriously strained relations, particularly with the press. The rift started when the southern California media urged that the Army team starring Blanchard and Davis be invited to the 1947 Rose Bowl instead of Big Ten conference champion, Illinois. One West Coast critic campaigning against Illinois said, "It will take more than the smell of Roses to dispel the odor of Illinois' participation."

Illinois quite naturally took umbrage at such slurs, and so did the rest of the then Big Nine. Illini coach Ray Eliot recognized a good gimmick toward team motivation when he saw one and reacted by barring all West Coast writers from traditionally open practice sessions. That really fanned the flames. The chasm deepened when Illinois crunched UCLA 45-14 and the Big Ten press chortled with glee.

Subsequent Big Ten visiting teams continued the lockout

of West Coast writers and added insulting new twists as they went along. Relations were not improved by the continued wallopings Big Ten teams handed the home clubs; they had won six of seven when State arrived on the scene.

James Denison, who was assistant to President Hannah for university relations, recalls how stiff and formal the Tournament of Roses committeemen were when they met the advance arrangements party of Michigan State officials at the Los Angeles airport. But no one could stay reserved long with the hearty back-slapping extroversion of MSC business manager Lyman Frimodig or the gusty geniality of Ralph Young. The bowl officials quickly broke down and enjoyed "the new kind of Big Ten people," as they themselves put it.

This was State's first year in the Big Ten, and East Lansing-ites were so new and green that feelings generated by an incident seven years ago meant nothing to them. Biggie Munn promised to hold daily press interviews at the Huntington-Sheraton Hotel, traditional home of the visiting Rose Bowl teams back through the years. And he kept his word.

Two other gestures broke the last barriers between the midwesterners and Californians. At a press affair for the benefit of photographers, writers, TV, and radio people in old Brookside Park, the practice field, Biggie's attention was called to the fact that several hundred people had gathered around the locked gate and were calling, "Biggie, open the gate! We're friends! Let us in!" Biggie considered a moment, ordered the gate opened, and ushered the grateful fans to the small cement grandstand. Then he told them about the Michigan State team and wound up by calling the players over and introducing them. The press was bug-eyed. Nothing like this had ever happened before.

The second wound healer was Munn's promise that all California practice sessions would be open or closed to the press on an equal basis.

"We have to get a job done," Biggie told Bob Voges of the Associated Press, "so some practice sessions will be closed. I mean closed to everyone—Midwest as well as Pacific Coast press. I see no reason to discriminate against any regional section of the press. What goes for one group will go for all."

Biggie followed through to the gratification of a dubious Los Angeles area press and welcomed all bona fide media people to workouts at Brookside Park.

158

Spartan regulars in Brookside Park. Line, left to right, Dohoney, Fowler, Bullough, Hallmark, Neal, Jebb, Quinlan. Backs, Wells, Slonac, Yewcic, Bolden.

The *Times'* Al Wolf, who was assigned to daily coverage of the Spartans, asked Biggie why he was doing this. Biggie endeared himself and all Spartans to the Californians by replying, "My experience with West Coast newspapermen on Michigan State trips and at East-West Shrine games has been very fine. I want to keep it that way. Besides, it's only fair for all writers to get in if any do."

Reactions of the West Coast writers to the Spartan team were most amusing. They had been advised beforehand that the MSC squad was quite small, but they did not quite believe it. They thought all Big Ten teams just had to be big and powerful.

"Midgets. Comparative midgets," wrote Dick Hyland in the *Times.* Sid Ziff, the *Mirror* sports editor, said, "When the Spartans lined up for the photogs yesterday everyone in the backfield except quarterback Tom Yewcic seemed to be standing in a hole. This must be the first college football team in his-

159

tory that has over-exaggerated its heights and weights in its listed roster."

The Spartans worked hard getting ready for the game, and they barked like trained seals as they inhaled too much of the unwelcome smog which shrouded Brookside Park most of the time. But they also had fun.

There was the standard visit to Disneyland with the UCLA team for a flurry of publicity pictures of the rival captains shaking hands and players posing with pretty members of the Rose Bowl queen's court.

There was a roast beef eating duel at Lawry's, which State won, and a movie studio visit where players met Doris Day, Phil Silvers, Laurence Harvey, George Sanders, and Rex Harrison, among others.

The annual Big Ten club dinner was a huge spectacle with Bob Hope as MC and Bob Crosby and his orchestra providing music. Billy Wells met Debbie Reynolds, as he was longing to do. They had a post-game date, too, making some night club rounds.

On the serious side, the Spartans became heroes when a fire broke out in the Huntington-Sheraton Hotel.

Bob Shackleton, sports director of WKAR and WMSB-TV, recalls that he and various squad members were enjoying the Huntington's swimming pool on Sunday afternoon, December 20, when thick black smoke began pouring out from a fourth floor window.

"This looked like bad trouble," he related. "All of us thought of the many elderly people who are permanent residents of the hotel and who likely were napping in their rooms. A fire alarm was sounded, but it was quite a distance between the hotel and the Pasadena fire station.

"I arrived up in the fourth floor corridor of the hotel to find the hall completely blocked by smoke. The fire had started in a hall closet but was spreading rapidly through adjoining rooms.

"Various football squad members had beaten me to the scene. There, lying flat on the floor of the hall, were center Joe Badaczewski and fullback Evan Slonac, along with three other teammates. They were holding a fire hose and pouring water into the flaming area while red hot pieces of paint and plaster were falling on and around them. In order to prevent serious burns, other players joined in to relay cold, wet towels to cover

160

Billy Wells dated Debbie Reynolds.

the heads of Badaczewski, Slonac, and the others.

"Their quick thinking prevented what could have been a major disaster. The fire actually was under control before the hook and ladders arrived.

"Meantime, sophomore end Bill Quinlan and junior tackle Henry Bullough were alerting tenants on that floor to evacuate, knocking from door to door. One door was locked, yet they could tell someone was inside. They promptly smashed the door down and found an elderly invalid helplessly sitting in a wheel chair. Quinlan and Bullough picked up the chair and carried the woman four floors down the stairs to the lobby, where she was rolled to safety.

"Quarterback Tom Yewcic gave a helping hand, carrying hundreds of rolls of inflammable film from the photographers' room near the fire.

"There was no question in my mind, nor in any of those who were on the scene, that these young men prevented a major fire, one that could have caused great loss of life and property.

"The courage and quick thinking of that group of athletes shall go down as one of my greatest thrills in sports, even though the scene of action was not the stadium."

161

Other Spartans involved in the fire-fighting and rescue efforts were Gene Lekenta, Alvin Lee, Jim Jebb, Fred Rody, and student manager Keith Darby.

Biggie was appreciative of the all-out response of his players but still could say, tongue in cheek, "Get the first 22 men in the swimming pool."

Despite these and other distractions, such as Christmas celebration so far from home, practices continued well.

The little Spartans impressed people with their speed, obvious love of contact, and team play. LeRoy Bolden, the 163-pounder who hit like a fullback, was a particular favorite.

At the first scrimmage at Brookside one spectator suggested that, instead of all those "feather merchants," they should put in "that big guy with the satchel." Would that wise guy have been surprised? The big guy with the satchel was Dr. Jim Feurig, the Spartans' team physician. He was a former Green Bay Packer, still in pretty good physical condition.

Some shifts in State's lineup shook up the angle-hunting LA writers. They reported in bannered stories that Earl Morrall had moved in ahead of Tom Yewcic, Bill Ross was at Ferris Hallmark's guard post, Embry Robinson was in for Jim Jebb, and Ellis Duckett was in for Bill Quinlan.

Biggie declared there was no discipline involved. "We just want to give the boys some incentive. Keep them alert."

The usual regulars started the big game.

Around Christmas time, Biggie and UCLA's Red Sanders announced that the last week of drills for the Friday game would be closed to all press, for reasons of complete concentration rather than any secret moves. Biggie also had become unhappy with the facilities and security around Brookside and moved the team's practice sessions to the much superior East Los Angeles Junior College stadium.

Legions of fans from the Midwest poured in during the last week. Special luncheons, dinners, and even one breakfast—mostly for dignitaries, not the players—dotted the calendar.

Newspaper headlines continued to laud State, but most of the prognosticators wound up picking UCLA. Home town fans were still with State, though. A Western Union message 85 feet long and containing names of over 3,000 well-wishers arrived from Lansing. Rube Samuelson said in the *Pasadena Star News* that it was going to become the first million dollar game in football history.

There were rumors that this was to be Biggie's last game as head coach and that he would soon move up to succeed Ralph Young as athletic director. Top MSC officials said "no comment," but press reports daily became more positive.

The big day dawned cool and clear, except for the haze of smoke from forest fires somewhere in the nearby Sierra Madre range. By game time the temperature was 70 degrees, skies clear, the field in perfect shape.

Everything was normal, including State's lousy start. Fourteen times in its string of 32 victories in 33 games, State had fallen behind. In all but one, it had come on to win. Could it happen again?

State came out in an unbalanced line with the players spread a good yard apart. It was supposed to be a surprise, but it did not seem to faze UCLA a bit. UCLA held the Spartans to just four first downs and 56 total yards in offense in the first half while rolling up 154 yards. They also intercepted a Yewcic pass intended for Bolden and recovered fumbles committed by Bolden and Morrall. But most importantly, they scored two touchdowns to lead 14-0 with less than five minutes gone in the second quarter. It looked like a complete disaster in the making except to the most optimistic Spartan fans, those who had been through this before and just "knew" their favorites would come back.

Billy Wells (14) was game's most valuable player.

With such tremendous players as Rommie Loudd, Jack Ellena, Chuck Doud, Paul Cameron, Bob Davenport, and Danny Villanueva manning the UCLA ramparts, the Spartan fans could have been whistling Dixie, but once again their faith was rewarded.

The spark that ignited the comeback was one of the great defensive plays in State's entire gridiron history. After UCLA's second TD, State still failed to move the ball. One first down was all it could muster before Yewcic punted to Cameron on UCLA's 12. The strong, talented UCLA All-America was downed on the 20.

UCLA faltered, and Cameron dropped back to punt from his own ten. Never in Red Sanders' head coaching career had a team blocked a punt against him. Ellis Duckett, State's lightning fast end from Flint, took care of that perfect slate right then and there. On a deftly executed play that had him dart into the Bruin backfield behind a block thrown by Hank Bullough, Duckett leaped high in the air and caught Cameron's solid boot on his chest. The ball hit the ground on the UCLA 7, bounced like a basketball back into Duckett's arms, and he ran it in for a touchdown. Slonac kicked the extra point, and in one magnificent moment State had turned the tide, gained the momentum, and started on its way to victory.

Ellis Duckett's blocked kick turned game around.

Biggie is credited by many of his idolizing players with adding impetus to their victory drive in the second half by an episode at half time.

George Alderton wrote about it this way in the *Lansing State Journal:*

"Calm reigned, finally, and the Spartan boss stopped at mid-room, fished a bit of paper out of his pocket, handed it to Captain Don Dohoney and said for all to hear:

"'I was up at dawn this morning. I sat in my room watching the sun rise, thinking about the game. Something came to me and I wrote it on this piece of paper. Captain Dohoney, will you read this to your team?'

"Dohoney, his face sweat-streaked and soiled, took the paper and read: 'Get off the floor in '54.'

"A snicker ran around the room, then a laugh. Then faces straightened, and Munn grinned. Humor, in goodly portion, even corny humor, has always been in his recipe for fun in football—for victory!"

Whatever the reason, State really took charge in the second half. Running their multiple offense, with emphasis this day on the split-T, the Spartans took the opening kickoff and struck with 14 straight running plays. Every single one gained yardage, and the result was a touchdown by Bolden on a one-yard smash. Slonac kicked the extra point, and the score was tied.

One thing that was different in the second half was Billy Wells' influence. In the entire first half Wells carried the ball only once—that time, early in the game for no gain. But Spartan press box spotters saw something in the UCLA defense, and in the second half Billy Wells became the workhorse, carrying the ball 13 times, seven of them in that opening drive.

UCLA was stopped cold, and Cameron quick-kicked for 59 yards. State threw it into high gear again and moved 73 yards on 14 plays for another TD, with Wells bolting into the end zone for the score from the two. Slonac converted, and State was ahead to stay.

Early in the 4th period UCLA's Cameron passed to Loudd for a score, making it 21-20 (State's favor). But the kick was no good, and UCLA was doomed.

Late in the quarter Wells put bonus points on the board with an all-time Rose Bowl record punt return of 62 yards for a touchdown. It also clinched him honors as the game's most outstanding player, by vote of the press box denizens.

Biggie gets victory ride.

But there was glory for all, and every one of the 44 Spartans on the Rose Bowl squad, 32 of whom got into the game, won a share for himself.

Those persistent reports that this would be Biggie's last game as head coach, at first considered frivolous gossip, soon proved out to be fact.

In staccato succession, early in 1954, it was announced that Ralph Young would retire as MSU athletic director, that Biggie would succeed him, and that Duffy would be the new head coach.

Thus concluded one of the most remarkable coaching eras in the history of college football. In just seven seasons, the stocky, slope-shouldered, jut-jawed, hyperaggressive Munn had forged a 54-9-2 record at MSC which projected the school and himself into national gridiron eminence.

Not the least of his manifold talents was the perfect timing of arrival and departure on the MSU coaching scene. He leaped on stage just as the burgeoning school was longing for a star to guide it. He bowed out at the zenith of success, a knack few people have possessed.

He demonstrated remarkable empathy with his athletes. They loved everything about him from the way he roared "jackass," "double jackass," or even a rare "triple jackass" at under achievers, to his ability to bend down and pick up four leaf clovers while seemingly engrossed in a hot practice scrimmage or press interview. Players couldn't wait to hear his next pre-game or half-time pep production. He was known to light torches, strew news clippings, distribute compasses, and shout rallying slogans like "just thirty minutes to play and a lifetime to remember." Many were corny, but they worked.

Other facts of his coaching genius were the ability to pick brilliant aides with convincing regularity, to spot and adopt immediately smart stratagems used by opponents, and to infuse everyone around him with his own winning ardor. This latter attribute amounted to a Munn-omania, and at times made him extremely difficult to work with. His temper eruptions when crossed were volcanic, leading associates to predict that some time a heart attack or stroke would hit him. One of the latter did, in 1971, just two days before the Michigan game. A second massive blow in March of 1975 took his life.

His credo, emblazoned at various places around campus and in his very heart, was:

"The difference between good and great is a little extra effort."

Actually for Biggie that phrase "little extra effort" was a vast understatement. Gargantuan effort was more like it.

After the battle. Biggie and the Light Brigade backfield.

Rags To Riches

Duffy Daugherty's inaugural season was ruined 48 hours before the opener at Iowa City.

State had suffered severe personnel losses from the superb 1953 team. Don Dohoney, Bill Quinlan, Tom Yewcic, Evan Slonac, Billy Wells, Larry Fowler, and others were gone. But one star of the first magnitude, LeRoy Bolden, was back for his senior season, and around his abundant talents the offense was built.

The team held its final workout in Spartan Stadium Thursday afternoon prior to going to Iowa. Part of the work was a passing drill. Bolden, an adept receiver as well as a marvelous runner, ran into the end zone for a pass. It came in high and long. Bolden leaped for it, hit the goalpost in midflight and was knocked unconscious. LeRoy really was lucky. He could have been killed, but he escaped with a badly bruised leg.

That damaged leg bothered him all season, however. He kept reinjuring it and was only a shadow of his old self. With a fully able Bolden, State probably would have had a winner that fall instead of a 3-6 loser.

Bolden played in the opener and even scored a touchdown, but Iowa sneaked past State 14-10.

The following Saturday, Wisconsin, with All-American Alan (The Horse) Ameche at fullback, capitalized on an official's blunder to win 6-0 at East Lansing. Once again Bolden figured in the incident. Despite the gimpy leg, he was playing both on offense and defense as athletes had to do in that era. He was knocked out on a tackle at the sideline and lay there just off the playing surface surrounded by photographers, fellow players, trainers, and the team physician.

Wisconsin huddled and came out for the next play. Spartan defensive back John Matsock saw State was shorthanded and tried to call an official's attention to the fact and stop the play. He was waved off, the ball was snapped, and Ameche stormed 28 yards for the only score of the contest.

Duffy attained his first coaching victory the following week at Indiana 21-14 to set the stage for his first go at Notre Dame. It was billed to be an intriguing matchup of Spartan speed against typical Notre Dame bulk and power. But a driving, relentless rain made the Notre Dame field a dismal swamp in which the Irish sloughed to a 20-19 victory. The *Detroit Times* headlined its story, "Mud Stalled Fleet Backs. Experts Blame Rain For Spartan Loss."

So now there were three losses by a total of 11 points in the first four games. Then a couple of weeks later Bob McNamara, a talented Minnesota back, picked a fumble out of the air and ran it 40 yards for the clinching score in a 19-13 loss at Minneapolis.

State closed the unhappy campaign with a 40-10 victory over Marquette, a game most notable for the fact that a big sophomore from Flint named Clarence Peaks flashed the first signal of coming greatness. He carried the ball just six times but accumulated 150 yards. One of his carries was for 65 yards; another, for 53. Morrall had been getting the usual criticism leveled on the quarterback of a losing team, but he sparkled in this game. He connected with John (Big Thunder) Lewis for 59 yards, Lewis again for 63, and Planutis for 62. All three were for scores.

It was an inauspicious beginning for a new coaching regime, to put it charitably. The only victories had been over chronic losers Indiana, Washington State, and Marquette. Spartan fans were spoiled by a solid diet of seven straight winning seasons under Munn and quickly became perplexed, grumpy, and carping. The press did not become unduly critical, however. Many media people were rooting for Duffy to make it because they personally liked him so much. His fresh charm and humor despite adversity were in his favor.

During the season Biggie became upset by the losses and what some Spartan zealots felt was bad coaching. He entered a coaching staff meeting in Spartan Stadium and began criticizing Duffy's staff members. Then came what must have been the

Duffy's first staff may have been best ever assembled anywhere. Kneeling, left to right, are Burt Smith, Sonny Grandelius, Duffy, and Dan Devine. Standing, Bill Yeoman, Bob Devaney, and Don Mason.

shock of Biggie's life. Duffy told him to shut up and get out, that he was the head coach and not Biggie. Biggie left, angrily.

That confrontation had two consequences. It established Duffy as a head coach standing squarely on his own two feet and sowed the first seeds of ill feeling between the two which burst into the open several years later. The days of a father-son relationship were over.

Not much was expected of the 1955 season despite Duffy's chronic optimism. The official preseason prospects sheet from the sports information office put it this way:

"Michigan State's 1955 football team figures to have good offense but questionable defense, good backfield depth but shallowness on the line, fine speed but only fair size, spirit and desire but a heavy handicap of inexperience.

"All this points to an interesting team which could surprise some favored clubs but which isn't likely to produce a big winning season. State appears to be at least a year away from having a top-flight outfit again."

Only 16 lettermen returned, but what a sweet 16. In this number were quarterbacks Pat Wilson and Earl Morrall, fullbacks Gerry Planutis and Gary Lowe, halfbacks Gerry Musetti and Clarence Peaks, centers Joe Badaczewski and John Matsko, guards Embry Robinson and captain Buck Nystrom, tackle Norm Masters, and ends Jim Hinesly and John (Big Thunder) Lewis.

There also were some interesting sophomore prospects. Among these rookies were quarterback Jim Ninowski, halfback Walt Kowalczyk, end Dave Kaiser, tackle Pat Burke, and center and linebacker Dan Currie. Duffy and aides Don Mason, Bob Devaney, Burt Smith, Bill Yeoman, and Sonny Grandelius certainly struck nothing but solid gold in recruiting the freshman class of 1954.

Pat Wilson was figured to be ahead of Earl Morrall among quarterback returnees. There was a reason. Morrall played baseball in the spring of 1955 instead of working in spring football practice. Also there were sour recollections of the 1954 season. Then, too, Wilson's terrific spring performance led the coaches to think Pat was going to be No. 1 man at quarterback.

Earl's name was not even mentioned in a section of the printed *Football Facts Book for Press, Radio and TV* headed "Best Bets For Stardom." This section was written after consultation with Duffy as to which players he figured had the best prospects for outstanding campaigns.

It took Earl about one week of practice that fall to win back the starting job, and from there he went on to consensus All-American accolades. Duffy, the sports information staffers, and the press quickly jumped aboard his band wagon. Earl still remains living proof that a young man can be a "do it yourself" All-American through performance on the field. He certainly had no preseason ballyhoo.

Since at this writing Morrall is still playing football for the Miami Dolphins, a statement he made to a newsman back in the 1955 season has a certain wry humor:

"I've enjoyed every minute of the football I've played and wouldn't trade it for anything. I doubt very much if I'll be playing pro football. From now on I want to bear down on further engineering studies. I feel that I have a little catching up to do."

State began its season of destiny on an unimpressive note. It defeated Indiana at Bloomington 20-13. The Hoosiers had a poor team which finished ninth in the Big Ten at 1-5 and 3-6 overall. About the only bright spots were Peaks' good day of 95 yards rushing, a 64-yard punt runback by Jim Wulff, and some sharp passing by Morrall.

But for end Bob Jewett it was a day with special meaning. He calls Morrall the best player of his time and adds, "He threw me my first touchdown pass in 1955 against Indiana, which my father always remembered as the first touchdown scored by a Michigan State University team. We had just had our name changed from college to university."

That TD pass covered seven yards but was a mile long to Bob and his dad.

The following week State lost to a good Michigan team at Ann Arbor 14-7, at which point the chances of State's actually winding up in the Rose Bowl at season's end seemed very remote.

State led Michigan in some of the statistics, but generally was unimpressive. Morrall had two passes intercepted, and State lost the ball three times on fumbles. Sophomore Ninowski tossed a pass and fell into the standard pattern by having it inter-

Duffy with standouts, left to right, Buck Nystrom, Earl Morrall, Jerry Planutis, John (Big Thunder) Lewis.

cepted. Michigan's Terry Barr snuffed out two Spartan scoring chances by tackling first Kowalczyk and later Morrall inside the Michigan five.

Even the victory over Stanford by a nifty 38-14 count the following week could not have stirred any but the most optimistic among Spartan fans into believing wonderful things lay ahead. In the game Peaks scored two touchdowns, and Morrall hit on four of four passes. Outstanding plays included a 71-yard quick kick by Morrall and a 49-yard scoring aerial from Morrall to Lewis. Dale Hollern and Norm Masters were credited with causing Stanford muffs which resulted in TDs.

The BIG victory, the first of Duffy's coaching career and the one which galvanized super patriots and more casual fans alike, came the next Saturday. State smacked down Notre Dame 21-7 at East Lansing and returned to the big time in college football.

It was a good Irish team with quarterback Paul Hornung, fullback Don Schaefer, halfback Jim Morse, and many more. Notre Dame had not been scored on thus far in the season, but State quickly ruined that record. Spartan TDs were registered by Planutis, Morrall, and Peaks—all on short plunges. Morrall completed five of eight passes but had two intercepted. The Irish scored on a pass from Hornung to Morse, good for 40 yards. The score at the half was 7-7, but State put it all together in the final two periods.

State and especially Morrall finally found themselves. There was not another close game the entire season as the Spartans hurtled their way to glory.

Illinois succumbed 21-7 at East Lansing. Afterwards in the dressing room interview session, Duffy was asked by a writer what he thought of Morrall's play in the game. Morrall had completed five of eight passes for 136 yards and two touchdowns to Kaiser and Jewett, caught a pass, intercepted one, kicked off, punted four times for a 48-yard average, and starred defensively.

Duffy studied his questioner for a moment and then produced this "candidate" for understatement-of-all-time: "Well, you might say, if he doesn't get hurt, he'll make the traveling squad to Wisconsin next week."

Morrall indeed made the trip to Madison and piloted his team to a 27-0 conquest of the Badgers. Earl had another splendid day which featured two 53-yard punts, but the top honors went to Kowalczyk. The big, swift, and powerful sophomore, soon to be nicknamed "The Sprinting Blacksmith" by UCLA's Red Sanders, toted the pigskin ten times for 172 yards and two scores. One of his exploits led to a favorite Duffy story told many times on the banquet circuit.

"The week of the Wisconsin game," Duffy would relate, "I worked hard on Kowalczyk to quit that kid stuff of shifting the ball from one arm to another and trying to straight-arm people. 'That's for high school players,' I told him. 'Hang on to the ball!'

"So against Wisconsin Walt ran 72 yards for a touchdown and on the way shifted the ball three times and knocked loose three or four tacklers with the prettiest straight-arm I've ever seen. It just shows what great coaching can do for a kid."

The Purdue game the following week might be the only one on record in which a coach who just lost 27-0 said in all seriousness that he felt his team should have won. That coach was Stu Holcomb, the Boilermaker head man.

There were two unorthodox Spartan scores which Holcomb particularly had in mind. In the second quarter with the score still 0-0, Purdue recovered a Kowalczyk fumble on the State 18. The Boilermakers moved to the eight on three plays and seemed headed for a score. Then it happened. Purdue fullback Bill Murakowski started to run to his left and found Spartan defenders in close order drill coming at him. He decided to unload the pigskin to his trailer, Jim Whitmer. Bill tossed it wildly; Earl Morrall picked it off and set his course down field. Not noted for Mercury speed, he still went 92 yards for the score. Then later, in the third period, Spartan center John Matsko kicked off, raced down field in time to catch a Purdue fumble in the air, and ran it 21 yards for a score.

Purdue dominated most of the statistics, including such negative ones as ten turnovers. Seven of them were fumbles repossessed by State, and three were interceptions of Lenny Dawson passes.

State closed out the season with a pair of easy victories at East Lansing over Minnesota 42-14 and Marquette 33-0.

Against the Gophers, 14 backs carried the ball and six people scored. State thus had placed its 5-1 conference record in the books and now could sit back and see if that rated a Rose Bowl bid.

The Marquette game was memorable for some weird and

wonderful crowd conduct related to a football game being played 65 miles away at Ann Arbor. Ohio State and Michigan were meeting in their usual season ender, and the outcome of that game would dictate whether or not State would spend the holidays in California. Going into the finale, Ohio State was 5-0 in the league and Michigan, 5-1. The Wolverines had been upset two weeks before by Illinois 25-6. If Michigan won the Ohio State game, its resultant 6-1 conference mark would give it first place and certainly the Rose Bowl bid. But if Ohio State won (which it ultimately did 17-0), it would finish first with a 6-0 card; State, second at 5-1; and Michigan, third at 5-2. Under the no repeat rule then in effect, Ohio State could not be sent west as it had gone there after the 1954 season. So State almost certainly would be selected to go.

There was so much fan interest in the Ann Arbor game that the Michigan State athletic department agreed to waive its rule against radios in the stands for this one occasion. The attendance that day was 41,484, and it was estimated that at least one of every four patrons had a portable blasting away.

The result was a series of fantastic, funny crowd reactions in relation to the game being played before it. One time fans broke into a mighty cheer over some development at Ann Arbor just as a 15-yard penalty was being walked off against State. Several times the crowd exploded as State was huddling. A helmeted head or two popped up quizzically. But what really got Duffy's blood pressure surging was the discovery that his players on the sidelines were not following the game at hand. They were bending an ear toward the nearest radio in the stands.

State was leading by a precarious 6-0 count at the half, and Duffy realized fully that a poor performance against Marquette could negatively influence the conference athletic directors in their Rose Bowl vote. He read the riot act in the dressing room and invited anyone who was more interested in the Michigan-Ohio State game to change clothes and hurry down there. Sobered players got the message and scored 27 more points following intermission.

It was revealed after the game that Duffy had received a threat on his life if his team defeated Marquette by more than six points. The letter, typed and unsigned, came from Newark, New Jersey.

Duffy's typical reaction was to joke. "I told Bob Devaney, who sits on the bench with me, that I thought it would be a good idea if he wore a jacket with 'Head Coach' in large letters on the back."

Consequences of the excellent season were many, varied, and delightful. Four players—Morrall, Masters, Nystrom and Planutis—made All-Big Ten. The same four were named to one or more major All-Americas. Morrall and Masters both achieved consensus All-America status.

And State was named to go to the Rose Bowl. Despite the early Michigan loss, it was ranked No. 2 nationally in wire service polls behind Oklahoma. Ohio State was ranked fifth, and Michigan was out of the top ten.

Duffy was acclaimed "Coach of the Year" by balloting of his fellow coaches. He made it by the widest margin in the 21-year history of the poll, with good friend Bud Wilkinson in second. His overwhelming selection testified to the affection his coaching peers held for him as a person and also their admiration for the remarkable comeback from a 3-6 to an 8-1 record achieved by his team in one year's time.

State's multiple offense again was the talk of the country as it had been under Biggie. A widely used quote from Duffy

Front line bruisers—Embry Robinson, Norm Masters, Buck Nystrom.

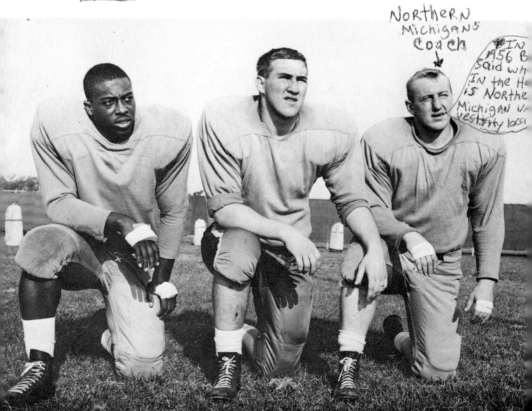

Trainer Jack Heppinstall completed 40 years' service in 1955.

was: "Our single wing is not as formidable as Red Sanders'. Our split-T is not as deceptive as Wilkinson's nor is our T as slick as Red Blaik's.... But we can hit 'em with anything."

Morrall rated near the top nationally for both passing and punting. He threw the ball 68 times during the regular season and completed 42 for 941 yards, a remarkable .617 completion percentage. But even more phenomenal was his yardage average of 13.9 on every throw, complete and incomplete. That stood in the NCAA books for many years as the record. Earl also averaged 42.9 yards per punt to finish second nationally and put his name in State's record book as the all-time leader.

Earl was frequently interviewed during the season and in its delicious aftermath. The handsome, brainy, reserved master field general once described the workings of the multiple offense in these words:

"It's really not overly complex. You might say we have only 10 or 11 basic plays. It's essentially a system of combinations which make for seemingly infinite variety. Ball carrying and blocking assignments are given in the huddle and designated by numbers.

"We'll use the single wing to get a back in what shapes up as a good blocking position or to put him in a good spot for catching a pass, just as you might use a flanker. If a team is ganging up on us inside, we'll spread it out with a split-T. We'll also favor the split-T when an opposing line is much bigger than ours. This gives us a better chance to drive past them.

"The biggest advantage of the system is its deceptiveness. We can keep them guessing about what's coming. We don't try to lure a team offside by shifting from the T because we know they're watching the ball."

Duffy revealed that Earl called practically every play in every game that championship season. "I sent in maybe three or four a game," Duffy asserted. "The rest of the time he was on his own out there."

Golden Toe

Michigan State won the 1956 Rose Bowl on a broken play.
What?

Dave Kaiser's fabulous 41-yard field goal with seven seconds left was a broken play?

That's right!

A broken play is one in which something goes drastically wrong. Usually it means disaster, but sometimes it can turn to gold.

Kaiser was in the middle of a practice swing of the leg when the ball arrived in holder Earl Morrall's hands. Kaiser's reflex reaction—there was no time for thinking—was to step back and swing through again, this time at the ball. He connected solidly, followed through perfectly, and the ball whirled end over end through the goalposts slightly left of dead center, 41 yards away.

It should be remembered that this was in the day before the collegiate goalposts were widened, and a kick of 41 yards was phenomenal under the most ideal circumstances. Dave certainly merited his new nickname, "Golden Toe."

It was a broken play in the press box, too. Jerry Planutis, who had had great days kicking extra points and field goals for State, this day had missed two field goal tries. So quarterback Morrall called on Kaiser to make the last ditch try. Almost everyone in the press box thought it was Planutis again and gave him credit for the winning kick. It took some time to get things straightened out and news stories and radio and TV announcements corrected. Even the official play-by-play report distributed in the press box named Planutis as the kicker.

The fact that it was Kaiser's first field goal ever was played up big. So was a colorful feature angle that Dave had forgotten

Kaiser's winning field goal.

his contact lenses and was unable to see his kick spinning home. That it was Dave's first field goal was true enough, but the truth about the contact lenses did not come out until later. He had not forgotten them at all. They were the old-fashioned cup type which irritated his eyes after a couple of hours. So he deliberately left them behind in the locker room. But he was farsighted and had no trouble following the ball in flight without them.

As Kaiser's name became a national household word, it was revealed that his true family name was Kajzerkowski. "Kaiser" had been hung on him and his brothers (several of whom also were fine athletes) by *Alpena News* sportswriters. They had gotten sick and tired of spelling out Kajzerkowski day after day and came up with Kaiser.

It was mentioned, too, that his high school coach was now a Michigan State assistant, name of Bob Devaney.

There was wild excitement over the way State won the 1956 Rose Bowl, but the experience started placidly. Fans' reaction contrasted sharply with what it was for the first Rose Bowl invitation two years before. The basic support and enthusiasm for the team was there, however, and plans were quickly made for six special trains to carry some 2,700 State students and faculty advisors to Los Angeles. Another 1,800 students planned to travel by plane and automobile.

Bob Voges of the Associated Press reported that "When some 2,700 Michigan State University students take off Monday for the Rose Bowl festivities in California, it will be the largest peace-time, non-military point-to-point mass movement by train in history." The AP said it had this on the authority of representatives from 11 major railroads, who pooled rolling stock to make up the six special trains.

A seventh special train also went west, carrying the band, cheerleaders, varsity squad players not picked for the official 44-man traveling squad, and other campus representatives.

When the team boarded its plane at the Capitol City Airport, some 500 Spartan boosters, among them Gov. G. Mennen Williams, cheered, danced, and sang the "Spartan Fight Song" with the MSU band.

The pace picked up quickly once the team arrived in California and the press began its usual spate of extravagant stories. Most writers said the 1956 Spartans were the best team ever to come out of the Big Ten.

Duffy followed Biggie's lead in his cordiality of two years before by announcing practice sessions would be open to all the press. The preceding December Woody Hayes had reverted to standard Big Ten policy of banning West Coast writers, but Duffy declared, "If I didn't feel I could trust the newspapermen, it would be a pretty poor reflection on both our professions. The job of a sportswriter is to write, so I figure my job's to help him."

However, Duffy went Biggie one better, much to the consternation of his assistant coaches. At the open house affair, meant mainly for the press to take pictures and talk to coaches and players, Duffy ran his team through dummy plays and explained them to some 3,500 spectators in the stands via a public address system.

"We showed them just about everything we used this year," he said afterwards. "I figure Red Sanders had us pretty well scouted, so what's the harm in showing the folks our stuff."

That was not what concerned the assistants. Duffy also showed some plays which had been put into the repertoire just for the Rose Bowl. One of the plays he revealed was later used to score a touchdown in the big game. Alderton recorded the play this way in his game story in the *State Journal:*

"Then came the play—a brand new one by the way. Morrall lateraled out to Peaks, who had a clean left flank sweep. He ran two or three steps, then stopped and fired a pass to John Lewis.

"Big Thunder took it on the run, behind the Bruin defense. It was beautifully thrown and perfectly timed. It was Peaks' fourth throw this season, and the second completed....

"John scored standing up and Planutis converted to make it 14-7 for State."

Duffy was applauded for his open practice sessions and frankness and cooperation with the media everywhere except, perhaps, in the environs of Ann Arbor and Columbus. But Duffy began to have some misgivings and expressed concern to close associates about how the folks back home might be reacting to his open door policies. If his team lost the game, he foresaw that Spartan fans would criticize him for not being tougher.

There were more immediate worries, though. His Spartans were plagued with injuries. Embry Robinson, a regular at guard, and Jerry Musetti, a letterman at halfback, were out of action. Robinson's knee injury was to give Dan Currie, a young Detroiter with a big future, the starting shot in the bowl game. Bob Jewett, Jim Wulff, and Archie Matsos were out of practice action for awhile, and Earl Morrall came down with a bad cold shortly before the team takeoff from East Lansing and spent some time in Olin Health Center. But then Clarence Peaks returned to practice in good health for the first time since being injured in the Notre Dame game, the fourth of the season.

Peaks was withheld from any contact work during practice, but Duffy said, "The best sight I've had since we arrived is Peaks back in tip-top condition. He looks like he did when we started the season."

The Los Angeles press noticed the light practices, and Furillo quoted Duffy as saying, "I can't take the chance on anybody getting hurt. I doubt if we'll scrimmage more than once or twice before the game with UCLA."

Duffy declared that his biggest worry outside of his team's physical condition was defensing the UCLA single wing. He had good reason to be concerned. State had faced the same type of offense against Michigan, and that was the one game it lost. Later it beat a Wisconsin team using the single wing by 27-0, but the Badgers had owned the ball an amazing 84 plays from scrimmage, compared to 43 for State. If UCLA could establish such ball control, it could win.

"We've got to fight that possession superiority," Duffy said. "The single wing is a grinding offense, and the Bruins use unit blocking (double teaming ends and tackles) like Ohio State. We know how dangerous that can be."

Media observers still asserted that this Spartan team was superior to the 1954 team on at least two counts. It was bigger physically, and it had a much stronger passing game with Morrall at quarterback and the likes of Big Thunder Lewis, Dave Kaiser, Bob Jewett, Tony Kolodziej, and Jim Hinesly to catch the ball.

When Al Wolf wrote in the *Los Angeles Times* that a former Big Ten coach said Morrall was not a "pro-type player,"

Spartan starters in 1956 Rose Bowl. Line, left to right, Kaiser, Burke, Masters, Nystrom, Badaczewski, Currie, Lewis. Backs, Kowalczyk, Morrall, Planutis, Peaks.

Duffy's hackles were raised.

"Earl Morrall," Duffy fired back via Al Wolf, "is the finest pro quarterback prospect I've seen at Michigan State in my nine years here." (That included Al Dorow and Tom Yewcic, both of whom played pro ball successfully.)

Duffy went on to say that Morrall was "an honor student, a good runner, a fine passer, a superlative kicker, a natural leader who never loses his poise, a smart play-caller and a strong, good-sized athlete."

He pointed out that although Earl had not thrown much in the 1955 season, he still had set an NCAA record for average yardage gained (13.9) on every pass he threw.

Developments over the years proved Duffy was right.

While the team was readying for the contest, the usual social activities were permitted—a Disneyland tour, a barbecue at a ranch in the San Fernando Valley, the much ballyhooed roast beef eating duel at Lawry's restaurant between the teams (but on different nights), and the Big Ten dinner.

Duffy and Red Sanders traded quips with Jack Benny on his television show the Sunday night before the game. Then there was a movie studio visit, this time to Columbia studios where players watched June Allyson working a scene.

Finally the day arrived for one of the most thrilling, tension-packed, fiercely contested, and ultimately controversial Rose Bowl games ever played. The weather was clear and warm, the field in excellent shape.

The first rousing play came before the 100,809 fans had reached their seats. UCLA kicked off to State, and Walt Kowalczyk ran the ball out of the end zone to the 12. On the first play from scrimmage Morrall tried a running pass, but defender Jim Decker intercepted it on the run and carried it back to State's 16. Four plays later UCLA fullback Bob Davenport ploughed into the end zone for the opening score.

If the Spartans were shocked, they did not show it. They took the ensuing kickoff and immediately drove to the UCLA 15. However they had to turn over the ball on downs. Indicative of the ferocious defense being thrown up by UCLA was the fact that the redoubtable Peaks was tossed for a loss of nine yards on State's final down to give the West Coast club the ball on its own 24.

The rest of the first period was given over to a defensive duel punctuated by punts until a questionable official's call gave

UCLA its second big break. Morrall, back to pass, was hit from behind by a UCLA defender. The ball fell free and was recovered by Bruin end Hal Smith on State's 36. Spartan partisans thought Morrall had started his passing motion and that the call should have been simply an incomplete pass. The officials ruled, however, that it was a fumble, and the ball belonged to UCLA.

Sensing an opportunity to put the game on ice early, the totally energized Bruins moved the ball to a first down on State's nine in eight straight running plays. An off side penalty against State helped in the drive.

State had to stop UCLA if it was to stay in the game, and somehow State found the resources needed to blunt the thrust. Davenport made one yard before being dropped by Spartan Pat Burke. Then Sam Brown tried an end sweep but end Tony Kolodziej smashed down the interference, and halfback Gary Lowe nailed the Bruin runner for a five-yard loss back to the 13. On the third down play UCLA finally elected to go to the

Ace running back Clarence Peaks gets repairs.

Heavy action in bowl.

air. Brown moved back to throw and found three Spartans going right with him—Norm Masters, Pat Burke, and Jim Hinesly. They smeared him on the 21. A fourth down field goal try was missed, and State had won the battle for survival.

From there, State swept 79 yards on 13 plays for the score which, along with Jerry Planutis' conversion, tied the game at 7-7. The big play in the series was a blast over left tackle for 30 yards by Walt Kowalczyk. That gave State a first down at the UCLA 17, and two plays later Morrall found Peaks on the goal line and clotheslined a pass to him for the score. That was it at the half.

State dominated the third period action with an 18-play

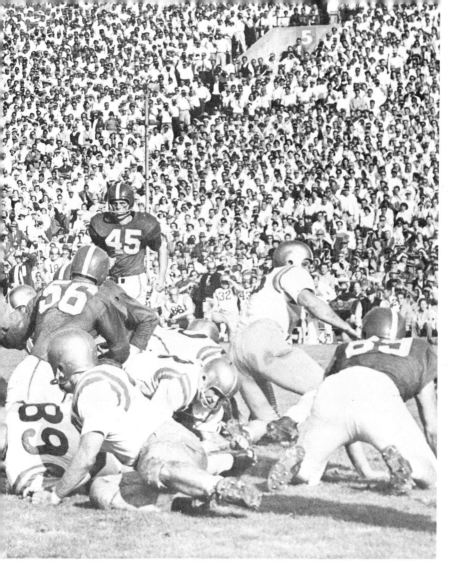

drive which covered 72 yards but ended short of pay dirt.
Planutis' field goal try missed, and UCLA regained possession
on its own eight.

The big play which Duffy had showed the fans on press
day a couple of weeks earlier was sprung early in the fourth
period. Morrall lateraled to Peaks, who flung a forward to Lewis
about the midfield stripe. Lewis ran it home almost untouched.
The action covered 67 yards.

That might have been the clincher, but UCLA had some
surprises left. One was a 47-yard pass play, Ronnie Knox to
Decker, for a first down on State's seven. Knox hit tackle twice,
and finally Doug Peters flung himself over center for the score,

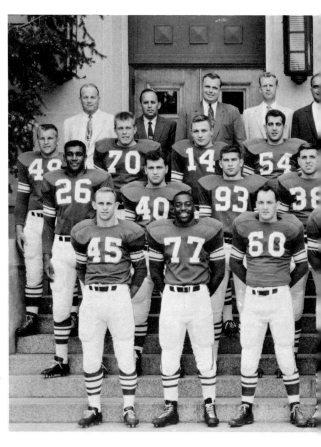

1956 Rose Bowl champs.

The extra point was good, and at 8:53 in the final period the count was tied again.

Fans by this time were either limp and exhausted or hysterical. But further excruciating assaults on their nervous systems were about to be inflicted.

State took off on a vigorous drive immediately after the kickoff. It was Planutis for 14, Peaks for 13, Peaks again for 9, Planutis for 10, and so forth. UCLA finally braced, a couple of pass attempts failed, and it was fourth down and 11 on the UCLA 24.

Planutis was called on for a field goal try and missed. It did seem this was going to end in a 14-14 tie.

Then strange things began to happen on the field. Five of the next six plays were nullified by penalties. First an unsportsmanlike conduct call was made against UCLA for coaching from the sidelines, so the Bruins took possession of the ball after

Planutis' missed field goal back on their five instead of the 20. Next, an intentional grounding rap was pinned on Knox, who had flung a desperation pass. Now the ball was on the UCLA one.

A punt was clearly in order, and Knox got one off to the UCLA 40. But there was another flag; the Bruins were penalized for interference by team captain Hardiman Cureton with Sparton receiver Clarence Peaks' opportunity to catch the ball. The ball was handed over to State on the UCLA 19.

Dennis Mendyk tried right tackle on the first play, fumbled, and the ball was recovered by Planutis. But now State was penalized for holding, and the referee marched the ball back to State's 30. Next Morrall passed to Don Zysk, complete on the 19. Officials let that one stand but moments later penalized the Spartans for delay of the game. There had been a momentary mix-up over getting set for the last gasp field goal try. That five-yard penalty moved the ball back to State's 24.

It was the decisive moment. The scoreboard clock was at the seven second mark and holding. The crazed crowd watched Morrall assume his one-knee-down holder's position seven yards behind center on the 31 yard line. Only the most observant would have noticed that the ball arrived too soon and that the kicker had to hop back and swing his leg again.

Kaiser said later he knew it was going to be good as soon as he felt solid contact with the ball. But just to be sure the official saw it that way, he turned and faced the referee before the ball had even reached the goalposts. A wonderful picture taken from the end zone stands shows the ball en route well above, but still short of, the crossbars. It also shows virtually every face watching the flight of the ball. Only one person has his back turned to the action; number 89 shows on the back of his jersey. It was Dave Kaiser watching for the referee's confirmation that he had made Rose Bowl history.

President Hannah and Tug Wilson congratulate Kaiser.

Some of the Los Angeles writers, most of whom had wound up picking UCLA to win after first building State to the skies, took out after the officials for what they called wresting the game away from the kids in the final moments. Especially blasted was the unsportsmanlike conduct call. But statistically, State had by far the better game. It led in total offense 381 yards to 197. It also led in first downs (26 to 20) and plays from scrimmage (72 to 60). Kowalczyk, with 88 yards rushing, was named the outstanding player of the game by the media. He and Jerry Planutis (with 66 yards rushing) both topped UCLA's best, Sam Brown, who had 63.

Morrall did not have a big day passing, with only four completions in 15 tries, but his successes netted 88 yards and one touchdown. Knox completed two of eight throws for 61 yards, and Peaks caught three passes and threw the big one to Lewis. Many Spartans played crucial roles in the great victory, and there was glory for everyone.

Bill Corum, the distinguished sports columnist for the International News Service, wrote in a bowl game review that "It was as good a football game, college or pro, as a fan could wish to see. A story-book finish that even Hollywood could not have duplicated with a script."

Good Times, Bad Times

Duffy was acclaimed by *Time* magazine in a cover story early in the 1956 season as "the master craftsman of the most intricate offensive in modern football," and the team was rated high nationally from the start.

Duffy joked with a preseason assemblage of the Lansing Downtown Coaches club in Spartan Stadium, saying, "You know, I've got a real problem this year. I'm expected to win football games with halfbacks named Blanche, Clarence and Dennis. Now I ask you, how can fellows with names like that play this rough game of football?"

His audience roared with appreciative laughter. They knew he was referring to Blanche Martin, a brilliant sophomore prospect from River Rouge; Clarence Peaks, the established star and a solid preseason choice for All-American honors as well as a Heisman award possibility; and Dennis Mendyk, the gawky, high-striding Ichabod Crane from St. Charles, Michigan. Any coach in the country would have mortgaged his stadium for them.

The 1956 Rose Bowl champions rewarded their fans with four straight victories at the outset. They were 21-7 over Stanford at Palo Alto, always a difficult place to win; 9-0 over Michigan at Ann Arbor, the usual location for the game (Biggie was, however, about to win his long fight to put the Michigan-MSU series on a home-and-home basis); 53-6 over Indiana at Bloomington; and 47-14 over Notre Dame at South Bend.

The intrastate classic was a typical bone rattler, with the score tied 0-0 at the half. Michigan was strong that season and had such stars as Ron Kramer, John Herrnstein, Jim Pace, and

Bob Ptacek.

"The coaches found the holes for us at the half," said ecstatic team captain John Matsko afterwards. Special tribute went to coaches Sonny Grandelius and Lou Agase, the main men on the press box phones for State.

Matsko was a major figure in those opening games. The blonde, stubby (5-10, 192), crew-cut senior center had produced the first big break for his team at Stanford by intercepting a pass which led to State's first score. At Michigan he booted a field goal, which proved to be all that State needed to win, and contributed another interception.

A giant in the Michigan contest was a 220-pound junior from Wierton, West Virginia, named Joel Jones. Recently switched from end to tackle, Jones made tackle after tackle and delivered crushing blocks offensively. He finished the day by tearing the ball loose from Michigan fullback John Herrnstein. Jim Hinesly recovered, and a few plays later State had its lone touchdown.

State's stampede over Notre Dame was one of its all-time offensive masterpieces. The Spartans sprang an unbalanced line left which it had not exposed previously, and that may have had something to do with it.

The field at South Bend was sodden from a three-hour rain in the morning, scarcely a good omen for a dazzling running show. The Irish, urged on by the Irish student cheering section in the northwest corner of the stands, scored first. Then Clarence Peaks, Dennis Mendyk, Pat Wilson, Jim Ninowski, Don Arend, Don Gilbert, John Matsko, and their cohorts took over.

Mendyk produced dazzling TD runs of 62 and 68 yards. He almost reeled off a return of a kickoff over 90 yards for a score, but a desperation effort by safety Paul Hornung toppled him at midfield.

Arend turned end on a 65-yard scoring gallop, and Gilbert and Peaks scored on short plunges climaxing long drives.

Peaks contributed two magnificent plays in a row. Hornung launched a long bomb toward Jim Morse in the third period when the game's outcome was still in doubt. It looked like a certain TD until Peaks streaked out of nowhere, tipped the ball away, chased and caught it, and set sail down field. He was downed on State's 22; however, the ball went back to the seven on a penalty. On the very next play the marvelous athlete from Flint broke through tackle, ran over several Irish defend-

Spartans stop Notre Dame.

ers, and raced 93 yards into the Irish end zone for what would have been the longest rushing play in State's history. It, too, was called back on a flag down at midfield.

But nothing could stop State. It amassed 369 yards rushing and 125 passing. All scores were made via running plays.

The time was ripe for a Duffyism and he told the press in the locker room: "I wasn't worried about getting our boys up for this one. They were so high this week that we had to shake the trees around the field to get them down for practice."

Voters in the wire service polls promptly moved State into No. 1 nationally. Fans were ecstatic, but they completely overlooked the developing calamity. State's injury toll had been mounting rapidly. It was not the numbers so much as the quality of men dropping by the wayside.

Brilliant halfback Walt Kowalczyk suffered a badly sprained ankle in preseason work and never was right that fall. Tackle Pat Burke, who had started every game as a sophomore in 1955, went out early with a knee injury. Bob Jewett, an excellent receiver, broke a bone in his foot and was sidelined. Dave Kaiser checked out with a badly sprained ankle and foot against Indiana. Numerous others kept on playing but were far below par with injuries.

Somehow it seemed that as long as Peaks continued performing, State could overcome anything. Wilfrid Smith, *Chicago Tribune* sports editor and one of the finest football writers and authorities on the game ever to batter a typewriter, wrote after the Notre Dame game that "Michigan State has one of the all-time great backs in Clarence Peaks." *Collier's* magazine had Peaks all set for the cover of its All-American issue. Special pictures had been taken on campus, and the cover art had been completed.

Then State went to Illinois. The Illini were having a miserable campaign despite the presence of some fine players like backfield ace Abe Woodson. "Goodbye Ray" signs festooned Champaign. The papers were critical of Coach Ray Eliot, and the alumni were disgruntled. It was a lot like the Purdue situation of 1953.

As members of the Spartan team party walked about on the turf in Memorial Stadium the day before the game, they noted how hard and rough the field was. There were great holes gouged out of the grass. Clumps of sod like huge golf divots lay about loose, and the place looked like a battlefield pockmarked with bomb craters.

The game started well, with State going ahead 13-0 by the half and Peaks giving another marvelous performance. He had carried the ball seven times for 42 yards and a touchdown. But best of all he had been stopping the redoubtable Woodson cold.

Then it happened. Early in the second half an Illinois pass play developed. Peaks, playing safety, backpedaled swiftly to cover anything long and tramped into one of the ruts. His knee collapsed, and he went down in a heap. The verdict was a serious knee injury.

With Peaks gone, Illinois rose and took charge. Woodson scored three touchdowns, two on runs of 70 and 82 yards, and Illinois won 20-13.

With the loss, State's No. 1 ranking went down the drain. So did the *Collier's* cover and Peaks' all but certain All-American status. Had the injury occurred just a week later, he would have been in safely for major national honors. Every Spartan fan who saw that game is convinced that there was no way that

*Faces of football. Old friends Dale Smith and Sam Williams
before and after 1957 Illinois game in Spartan Stadium.*

Woodson or anyone else could have scored three times against State had Peaks remained in the game. He had been the dominating figure on the field.

State did not completely collapse. The following week it beat Wisconsin 33-0, with Wilson throwing strikes to Tony Kolodziej for one score and other good gains, and Mendyk cashing six points on a brilliant 67-yard punt return.

Purdue proved tougher and more costly to State. The Spartans won 12-9 at East Lansing but lost Joel Jones and Kolodziej to injuries. Jones suffered a wrecked knee which ended his college career. State had a break in that game. Boilermaker quarterback Lenny Dawson had his arm in a sling and did not play. End Harold Dukes scored one TD for State on a pass from Jim Ninowski. The other was registered by Kolodziej on a recovered fumble in the Purdue end zone.

State now was 4-1 in the conference and still had a possible tie for the crown in view if it could win its last league test against Minnesota at Minneapolis.

It was not to be. State presented a patched up lineup on a bitterly cold day and was edged 14-13.

State bashed Kansas State 38-17 the following week to conclude a respectable 7-2 season, with center and team captain John Matsko winning well-deserved All-Big Ten laurels.

The 1957 Spartans were picked to top the Big Ten again and finish high nationally. As usual, it was Duffy's fault.

"The trouble with you is that you get carried away by my enthusiasm," Duffy cajoled a newsman prior to the start of the season.

The eternally optimistic Scotch-Irishman could not contain himself when speaking of his team's chances for the season. He would cite all the losses through graduation, the strengths of Michigan or Purdue or Ohio State, the overall defensive problems, and the many young players who might make mistakes. But then he would be asked about Walt Kowalczyk or Dan Currie or Dave Kaiser or Jim Ninowski, and it was "Katy bar the door." He not only never said a negative word about a player, he was hard put to be less than ecstatic about one of his athletes. They were the fastest, strongest, smartest, most marvelous young men God ever created or he ever coached.

Press people drank it all in and wrote it verbatim. Year after year the "skywriters," the band of newsmen who still fly from one Big Ten camp to another prior to the season to talk to the coaches, visit practices, sometimes interview players, and finally predict the outcome of the Big Ten race, almost invariably picked State to win the championship.

The skywriters were so wrong so often, it began to be embarrassing. Some newsmen groused that Duffy had been putting them on, that he was deliberately dishonest with them. But people who understood Duffy better countered this with suggestions that good reporters evaluate statements in relation to their source, and surely everyone knew that Duffy was the supreme optimist.

"Did you believe Frank Leahy when he said poor ol' Notre Dame would be lucky to make a first down?—Then how come you swallow everything Duffy says?"

But the newsmen generally believed Duffy, and one time that they should have been right was 1957.

This team, Duffy's fourth, came within one erroneous official's decision of winning the complete jackpot—the Big Ten title, the Rose Bowl assignment, and the national championship. The blown decision was confirmed the following week by the Big Ten office, with many apologies. Duffy complained bitterly to conference officials but kept his mouth shut publicly, as it was decreed coaches should.

The penalty came on a touchdown plunge by Kowalczyk early in the second quarter of the Purdue game. A Spartan lineman was charged with having sustained a block after the whistle had blown the play dead. The infraction occurred after the score had been made, and the penalty should have been assessed on the ensuing kickoff. Had the TD been allowed, the score would have been 13 or perhaps 14-0, and the entire complexion of the game would have been changed. As it was, a relieved Purdue team scored late in the second period and left the field at the half with a 7-7 tie. The Boilermakers went on to win 20-13.

State had opened its 1957 season with resounding victories over Indiana (54-0) and California (19-0) and an eye-popping 35-6 conquest of Michigan.

Twenty-one players had carried the ball against Indiana. Jim Ninowski bingoed on six straight passes, and Blanche Martin scored two touchdowns.

Ninowski devastated California with nine pass completions in 14 throws, including touchdown heaves to Sam Williams, the blonde junior giant from Dansville, and Dave Kaiser. A Mike Panitch to Art Johnson pass accounted for MSU's other TD.

Michigan was shaken to its foundations by State's offensive rampage that included a 113-yard rushing performance by Kowalczyk, touchdown heaves by Ninowski to Williams and Jewett, and a 62-yard TD run by Art Johnson. It was the worst chastising ever administered to the Wolverines by their East Lansing country cousins.

State struggled after the bitter Purdue disappointment and barely squeezed past a testy Illinois team in Spartan Stadium 19-14. The Spartans hurt themselves with six fumbles, four of them lost to the enemy, but Blanche Martin saved the game. He returned a punt 86 yards for a touchdown. He ran the ball

Blanche Martin could fly.

north along the east sideline until apparently trapped at midfield. Several Illini crashed into him, and the play seemed ended. However, the whistle did not blow because Martin was still on balance and had not been tackled—only blocked to a momentary stop. Suddenly he sprang free and sprinted into the clear before relaxed Illinois defenders could react. Martin also scored another touchdown from two yards out, and Kowalczyk broke loose for a 36-yard canter to score.

The rest of the games were breezes, two touchdowns or more over Wisconsin, Notre Dame, Minnesota, and Kansas State to close out an 8-1 season. State's 5-1 in the league was second to Ohio State's 7-0. But the Bucks had dropped a non-conference or "exhibition" game, as Woody called the ones he lost. Had MSU defeated Purdue, it would have been 9-0, and its top national ranking and conference championship tie probably would have sent it to Pasadena. (MSU and OSU did not play

All-American Walt Kowalczyk almost loses his head.

Spartan Stadium was doubledecked in 1957.

each other that year.)

Two Spartans attained All-America laurels that fall—
Kowalczyk and Currie—and six made All-Big Ten—Kowalczyk,
Currie, Jim Ninowski, Pat Burke, Ellison Kelly, and Sam Wil-
liams.

All of them deserved their honors, but there was another
Spartan who somehow got left out, probably because so many
others were cited and he still had a year left. Martin had starred
in game after game, capped by his performance against
Minnesota. In that one he carried the ball just six times but ate
up 134 yards.

"It was quite an experience," Martin said. "It was the first
time I'd gotten past 100 yards rushing, and that was still quite a
thing then.

"Today the ballcarriers run 20 or 30 times a game, but if
we carried the ball ten times in 1957, we figured we'd put in a
hard day's work."

"The big ones were veer traps," he recalled, using a word—
"veer"—which was to be in vogue a decade later. "All you had

201

to do was get by the end, and you were gone," he added.

Martin today is a dentist in East Lansing and chairman of the university's Board of Trustees.

Duffy called the 1957 team the greatest he had coached. Others agreed. After all returns, including the bowl games, were in, State wound up third in the nation behind Auburn and Ohio State.

Twenty seniors, including many stars, finished their careers that 1957 season. It should have been a forewarning of rough weather to come, but by this time State partisans and most of the media looked upon victories as the Spartans' natural, inevitable due.

Duffy opened in good form with a practical joke on the skywriters, which was recounted all over the land.

Woody Hayes had ordered the touring skywriters off the Buckeye practice field. "I wanted to give the players hell for some of their mistakes, and I never do it in front of outsiders," he explained later. "I don't believe in whipping them in the newspapers."

The same writers stopped at East Lansing the next day. When they reached the practice field, they found that Daugherty had ordered the gate locked. They groused impatiently for a few minutes, and finally Duffy poked his head out.

"I kept you guys waiting," he said, "because I wanted to praise my players for their good work, and I didn't want to do it in front of strangers."

That also was the fall that Duffy announced to the world that "Football is not a contact sport. It's a collision sport. Dancing is a good example of a contact sport."

The team started with an easy 32-12 conquest of California, a frustrating 12-12 tie with Michigan, and a 22-8 rout of Pittsburgh. All three games were at home.

Dean Look starred in the opener with California by running for 103 yards on 18 carries and connecting with quarterback Greg Montgomery on a 57-yard scoring pass. Montgomery also found rugged sophomore end Fred Arbanas with a 27-yard scoring toss.

The Michigan game was a defensive battle in which Look made the big play, a 92-yard punt return for a score, thanks to crunching open field blocks by Mike Panitch, Archie Matsos, and Dick Barker.

Then weaknesses began to show, and State dropped five

202

straight games before closing out with an easy victory over Kansas State. The record was 3-5-1.

A general lack of depth, quarterbacking problems, and injuries had taken their toll. The prospects piece in the preseason facts book for press-radio-TV had forecast the difficulties with the opening statement that "The biggest rebuilding job in years faces Michigan State's football forces."

Missed most that year was power running back Blanche Martin, who was out with a knee injury suffered in spring drills. Some players had been stars, however. Sam Williams, captain that year, played a brilliant game at end and won well-deserved All-Big Ten and All-America honors. Lineman Ellison Kelly joined Sam in conference recognition. And there were promising sophomores such as Herb Adderley, Fred Arbanas, Fred Boylen, Al Luplow, Ed McLucas, George Perles, Mickey Walker, and Tom Wilson.

Irrepressible Duffy still found something to joke about. A favorite story that winter told of a letter he had received at season's end.

"I didn't mind that the guy wrote me from Detroit," Duffy would say, "just telling me I was a bum and questioning my ability as a coach. But I objected to the swiftness with which the post office department delivered the letter. It got there in the usual time—with just the address 'Duffy and Dope' on it."

But there were serious developments that year which even Duffy could not laugh off. They were triggered by a 39-12 loss suffered at Minnesota in the next to the last game of the season, a loss which consigned the Spartans to the Big Ten basement. Biggie Munn was terribly embarrassed by the team's play before his home town and old school people and talked to Detroit newsmen in a Minneapolis restaurant.

Pete Waldmeir reported in a front page *Detroit News* story under an eight-column banner the next day that Biggie had said, among other things:

"I've been in football since I was 14 years old and I've never been dumb enough to think that you can win them all. But when you throw the game away like we did today by losing the ball ten times, it's terrible...just terrible.

"It was the most futile display I've ever seen. Utter futility. I've never taken losing so bad, but I cried after this one.

"When you have scratched and crawled a tenth of an inch

at a time to build an empire, although it's a small empire, it takes a lot out of you to see it crash."

Biggie's remarks brought the rift between him and Duffy into the open.

President Hannah moved swiftly into the picture, met with Munn and Daugherty, and issued a statement in which he said:

"I had a long and profitable discussion with Director Munn and Coach Daugherty and was gratified to have them confirm my belief that reports of differences between them have been greatly exaggerated.... There has been no loss of confidence in their ability or their dedication to the best interests of the university. They are united in their determination to restore the fortunes of the Spartans....As far as I am concerned, and as far as Mr. Munn and Mr. Daugherty are concerned, this is a closed incident, and there will be no additional comment."

The press fulminated over what they called Hannah's "gag rule," but things gradually quieted down. The wounds, however, were deep.

Duffy was a much more sensitive and serious man beneath his facade of affable Irish wit than most people realized. He was hurt by the episode but never fired back publicly. He kept the jests going while determinedly preparing to bring the Spartans back into gridiron prominence.

Duffy astonished everyone by announcing that Dean Look was going to be the Spartan signal caller in 1959. Dean had never played quarterback in his life and had not even worked at the position in spring drills. He was a brilliant outfielder with the baseball team and received—but turned down—a major league offer of over $50,000 (big money in those days). He also was State's best returning running back.

One Big Ten coach said of the move, "If Duffy brings this off, it will be the coaching job of the year."

State's renowned multiple offense was enriched by the addition of a double wing formation featuring an unbalanced line, a man in motion on nearly every play, and the quarterback operating from the T-position behind center.

Whether these two decisions were responsible or not, the fact remains that State's 1959 team surged back victoriously. Its final 5-4 record was better than it sounds as the Spartans went 4-2 in the Big Ten, beat both Michigan and Notre Dame soundly, and nearly wound up in the Rose Bowl.

Dean Look, an alumnus of Everett High School in Lansing,

responded to the challenge of becoming a quarterback. Shortly after Duffy made his startling announcement, backfield coach Bill Yeoman had taken over. "Dean," Yeoman told his willing charge, "you think you are close to your wife. Starting September 1 you will think you divorced her and married me."

The odd couple marriage worked so well that Look made the *Look* magazine—Football Writers All-American team that fall as well as All-Big Ten. Late in the season Duffy proclaimed him "as good a quarterback as any we've had."

Some of Look's brightest achievements were a 52-yard TD pass to Fred Arbanas in the 19-0 victory over Notre Dame and a touchdown scored personally and another on a pass thrown to Don Stewart in the 34-8 romp over Michigan. In the Michigan game halfback Bob Suci produced State's all-time interception return of 93 yards.

On the final weekend of the season, State played and lost to Miami of Florida on a flooded Friday night in the Orange Bowl, but it had its 4-2 league record in the bank. The following day Spartan players, coaches, and team party members rested in

Dean Look runs against Michigan.

the lobby of a Miami Beach hotel and watched a televised game between Wisconsin and Minnesota, which would clarify the Rose Bowl picture. Wisconsin went into the game with a 4-2 league mark and was tied for the lead with MSU. Minnesota was 1-5 and in the Big Ten cellar. If it pulled an upset, State would be the conference champion and most likely would get the bowl bid.

Everyone in the hotel lobby rooted lustily for Minnesota, but a few there were relieved when Wisconsin rallied to win and get the Rose Bowl call. Their thoughts were: "Take a 5-4 record to the Rose Bowl? Can you imagine what the national press vultures would do to us? They'd pick us clean. At least Wisconsin would go with a 7-3 slate. Please Lord, not this time. Let us wait a year." As it turned out, Wisconsin lost in the bowl to a strong Washington team 44-8.

Duffy may have felt some pressure that season, but he never lost his sense of humor. He had warmed up for the new season early in September. A jammed safety valve in a dormitory steam boiler near the practice field caused a loud and persistent hiss of steam. Duffy listened intently for a few minutes and then commented to bystanders: "The alumni are warming up early this season, aren't they?"

He also claimed he had received a letter from an alumnus saying: "Remember, Duffy, we're with you win or tie."

An especially poignant Duffyism, in view of the troubles he had the year before, was his comment when he learned that Biggie had been elected to the Football Hall of Fame. "You can credit me for getting Biggie into the Hall of Fame," he said. "After six years of my coaching they appreciate what a great coach he really was."

But probably the most often repeated and frequently borrowed gem was one involving a couple of giant freshman linemen named Ed Budde and Dave Behrman, both of whom later achieved All-American and went on to pro success.

"I have a couple of big freshmen preparing for a special job next fall," Duffy declared. "At the end of each game, win or lose, they are to hoist me to their shoulders and carry me off the field. Then fans in the stands will say, 'Look, there goes old Duffy again. He might not be much of a coach, but his players sure love him.'"

Winners But No Cigar

The good 1959 team which came so close to being an outstanding one established a pattern for Spartan clubs which endured four more years, through 1963. All teams were consistent winners, and they boasted outstanding players. Neither Notre Dame nor Michigan beat any of them, and high national ranking was the norm. Yet none achieved a conference championship or went to the Rose Bowl. Something always seemed to happen to frustrate the most valiant efforts.

The 1960 club, which wound up 6-2-1 and 13th in national rankings, fell out of the Big Ten race early with a heart-breaking loss to eventual conference co-champion Iowa. The Spartans had fought the favored Hawkeyes to a standstill in Spartan Stadium. With less than three minutes to play they led 15-14, had possession of the ball, and were driving deep in Hawkeye territory.

Then quarterback Tommy Wilson and fullback Ron Hatcher got mixed up in a routine play-from-the-belly series. The ball popped into the air, and Iowa linebacker Joe Williams snatched it and ran 67 yards untouched for a game-reversing score. To compound State's frustration, Iowa scored again following an interception of a desperation Spartan pass, to make the final count an unreal 27-15. Ironically, Iowa's Williams was out of position. He had been blocked so viciously on two preceding plays that he had moved inside to avoid another man-handling. And that was exactly where the fumble occurred.

There was luck for the 1960 Spartans, too. In the opener at Pittsburgh, end Mike Ditka registered the Panthers' TD on a pass reception. Later a Tommy Wilson aerial was tipped by a

Pitt defender right into the hands of Spartan end Jason Harness, who went for 66 yards and State's touchdown to make the final score 7-7.

Then State ran its unbeaten string over Michigan to five at East Lansing. The score, 24-17, was completely representative of the closeness of the game. Charon was the Spartan offensive star with 124 yards rushing and one touchdown.

Notre Dame was humbled 21-0 with Wilson passing 52 yards to Don Stewart and 23 yards to Herb Adderley for scores, and Ike Grimsley cantering 35 for another. That victory, the fifth straight over the Irish in a string which was to reach eight before snapping, brought a stampede of newsmen to the Notre Dame Stadium dressing room to interview Duffy. They caught him just as he was stepping out of the shower.

Duffy smiled graciously, reached for a towel, and announced, "I think this is the best showing I've made all year."

State beat Purdue 17-13 with Art Brandstatter, Jr., contributing nine crucial points on a touchdown pass reception from Wilson and a field goal. The Spartans were down 7-3 at the half and had been guilty of several fumbles. As Duffy and his team were leaving the field for the dressing room at half time, the Michigan State drum major dropped his baton. A disgruntled Spartan fan roared, "Looks like Duffy is coaching the band now, too."

Fullback Ron Hatcher had the kind of a day every player dreams about against Northwestern that fall. State won by the skin of its teeth 21-18, with Northwestern on the Spartan two when time ran out. Hatcher carried the ball ten times for 109 yards and scored touchdowns on runs of 32 and 51 yards. Gary Ballman contributed the other on a 51-yard ramble.

State had played miserably in the first half against the Wildcats, a frequent habit of Spartan teams throughout the years, and at intermission Duffy really blistered his players.

Student manager Jim Arbury recalls that Duffy's harangue went like this:

"We bring you to Chicago, put you in the best hotel, serve you the best food, show you some of the finest entertainment there is, and treat you like kings. And what's your response? You play like bums. OK, if you want to play like bums then we will treat you like bums. If you lose this game, the next road trip we have, we are going to have hamburgers and we are going to travel there by the worst possible means of transportation and we are going to sleep four men to a room in a flophouse."

Duffy's message clearly hit home and was typical of his approach to things. As Arbury explained: "It was obvious that Duffy was mad and disgusted with everyone. But there was enough humor laced into the speech that everybody sort of got their spirits lifted."

The 1960 season closed with a 43-15 victory over a Detroit Titan team in Spartan Stadium. Fred Arbanas, co-captain that fall with Herb Adderley and Freddie Boylen, closed out his collegiate career that day with two pass receptions for touchdowns.

This was a game scheduled because of pressure by some Detroit area legislators years before. The bait they dangled was their support of Michigan State's bid to have its name changed from Michigan State College to Michigan State University. It

1960 team had tri-captains, Fred Boylen, Herb Adderley, Fred Arbanas.

was the first time State had met the Titans on the gridiron since 1934 as the once lively series had been dropped after some row-dyism on campus and in town.

The next season brought a 7-2 record, which would be happily accepted by most schools, but all that 1961 record got Duffy was an effigy hanging and a lot of criticism. Spartan hopes soared during five straight victories over Wisconsin (20-0), Stanford (31-3), Michigan (28-0), Notre Dame (17-7), and Indiana (35-0) in the openers. Fans thought that this was indeed going to be the BIG year. Then came a 13-0 loss to Minnesota at Minneapolis and a 7-6 fumble-marred defeat by Purdue at Lafayette. The fact that both the Gophers (second in the Big Ten at 6-1 and 8-2 overall) and the Boilermakers (4-2 in the league and 6-3 in all games) were excellent teams meant little or nothing to the disappointed.

State went on to win its final two league games over Northwestern and Illinois, to wind up eighth in national ratings and third in the conference.

Most impressive about the 1961 Spartans was the defense. No opponent made more than 13 points, and all nine of them put together garnered only 50. One can understand why when the names of players are recalled. Working in the front line trenches were such as Dave Behrman, Ed Budde, Dave Manders, Matt Snorton, Art Brandstatter, Jim Bobbitt, George Azar, Ernie Clark, Charlie Brown, Tony Kumiega, and Pete Kakela. Behind them were Wayne Fontes, Lonnie Sanders, George Saimes, Carl Charon, Bob Suci, Gary Ballman, Herman Johnson, and others.

By this time, the once strict substitution rules had been modified to the point that a degree of platoon play was possible, but offensive units had to be prepared to go defensively at times and vice versa. The Spartans made several magnificent goal-line stands that fall and led Duffy to remark: "I like those goal-line stands of ours, but I wish they would make them up around the 50 yard line where I could see them better."

Ed (Rocky) Ryan, captain of the 1961 team, has special reason to remember the Wisconsin opener. He was a defensive specialist, the fellow who moved in for the quarterback when the ball went over to the opposition. Rocky liked this chore. He was a hard-nosed, blood-and-guts type of player who delighted in combat.

Against Wisconsin, one of his assignments was to keep a

giant end named Pat Richter (6-6 and 230) under constant surveillance. Rocky did his job so well that after the game Richter sought out Spartan players outside their dressing room and inquired, "Who was that guy who nearly busted me in half? I've never been hit like that."

Ryan had hit Richter so hard that he popped fillings out of his own teeth and had to have them repaired the next week.

Tension before a major game can be almost unendurable for players, so coaches often seek to break it and keep the team loose. Duffy found a way right before the Michigan rout.

Student manager Jim Arbury, who was all of 150 pounds stretched thinly over six feet, was stripped to the buff before a

Duffy gags it up with All-American linemen Ed Budde and Dave Behrman.

locker in the stadium dressing room when Duffy blew his whistle.

"Duffy proceeded to make a speech about how much money the school was spending on its training table for its athletes," Arbury recalls. "Then he pointed to my skinny body and talked about what a tremendous job it had done for me. As I turned a slight shade of purple, the other people in the room burst into a loud roar of laughter. That loosened them up!"

But there was more, Arbury says, and gives credit to All-American fullback George Saimes for what happened.

"I really think that game was won in the long tunnel that leads from the dressing rooms down to the field at Ann Arbor," Arbury recalled. "The Michigan players were standing down at the end of the tunnel waiting for the 'Star Spangled Banner' to finish before running onto the field. Our team was behind them.

"Now Saimes had always taken offense to the way Michigan people called us 'cow college' and said loudly that if they thought we were farmers then that was what we would give them. He proceeded to burst into a series of barnyard sounds—a cow, a horse, a pig. Everyone else broke in, and it sounded like the Chicago stockyards in that tunnel. The entire Michigan team turned around to get a look at what was coming at them, and I think that we really intimidated them."

Gary Ballman, George Saimes, and Sherman Lewis scored touchdowns by rushing, and Pete Smith passed for a fourth to Carl Charon. Art Brandstatter hit all four extra points.

"Imagine that," Duffy mused when told a crowd of 101,001 people had been announced in the press box. "Why, Lady Godiva wouldn't pull half that crowd. People just aren't interested in looking at white horses."

Fourteen of the 22 men on the first offensive and defensive units completed their eligibility in the 1961 campaign, including such standouts as Art Brandstatter, Dave Manders, Gary Ballman, Ron Hatcher, Tony Kumiega, and Rocky Ryan.

State's depth was decimated, and in 1962 Duffy moved to compensate by abandoning the two platoon system and going to a first team, second team, type alignment.

"We are going to have to get our best 11 players on the field at one time," he explained. "Platooning is a luxury we won't be able to afford this fall."

As it had in 1961, State was using a "bi-line" system under which the entire repertoire of plays was geared to go off from either a balanced line or a line unbalanced either left or right. It was believed this was a first in the history of college football.

The Spartans had not lost all their outstanding players. There were men such as Dave Behrman, Ed Budde, Jim Bobbitt, Sherman Lewis, and George Saimes on the first unit at the start of the season.

After a staggering start in a 16-13 loss to Stanford at Palo Alto, the Spartans got rolling with the same awesome power the early 1961 team had shown. It simply crushed North Carolina 38-6, Michigan 28-0 (for the second year in a row), Notre Dame 31-7, and Indiana 26-8.

Injuries had taken some toll, but circumstances did not appear too desperate even with Minnesota and Purdue coming up. Both were met at East Lansing and—disaster—both dumped the favored Spartans. Minnesota won 28-7 with those marvelous tackles, Bobby Bell and Carl Eller, playing superb defense. Purdue prevailed 17-9 despite close statistics, but four lost fumbles hurt State severely in that game.

Northwestern was toppled 31-7, but Illinois squeezed past the Spartans 7-6 in a defensive struggle at Champaign.

George Saimes and Ed Budde achieved All-American, as had Dave Behrman in 1961. This time Behrman missed All-American but made All-Big Ten for the second straight year, along with Saimes.

The 1962 campaign had been dotted with brilliant performances and exciting games. Stocky little halfback Ron Rubick set a Spartan record by rolling up 207 yards rushing against North Carolina. He also scored three TDs.

Michigan could get only 112 yards total offense against State. In contrast, Dewey Lincoln netted 139 yards rushing to lead State's offensive charge. Strangely, he scored no touchdowns, but Sherman Lewis registered three six-pointers.

Against Notre Dame, Saimes rushed for 153 yards and Lewis for 123. The Irish could accumulate only 123 yards offensively. Saimes scored three touchdowns and pulled the same feat again the following week against Indiana, to throw his All-American drive into high gear.

Curiously, Saimes' name appears nowhere among all-time outstanding performances in State's record book. Yet anyone who saw him in action would endorse him as one of the super backs in the school's football history. He had no glittering specialty but was a consummate all-around back, able in block-

All-American George Saimes was popular favorite.

ing, tackling, running, pass receiving, defense—you name it. He rarely made a mistake.

Although there was little to laugh about in the 5-4, 1962 season, Duffy was equal to the challenge. He told his postseason audiences that he had been trying to emphasize the vital importance of good blocking fundamentals when he asked a burly lineman at practice, "Where are more football games lost than anywhere else?"

Duffy swore that the lineman replied, "Right here at Michigan State, coach."

All four seasons from 1959 through 1962 were winning seasons, with their successes and frustrations, but they paled in comparison to the 1963 experience. It took a presidential assassination to foul up this one.

The Spartans, paced by Sherman Lewis in his fabulous All-American year, rolled through eight games to a 6-1-1 record. The lone loss was by 13-10 to Southern California in the Los Angeles Coliseum in the second game of the season. The tie was with Michigan 7-7 at Ann Arbor the week afterwards. State was 4-0-1 in the Big Ten going into the season finale in Spartan Stadium against second place Illinois, which was 4-1-1 in league contests.

The day before the game, Friday, November 22, 1963, Pres. John F. Kennedy was assassinated in Dallas. Numerous weekend football games were postponed or cancelled in the immediate reaction of national grief and shock.

Some Big Ten games were called off at once. Others, it was announced, would be played as scheduled, among them the Ohio State-Michigan game and the Illinois-Michigan State contest. By Saturday morning, however, pressures from faculty, alumni, government officials, and lay public forced a reconsideration. A few hours before game time all Big Ten action that day had been postponed.

The Big Ten title game between State and Illinois was rescheduled for Thanksgiving Day, the following Thursday. Illinois coaches were joyful as they took their club back home, they said later. They had felt their team was not emotionally keyed for the game, and this delay looked to them like a reprieve from disaster. Spartan coaches, conversely, felt their club had never been more eager and ready. To let off steam, the team ran through a dummy scrimmage that Saturday afternoon in the indoor baseball arena of the Men's IM building and simply exploded with spirit and ferocity.

But State was flat in practice the following week and never regained the fine competitive edge it had had on Saturday. However the Illinois team—again by the word of its own coaches—started rising and reached an excellent emotional pitch for the game.

Illinois won 13-0, thanks to great defensive work by Dick Butkus and his steamed-up teammates. State committed seven turnovers and never got rolling. Lewis, a potent game-breaker in earlier games, was controlled by an especially designed defense. Illini Jim Grabowski scored the game's lone touchdown following a Spartan fumble on its own 14. State's most serious threat was aborted on the Illini 11 yard line when Butkus nailed fullback Roger Lopes, forced a fumble, and personally fell on the

Squirmin' Sherman Lewis.

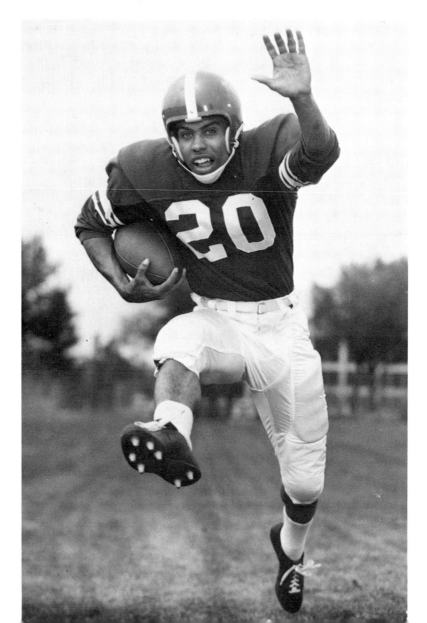

ball. Illinois went to the Rose Bowl and walloped Washington 17-7.

Despite the final disappointment, it was quite a big year for State and especially Sherman Lewis. The tiniest Spartan, 5-9 and 154 pounds, made a hatful of the major All-Americans by a brilliant performance which included five remarkable plays of 84 or more yards. There was an 88-yard touchdown pass reception from Steve Juday in the Southern California game, which remains as the longest such play in State's history. The Northwestern game featured Sherm's 87-yard run from scrimmage and an 84-yard punt return. In the Spartan record book the run is tied for third with the jaunt by George Guerre against Iowa State in 1947. Sherm's 85-yard run from scrimmage against Notre Dame is State's fifth best as is his 87-yard pass play against Wisconsin with Juday again on the pitching end.

It was Lewis' impending departure from the Spartan scene that gave Duffy the material for one of his most memorable one-liners:

"Sherman Lewis is a great football player with just one weakness," he told startled newsmen, who thought he was about to criticize a Spartan player for the first time in memory. "He's a senior," Duffy concluded.

Lewis and his fellow co-captain of the 1963 team, Dan Underwood, both made All-Big Ten. A few years later they were to return to their alma mater as fellow assistant coaches.

One enthusiastic Spartan guard named Earl Lattimer parlayed an unusual antic into an All-American rating on the *New York Daily News* team. He occasionally would turn from the huddle and somersault into his position. It may have annoyed opponents, but it enchanted the fans. They never knew when it was coming next and gave him an ovation every time he did it. It was just what a nameless, faceless lineman needed. Word spread around the country and undoubtedly helped Earl get the notice as an All-American hopeful.

When the 1963 season ended, Bump Elliott, onetime Wolverine All-American back and now head coach at his alma mater, paid Duffy a beautiful compliment when he said, "I think, taking everything into consideration, including solving problems of team personnel, depth, and experience, that Duffy performed the finest coaching job in the Big Ten this fall."

Duffy's Masterpieces

Great achievements in any field almost always come as the result of long, tedious, unrelenting effort. Overnight miracles are as rare as perfect 100-carat diamonds. Duffy Daugherty's masterpieces—the 1965 and 1966 teams—started taking form in the recruiting harvests of 1962 and 1963.

Duffy had achieved a national reputation as a Pied Piper among recruiters. Sometimes the praise was blunted by adding, "but he's not much of a coach,"—to Duffy's chagrin. But no fair-minded and knowledgeable football observer could quibble with the 1965 and 1966 results—those were well-coached as well as superbly talented teams.

Coaches rate recruiting as being up to 80 percent of the total job. In 1962, Duffy and his aides had acquired Steve Juday, Don Japinga, Ron Goovert, Harold Lucas, Buddy Owens, Tony Angel, Don Bierowicz, Eddie Cotton, Boris Dimitroff, John Karpinski, Bob Viney, Jim Garrett, Jim Proebstle, and Don Weatherspoon. In 1963, they came up with Clint Jones, George Webster, Gene Washington, Bubba Smith, Dick Kenney, Pat Gallinagh, Phil Hoag, Jerry Jones, Jeff Richardson, Jim Summers, Charley Thornhill, Jerry West, Larry Lukasik, and John Mullen. These players became the muscle and spirit of two tremendous teams which won 19, lost one, and tied one.

As sophomores and juniors, all were aboard the 1964 team. This team proved to be the third loser in Duffy's head coaching career, but the recruits were in various stages of development. Some had begun to achieve status, though. Clint Jones and Eddie Cotton were among the rushing leaders that fall.

Juday was the established quarterback with 894 yards and nine touchdowns through the air, and fleet Gene Washington became the all-time Spartan passing leader for one season with 35 catches good for five touchdowns.

Despite an overall 4-5 record and losses in the final two games to Notre Dame (34-7) and Illinois (16-0), both on the road, the feeling was abroad that big things were underway at East Lansing. How else could one explain the fact that for possibly the only time in the history of football polls, a losing team achieved a top 20 rating. State did it, ranking 20th in the final UPI standings selected by a national panel of coaches.

State opened the season against North Carolina and lost 21-15. Gene Washington and Clint Jones presented their first collegiate credentials in that game, Gene with four pass catches for 47 yards and one touchdown and Clint with 83 yards gained and a 42-yard scoring scamper.

Next State bopped Southern California 17-7 at East Lansing, with two sophomores again figuring prominently. Hawaiian barefoot place-kicker Dick Kenney toed a Spartan record 49-yard field goal, and Washington snatched two more passes, one for 22 yards and a score.

Then Michigan won for the first time in nine years by a 17-10 count at East Lansing with two touchdowns in the fourth quarter. Next Indiana scored one of its rare victories over State

Clint Jones finds daylight.

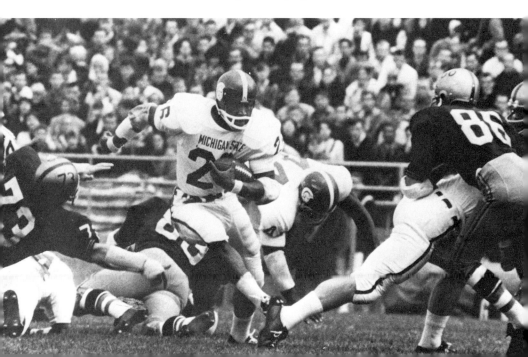

27-20 at Bloomington. So with four games gone, the young Spartans stood 1-3. Juday, incidentally, had one of his biggest days at Bloomington, completing a Spartan record 16 passes against the Hoosiers, one each to Tom Krzemienski and Gene Washington for touchdowns.

A senior halfback who had languished in the shadow of All-American Sherm Lewis for two years broke into stardom. Small, lightning swift, and elusive Dick Gordon, whose greatest days were to come as a wide receiver in pro ranks, suddenly had fans asking, "Where has he been all this time?"

Dick paced State to three straight victories with phenomenal performances. Against Northwestern he rushed for 105 yards, caught two passes, and scored one touchdown. Against Wisconsin, he rushed for 199 yards, including a 74-yard beauty for a score and a non-scoring foray of 57 yards. Finally, against Purdue, Dick ran for 145 yards, caught four passes, and scored two TDs.

The 1964 season closed out with two more losses, to Notre Dame and Illinois, but sportswriters, sportscasters, fans, and coaches had seen enough to know things were really happening

Stars in 1964 were Dick Gordon and Jerry Rush.

Circus catch by Gene Washington.

in East Lansing.

Dick Gordon and Jerry Rush (a bruising offensive tackle) made All-Big Ten. Dick also produced a rare double by being placed on the All-Big Ten Academic team. Gene Washington made the latter selection, too.

As usual, Duffy amused a national audience with widely reported quips. When he was asked by an earnest reporter who he was happiest to see returning to his team that fall, Duffy replied: "Me!" When he tipped over a cup of coffee on a table filled with play diagrams and coaches' notes, Duffy surveyed the mess, shrugged, and commented: "Oh, well, we have to learn to play on a wet field anyway."

Fans had responded enthusiastically to the exciting young 1964 Spartans. The four-game home schedule of Southern California, Michigan, Northwestern, and Purdue drew the

221

all-time average attendance at MSU of 72,520 people per game.

Selectors who otherwise might have plumped heavily for MSU to be a major conference and national power in 1965 were frightened off when they looked at the schedule. The 1964 agenda had been rated the nation's toughest, but this one was worse. After preliminaries with UCLA and Penn State, it called for meeting the top four Big Ten finishers of 1964 right in a row. In the order MSU was to confront them, they were Illinois, Michigan, Ohio State, and Purdue.

"Playing that gang will be like trying to swim up a waterfall," Duffy opined. "You can go like the dickens and still fall behind."

But this year State was ready, willing, and able to play anyone. Its stone wall defense was well-nigh impregnable. Its offense, while unpredictable, managed to get enough points on the board to win those six games by anywhere from four to 27 points. At the end Duffy and company were rated No. 1 on both wire service polls.

Every Saturday had its memorable moments.

The UCLA encounter at East Lansing was a Hawaiian Holiday. All Spartan points in a 13-3 victory were scored by islanders Bob Apisa and Dick Kenney. Apisa, a powerful and very quick fullback, bolted for the game's only touchdown on a 21-yard smash, and barefoot Kenney added the other seven markers on a point after touchdown and two field goals.

At this point *Look* magazine gave a big spread to the Spartans under the headline "Duffy's Hawaiian Punch!" Asked how all those fine Hawaiian athletes came to Michigan State, Duffy replied, "Well, first of all, they swam to California."

Penn State went down 23-0 at State College, Pennsylvania, leading Nittany Lion coach Rip Engle to aver that MSU had "the best football team we ever played."

The definitive blow was delivered early when Mike Irwin, the Lions' fastest back, was apparently loose for a touchdown on a kickoff return. He was hauled down from behind by Bubba Smith, and then Penn State wilted.

Illinois gave State a pretty good struggle, leading 10-9 at the half, but finally bowed 22-12, thanks to Kenney's 47-yard field goal and touchdowns by Clint Jones, Apisa, and Washington.

Michigan felt the developing power of State's defense and collapsed 24-7. Bubba, Don Bierowicz, Buddy Owens, Bob

Viney, Harold Lucas, Ron Goovert, Big Dog Thornhill, George Webster, Jerry Jones, Don Japinga, and Jesse Phillips, et al., combined to destroy the Wolverines' running game. The final Michigan total was minus 51 yards on the ground. The last 29 times the Wolverines had the ball, except for punts, they opted to pass.

Ohio State fared no better. Woody Hayes' revered "three yards and a cloud of dust" offense wound up minus 22 yards and a heck of a wreck. The Buckeyes never tried to run in the second half, ending up throwing an incredible 29 passes in succumbing 32-7. They made zero first downs rushing.

Two superb plays marked this game. Ohio State elected on its second scrimmage play to try Bubba for size. It sent an end run his way; fullback Tom Barrington carried the ball behind a pair of husky blockers who were zeroing on Bubba. But the biggest Spartan piled up both escorts with one mighty plunge, and Barrington fell over the top of the stack for a six-yard loss. That set the tone of the game. Moments later on the Spartans' second offensive play of the game, Clint Jones ran into a hopelessly jammed-up right side, moved into reverse, and swept down

Trainer Gayle Robinson finds Bubba Smith is too big.

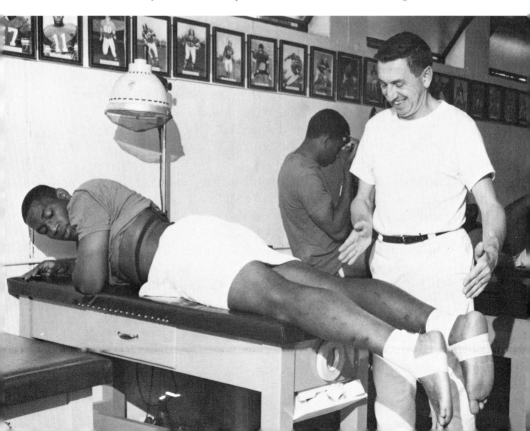

the left side for 80 yards and a score. Key blocks were thrown by Jerry West and Eddie Cotton.

Juday hit on 11 of 19 passes for 151 yards and one touchdown, and Washington caught six passes for 83 yards. Jones gained 132 yards rushing and Apisa, 114. Five times Ohio backs were dumped for losses, one for a safety executed by Owens and Goovert on Buckeye quarterback Don Unverferth.

But the major challenge that year was not Michigan or Ohio State, but Purdue. The Boilermakers had Bob Griese at quarterback and several fine pass catchers headed by Bob Hadrick and Jim Finley. They came into the Spartan game at Lafayette with a 2-0 Big Ten slate and a 4-0-1 record overall. Their tie game was with Southern Methodist.

Purdue started as though it was going to obliterate State. It completely dominated the first half action and went into the locker room with a 10-0 lead. Griese had never been sharper. He completed 13 passes, one to Hadrick for a touchdown, and personally kicked the extra point and a field goal.

The third period was scoreless, but early in the fourth State put together a drive which produced a six-pointer by Apisa on a short plunge. A fake extra point kick and a Juday pass to Jones made two more points and closed the gap to 10-8.

Then Purdue could not move and punted. Spartan Drake Garrett made a fine run back to the Boilermakers' 39. State's winning drive took nine plays plus a 15-yard penalty. (Purdue vehemently protested that penalty for a personal foul committed on Juday.) Jones ran in from eight yards out behind blocks by Apisa and guard John Karpinski. It was close, the only real cliff-hanger of the fall, but it was a victory.

Northwestern was dismantled 49-7 with Apisa scoring three times and Jones, twice. The Wildcats scrounged 79 total yards offense, just seven on land.

Iowa gave up five touchdowns in losing 35-0 and netted one yard rushing. Four of State's TDs were by Jones on runs of sixteen, six, three, and four yards.

Then Indiana expired 27-13 with Washington catching six passes, three good for touchdown jaunts of 27, 43, and 4 yards. Dwight Lee had himself a day with 103 yards on 23 carries.

The visit to Notre Dame closed out the 1965 season. The Irish kept things reasonably respectable with their 12-3 loss to the Spartans on a cold, rainy day at South Bend. Once again State's defense was awesome. The Irish lost 12 yards rushing

224

and gained 24 passing, for a net of 12 for the day. But Ara Parseghian's club had defensive muscle, too, mounted by such as Alan Page, Kevin Hardy, Jim Lynch, Tom Regner, and Nick Rassas. State's only scores came on a three-yard run by Jones and a 19-yard Juday-to-Lee pass.

That was it! The perfect 10-0 season was clearly the most splendid in State's history and one of the most impressive produced by any team, any time.

Honors and plaudits cascaded on individual players, the team, and Duffy in a torrent perhaps without precedent in college football annals. And deservedly so. State led the nation in rushing defense, permitting an average of just 45.6 yards per game against the strongest possible opposition. It paced the Big Ten in both offense and defense, finishing among the national leaders in total offense, rushing offense, and total defense. It permitted fewer points per game (6.2) than any other team in the land.

Quarterback Steve Juday wound up with 12 Spartan passing records in hand. His favorite receiver, Gene Washington, claimed Spartan season and career marks for pass receptions and total yardage gained through passes.

And there was more. Eight Spartans—Jones, Washington, Webster, Smith, Juday, Goovert, Lucas, and Apisa—made All-American. The first seven plus Don Japinga made All-Big Ten. And four—Jim Proebstle, Japinga, Juday, and Bierowicz—made the Academic All-Big Ten team, with Japinga and Bierowicz also making Academic All-American.

There was one more honor for a player. Juday was granted a National Football Hall of Fame Graduate Fellowship.

UPI named State national champion then and there, while AP decided to hold off its final balloting until after the Rose Bowl.

The team received other major awards: the MacArthur Bowl by the National Football Foundation and Hall of Fame (emblematic of the national championship), the Robert Zuppke Award, and "Team of the Year" awards by the Helms Athletic Foundation, *Sporting News,* and the Washington Touchdown Club.

Duffy was voted Coach of the Year by the Washington Touchdown Club, the Football Writers Association, *Football News, New York Daily News,* and *Sporting News.* State was named unanimously to go to the Rose Bowl.

Dick Kenney never said ouch!

There should not have been anything to mar Duffy's jubilation, but he had several gripes. One was the loss of first string center Walt Forman at the end of his junior year—to medical school because of his excellent grades. "We've learned our lesson," Duffy grumbled, but with a wink. "We'll never recruit anyone that smart again." And Dick Kenney's barefoot kicking caused him some distress, too. He had to tell Dick to cut his toenails, Duffy barked, because "he was scratching up all our footballs."

The funniest line that fall came from a player. Sophomore defensive back Drake Garrett, who wound up as State's only three-time winner of the Oil Can Award for spirit and humor, was knocked out in one game. When he finally emerged from the fog, he said to the worried faces hovering over him, "I'm okay, but how are my fans taking it?"

Roses With Thorns

Michigan State's third Rose Bowl venture in a period of 13 years began with great joy, adulation of players and coaches, and frantic preparations for journeys west. A major bowl experience is traumatic for an institution, particularly one nearly 2,000 miles from the scene; regular university functions nearly cease or are badly disrupted as the bowl arrangements are made. An estimated Spartan army of about 14,500 people eventually moved out for the game. Included were more than 8,000 students and faculty members, some 2,200 alumni, and about 3,800 season ticket holders who received priority shots at bowl game ducats. University-sanctioned tours handled some 3,200 persons via eight jet planes, two trains, and six buses. And local businessmen grumbled under their breath as they saw all that money going to California, which otherwise would have been spent with them during the Christmas buying binge.

The team set up training camp in the fine stadium of East Los Angeles Junior College once again. Duffy followed Spartan precedent by opening the gates one day to the general public and hanging out the daily welcome sign to all press people. The traditional rituals of a joint visit by the two teams to Disneyland, the prime rib feast at Lawry's, the Hollywood studio visit, the gala Big Ten dinner—all were performed. Comic Bill Cosby, baseball star Maury Wills, and the pop ensemble "Back Porch Majority" headlined the Big Ten banquet.

Superlatives heaped on the first two Spartan Rose Bowl teams by the California press seemed wishy-washy compared to the hyperbole they concocted this time. While the UCLA team was virtually ignored except for brief training camp reports, the

228

Spartans were reading this about themselves:

"I've just come back from the Michigan State football practice," said Sid Ziff in the *Los Angeles Times.* "Good grief! They're even bigger than I expected. If they changed uniforms their defensive line could pass for the Green Bay Packers."

Syndicated columnist Jim Murray said, "Looks like a casting call for a remake of 'King Kong'—44 guys bucking for the lead in 'The Creature That Ate Europe.'

"Their front line," he continued, "is so big that when they ran a picture of it on the front page of the *Detroit Free Press,* they had to make it 'Continued on Page 11.' Even then, they only got to the left guard."

Such a one-sided presentation in the press was a well-established practice in California, and not without some reason. The West Coast's Rose Bowl entry had been whipped in 15 of 19 games against the Big Ten, twice by Michigan State teams. And this year MSU came as the most glamorous team ever to show for the game, the undefeated national champion in the UPI and No. 1 in the AP, pending the final vote after the Rose Bowl. There were eight All-Americans aboard State's team and such gargantuan physical specimens as Bubba Smith, 6-7 and 267, and Harold Lucas, 6-3 and 286. State also had defeated UCLA 13-3 in the regular season opener at East Lansing and had ploughed brilliantly through a very tough schedule, while the Bruins had had some trying moments, including a loss to Tennessee and a tie with Missouri.

The California press people denied any ulterior motive in their praise for the Big Tenners, claiming they were simply writing for readership and at most could perhaps be accused of trying to be hospitable to the visitors. But Duffy was not blind to the damaging psychological potential of such praise. Even Paul Zimmerman, the straightest-writing Los Angeles newsman of his day, led off his eight-column-spread story in the *Times* the morning of the game with, "Oh, the monotony of it!"

Meanwhile, UCLA was getting such short shrift in the press that UCLA coach Tommy Prothro, who basically cherished the underdog role, was moved to tell writers, "It is embarrassing for me to be in the Rose Bowl two years in a row with teams that you do not think belong. I promise you there is more talent on my UCLA team than you think. We may be in over our head Saturday, but Duffy and his group will have to show us." Spartan coaches sensed several days before the game that

1965 Rose Bowl and national championship team.

something was going wrong. Practices were not as enthusiastic and intense as previously, and spirit seemed to be forced. There was a development at the Rose Bowl kickoff luncheon the day before the game which may have had influence on the contest:

Ziff told about it in a post-game column:

"J. D. Morgan, UCLA's athletic director, put questions to MSU's co-captains, Steve Juday and Don Japinga. They were the kinds of questions that had both boys putting their foot in their mouth and thoroughly enjoying it.

"As a matter of fact, those boys were delightfully entertaining and to the audience what they said was purely amusing. But to the UCLA players they must have sounded terribly egotistical. It was like pouring more coal on the fire. It made them (UCLA) that much more determined to win."

How pained Duffy looked at some of the answers, especially when Juday replied to one of Morgan's artfully leading

230

questions, "Oh, this Spartan team didn't need any coaching or leadership." He may have been kidding, but it sounded cocky.

The Spartan Marching Band had an omen that this New Year's Day was not to be a total joy; it was routed out of bed by a false fire alarm at 3:00 a.m., New Year's morning. But it came on to star in the parade and at the game.

To Spartan loyalists it is soul stirring to hear the band's distinctively rich, full-bodied sound growing louder and louder in the distance and then see the green flood engulf Orange Grove Avenue past the main reviewing stands.

The colorful parade provided a stimulating prelude to the main event—the big game in the nearby Arroyo Seco (Spanish for arid gorge).

The usual throng of over 100,000 people sat in on a score-less sparring match with few thrills for nearly the entire first quarter. Then a UCLA pass interception on its own 14 and a

42-yard run back by defensive ace Bob Stiles opened the gate to ultimate victory, although no one realized it at the time.

In fact, State seemed to have weathered the blow when its defense held and forced a UCLA punt. It was a routine, spiraling boot, the likes of which Don Japinga had fielded flawlessly many times in many games. But this one he fumbled on the MSU 7, and UCLA recovered on the six. The Bruins leaped to the attack and on two carries by quarterback Gary Beban went into the end zone for a touchdown on the first play of the second quarter. The extra point was good.

State was stunned and shaken, and UCLA was wild with jubilation. The big oval rocked with Bruin cheering. It was the perfect moment to throw a surprise at the Spartans, and UCLA coach Tommy Prothro had one pre-planned for just such a situation. The Bruins worked a perfect squib kick which they recovered on State's 42. Six plays, including two big ones—a 21-yard run up the middle by Mel Farr and a Beban-to-Kurt Altenberg pass for 27 yards—moved the ball to the one. Beban plunged for the score once again, and the kick for extra point was good. The Spartans were down 14-0 and already beaten, although nearly three quarters remained to be played.

State put together a long drive near the end of the first half, but it ended with Dick Kenney missing a 23-yard field goal try.

The third period brought more frustration for State as UCLA fought a grim holding action. Only seven minutes were left on the clock in the fourth period when the Spartans finally, belatedly, exploded. Taking the ball on their own 20, they worked seven plays, including a 42-yard aerial from Juday to Washington and a 38-yard run by Apisa, for the score. A missed two-point conversion attempt on a fake kick and pass by Juday hurt badly.

But State was not dead yet. With time now a big factor, the Spartans put together a final effort to salvage the game. They drove 51 yards on 15 plays to score a second touchdown. The counter was registered by Juday on a sneak from about half a yard. Then came a second try for two points which would tie the game, but UCLA's Bob Stiles stopped Apisa short of the big stripe, which iced the game. It was UCLA's first Rose Bowl victory in five tries.

A day or two afterwards the news was reported that huge Harold Lucas, All-American middle guard on the Spartans, had

UCLA's Gary Beban runs wide pursued by State's George Webster (90) and Don Bierowicz (65). Other Spartans are Don Japinga (14) and Big Dog Thornhill (71).

signed a fabulous contract with the St. Louis Cardinals of the National Football League. This was the day of the hot and heavy bidding war between the NFL and the AFL, and the Cardinals had beaten the Boston Patriots of the new league for Lucas' services. Reports were that he had signed for $350,000 on a five-year, no-cut contract.

Some months later, shortly after the pros began their summer football practice, there was even more astonishing intelligence: Lucas had walked out on the contract, had returned home, and was working in a Detroit factory.

Told of the incredible development, Duffy pondered it silently a moment, sighed and said, "Poor Harold, he'll spend the rest of his life trying to explain why—probably as long as I'll be trying to explain how we lost the Rose Bowl game."

Duffy did offer explanations—but never alibis.

The ultimate response appeared to be that it just was not Michigan State's day, that nothing seemed to go right for MSU, that the deserving team that day had won.

"There were a dozen turning points in the game," Duffy commented to the press. "The fumbled punt, the first downs we missed by a couple of inches, the missed field goal try, and some more. We don't have any alibis, and we certainly don't want anyone to put the blame on one or two of our players for the defeat. When we were winning, we always said it was a team victory. Our defeat was the same thing—a team defeat."

Others had explanations.

"The Spartans, after 10 straight victories, didn't believe they could lose," wrote Al Cotton in the *Jackson Citizen Patriot.* "UCLA, tired of reading that it was in a hopeless position, simply proved the oldest adage in football: Desire is still the biggest thing in the game. It covers almost everything. Even Michigan State players admitted UCLA's Bruins had more of it. It made them react faster, play just a bit harder and throw back the Spartans' last minute bid for a tie."

"I think hoopla caught up with them," wrote Joe Falls in the *Detroit Free Press.* He went on to say, "Duffy thinks his players weren't high enough. I think they were too high."

Clark Shaughnessy, the famous football coach, was quoted in a column by Sid Ziff in the *Los Angeles Times* as saying, "Michigan State didn't get up for the game until it was too late. You can't criticize Duffy Daugherty. He was kind of up against it. All that talk about his GREAT team contributed to its undoing."

Team co-captain Don Japinga was quoted by Pete Waldmeir in the *Detroit News.* "We let down subconsciously. We kept telling ourselves that UCLA was tough but everywhere we went people said we would win easy, by 30 points. Deep inside, I think that got to us."

It was a great football game but a sad postlude to a tour de force of ten straight regular season victories by a tremendous Spartan team.

Game Of The Galaxy

Football authorities will tell you that a senior-dominated team which already has achieved major success is a prime candidate for letdown and a disappointing season. The junior-loaded, still hungry team is the one which most often produces outstanding results, they say.

State's 1965 club was packed with junior standouts—five All-Americans and five All-Big Tens—and won big. The 1966 team, then, should have been a candidate for disaster. It had four senior All-Americans and four senior All-Big Tens from 1965 still aboard. However, it also won big.

Perhaps Duffy's recipe for success was more accurate and dependable. It said simply that to succeed brilliantly, a team must have a solid core of blue chip players, men with game-breaking potential, and it did not matter what class in school they were in. It was not the good players but the great ones that made the difference, Duffy's theory goes. That formula fitted both the 1965 and 1966 teams and all the other top ones in State's gridiron history like a leotard.

Losses from the 1965 team were heavy—Juday, Goovert, Lucas, Japinga, Owens, Bierowicz, Viney, among others. But there were some super athletes back again. Duffy built his new team around Bubba Smith, Clint Jones, Gene Washington, George Webster, Bob Apisa, Jerry West, Jesse Phillips, Charlie Thornhill, Tony Conti, Nick Jordan, Jimmy Raye, Dick Kenney, and others, and they were letdown-proof.

MSU opened at home against a North Carolina State team coached by Earle Edwards, a former Spartan assistant who revived a nearly dead football program at N.C. State. He had a

235

good club, well prepared, but it did not have a chance as the Spartans punched out a 28-10 victory. Clint Jones was brilliant with 129 yards rushing, topped by a 39-yard TD caper in which he brushed off four Wolfpack tacklers. Raye started to make believers of critics who thought he would never come close to replacing Steve Juday. He hit on six of ten passes.

Against Penn State the following Saturday at East Lansing, Raye led the way in a 42-8 rout of the Nittany Lions with brilliant passing which included TD bombs of 36 and 50 yards to Gene Washington.

Illinois at Champaign proved to be tough as always on its home turf, but it finally succumbed 26-10. There were several memorable plays, including a 95-yard punt return by Spartan sophomore Al Brenner, which is still the Big Ten record. Defensive end Phil Hoag recovered three Illini fumbles. One, which he took in the air, he lateraled to Pat Gallinagh who ran it 40 yards for a touchdown.

Apisa, the much-injured Hawaiian fullback, had a big day in State's 20-7 defeat of Michigan. He pounded 140 yards on 18 carries and scored one touchdown. The Wolverines were stopped with just 47 yards rushing.

Jimmy Raye fires against Penn State.

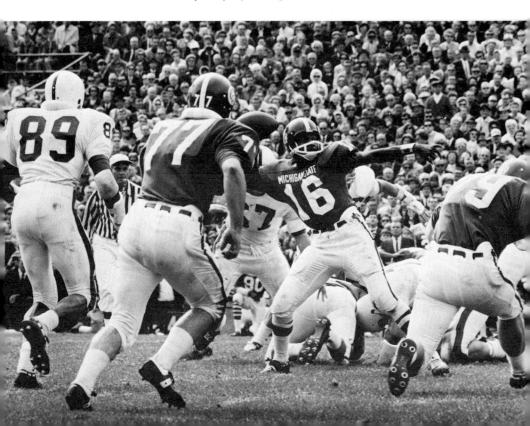

At this point of the season, State was firmly ensconced atop the national ratings by both the AP and UPI.

Then it ran into cataclysmic bad weather at Columbus. The rain was torrential, the winds cyclonic, the field a quagmire. Much of the contest was an exercise in futility. The Bucks scored first on Spartan center Ron Ranieri's bid for the all-time longest incomplete center snap. He fired one over the upstretched hands of punter Dick Kenney that carried more than 40 yards out of the Spartan end zone for an automatic safety.

That was the total scoring for the first half. MSU, unable to move for a touchdown and sensing that a field goal might win the game, had Kenney try boots of 40, 47, and 49 yards. He missed all of those but finally, in the third period, clicked on a 27-yarder.

The Spartans' 3-2 lead stood up until the fourth period when Ohio State hit a 50-yard scoring bomb, Bill Long to Kim Anderson, and seemingly had the victory locked up 8-3.

The Spartans, however, rose to the challenge, the certain mark of greatness in a team. Led by quarterback Jimmy Raye, State started an 84-yard scoring drive. For 16 plays, consuming seven minutes and 44 seconds of playing time, MSU assaulted Ohio State and the elements. Raye fired seven passes and was on target with all of them, but only four were caught. Washington caught a 28-yarder, Brenner caught two for 14 and 17 yards, and then Washington caught one for ten yards and a first down on the Buckeyes' two. Raye sneaked for a yard, again for two feet, a third time for no gain. It was fourth down and the moment of truth. MSU went with Apisa, and the lame Hawaiian blasted through the line for six points. Then came a Thursday play. Barefoot kicking specialist Dick Kenney took his usual ready position with fellow Hawaiian Charley Wedemeyer down for the snap. Only this time, the ball—incredibly, as far as Ohio State's scouting report was concerned—spiraled into Kenney's hands, and he dropped back to pass while various receivers squirted around the end zone. Unobtrusively, Wedemeyer joined the action, and Kenney lofted the ball to him for two points and an important three-point lead at 11-8.

The two-point conversion was the turning point of the game, not the preceding touchdown.

"It meant a field goal would not win for Ohio State," Duffy explained to the press later. "It changed their strategy because they were not playing for a tie."

Al Brenner moves against Michigan.

The ultimate irony was that, despite its superb victory surge against a grimly resolute Buckeye team on a horrible day, MSU lost its No. 1 rating to Notre Dame, which had waltzed to a 32-0 victory over North Carolina on a fair day at South Bend.

Thoroughly aroused by the close call at Columbus and loss of its No. 1 position in national ratings, State roared back the following Saturday and manhandled an excellent Purdue team 41-20 at East Lansing. Apisa had a tremendous game with three touchdowns, two on power runs and the third on a pass from Raye.

The Boilermakers were to finish second behind State in the league with a 6-1 record and go on to the Rose Bowl and a 14-13 victory over Southern California. Jack Mollenkopf's finest team had quarterback Bob Griese in his senior season, some able receivers, and the usual monstrous Purdue line.

Next came a trio of walkovers. Northwestern was scuttled 22-0, Iowa was minced 56-7, and Indiana surrendered 37-19. Noteworthy in the Iowa game was the all-time Spartan record of 268 yards rushing reeled off by Jones against his favorite fall guys. He scored three times on runs of 70, 79, and 2 yards.

Like the freight train rumble of an approaching tornado which gradually amplifies into an engulfing roar—that is the way the 1966 Notre Dame-Michigan State football game grew in the national consciousness.

The November 19 date in Spartan Stadium had been on the books for some years, long before anyone knew what kind of season the teams would have in 1966. What happened was that Notre Dame began bashing opponents. After an opening victory against Purdue (26-14), the Irish disposed of seven straight foes by margins of 24 to 64 points. Only two so much as worked up a score on Ara Parseghian's colossus. State, meantime, had been winning steadily but less overwhelmingly. Most observers felt State had a much more demanding schedule, however, and it had flattened nine rivals with only one close call (that at Ohio State).

As this pattern developed, it began to dawn on people that a great collision loomed ahead. Ted Smits, AP sports editor and a onetime Michigan State student, did a bit of quick research about midseason. He then proclaimed that if both teams went unbeaten down to their meeting, it would be the first time ever that the two top-rated clubs nationally had squared off in a late season contest for all the laurels.

That did it. The lid was off, and the mounting hysteria was incredible. The game of the year quickly grew into the game of the decade, the century—the most important in the history of football.

The mass information media were caught up in the mounting excitement weeks ahead of time. The battle for tickets was on, and scalping business reportedly was brisk despite the fact the game was to be on regional television and available without charge to most of the nation's population. The few areas of the country which were not going to get the game were screaming bloody murder. One Southerner filed a law suit in which he declared his right to see the big game. Altogether, fans raised such a ruckus that the NCAA relented and told ABC-TV it could telecast the game nationally, although delayed in some areas.

The contest was popularly dubbed the "poll bowl" and was ballyhooed by ABC-TV as "the greatest battle since Hector fought Achilles." The network said it had received about 50,000 letters demanding that the game be shown nationwide. Beano Cook, ABC-TV's colorful publicity director, declared, "We're putting out enough material to make *Gone With The Wind* look like a short story."

One Ohioan acquired a ticket for the game and got his name in newspapers all over the map when he wrote MSU athletic ticket manager Bill Beardsley: "If President Johnson phoned or wrote you asking for a ticket, I'm sure you would be able to send him one. Well, President Johnson will not be there, I'm certain. So why not send me the ticket you would have had for him." He also enclosed $5, the regular ticket price.

"While I want it clear that this gimmick is going to work only once," the amused Beardsley told the press, "I plan to do the very best I can to get him a ticket." The Ohioan got President Johnson's seat, on the 48 yard line.

A Saginaw beer store owner said he was willing to sell his prosperous business for four game tickets plus $1,700 for his stock and $4,000 for the store's good will. He so advertised in a Detroit newspaper.

Bars in the Lansing area and, indeed, all around the country put in extra stocks of booze for celebrating or mourning patrons. Bookie business was booming. One famous odds maker announced Notre Dame the favorite at from 3½ to 5 points. A legitimate Detroit banker said, "Dealers around here (Detroit's financial district) this week are trading the Notre Dame-Michigan State game heavier than any other issue."

A sellout had been announced in midsummer, and by the time the last MSU student was jammed in, the crowd reached a Spartan Stadium record of 80,011. That figure was 4,000 beyond the normal sellout of 76,000.

Media people began making requests for press credentials and rooms far ahead of the game. By the week of the classic contest, every nook and cranny of the commodious press box had been booked. More than 300 writers were assigned to the main press deck. An emergency fourth row of seats—laboratory stools borrowed from campus buildings—held over 80 of them. Many stood. With radio and television teams and photographic teams, the total working media count was 745, believed to be the largest assemblage ever to work a college game anytime, anywhere. Big name writers came from every sector of the country for this game.

The daily press conferences with Duffy began on Monday, and work to get ready for the media people progressed. Western Union set up press box operations. Extra telephones were installed. Every available rental car in the Lansing area was checked out, and a special bus service was begun by the university Wednesday to pick up media people at their hotels and motels, bring them to the stadium for the press conference and practice, and take them home again. Daily bulletins were stacked up in the press box so newly arriving newsmen could catch up quickly on what had gone before.

Duffy was at his charismatic best. He fielded every question with honesty and wit and even regaled the sophisticated newsmen with the Barnesboro High School alma mater and "My Sweetheart's a Mule in the Mines."

Student bodies at both schools whooped it up in a fashion reminiscent of innocent, naive days of yore. There were massive pep rallies and bonfires and buttons and bumper stickers. "Kill, Bubba, Kill" signs sprang up around East Lansing. A student auto had its hood gaudily emblazoned with the words, "Even the Pope has no hope."

ABC-TV headquarters in New York received a barrage of telephone calls protesting the showing on camera of a student sign saying: "Hail Mary Full of Grace, Notre Dame's In Second Place."

With all of that hoopla, the game itself might have been a big letdown. But it was not; it was loaded with tension. Almost every play brought the crowd roaring to its feet. Only the result, the now famous 10-10 tie, was disappointing to virtually everyone. But even that fact made its positive contribution. The enduring argument over the manner in which the game ended in a tie has insured its immortality as long as football remains a favorite bull session subject.

The very names of the key combatants tell what a great college football game it was. For Notre Dame, Terry Hanratty and Coley O'Brien were at quarterback; Jim Seymour, at end;

Tom Regner, Paul Seiler, and George Goeddeke, on the offensive line; and Rocky Bleier and Larry Conjar, in the backfield. On defense there was an awesome crew headed by All-American Alan Page, Kevin Hardy, Pete Duranko, Jim Lynch, and Tom Schoen.

The weather was as good as could be expected for late November—cloudy and cold, the temperature in the low 30's.

The first quarter was a defensive joust with no serious scoring threats. The main development of consequence was a shoulder separation suffered by Hanratty midway in the period. He had rolled out right, was turned inside by Webster, and smashed by Bubba and Charley Thornhill. This brought in Coley O'Brien, an entirely different kind of quarterback. He was a very good scrambler and played effectively against a Spartan defense which had been tuned to stop Hanratty's less versatile talents.

Late in the first period, a 42-yard Raye-to-Washington pass play started the Spartans on their lone touchdown drive of the day. The ball was on the Irish 31, and nine running plays later, fullback Reggie Cavender plunged into the north end zone from the four behind a fine block by Clint Jones. Kenney added the extra point.

When Notre Dame could not move the ball, Hardy punted dead on State's 19. From there State drove to the Irish 30, and Kenney popped a 47-yard field goal through the uprights for a 10-0 Spartan lead.

That seemed to arouse the Irish offense, and it struck back with vigor for the first time in the game. Tom Quinn ran back Chatlos' kickoff 38 yards to the Irish 46. After one incomplete pass, O'Brien proceeded to make three aerial strikes in a row for a touchdown. The first was to Bob Gladieux for 11; the second, to Rocky Bleier for 9; and the bomb, to Gladieux at the goal line 34 yards away. The extra point made it 10-7 at the half.

The third period was nearly a carbon copy of the first. Neither team could get an offense going until late in the period when the Irish started a serious push. It culminated on the first play of the fourth period with a 28-yard field goal by Joe Azzaro that made it 10-10.

The marvelous defenses of both teams took over again, and in the remainder of the game there were only three earned first downs, two by State and one by the Irish.

When, in the final minutes, Notre Dame took over on its

Reggie Cavender (25) scores against Notre Dame.

own 30 and ran out the clock on six straight running plays—obviously settling for a tie rather than trying to win—there was controversy.

The Irish action drew boos from the fans, taunts by Spartan players to their opponents on the field, and consternation in the press box.

"Why wouldn't they have tried at least one pass, a long one that would have been as good as a punt if intercepted?" was a typical exclamation.

Parseghian spent most of his post-game visit with the press in the Irish dressing room explaining his refusal to take any chance at all.

"At that stage, your strategy is dictated by the fact that you don't want to lose the game," he said, as reported by Dave

Anderson in the *New York Times.* "Interceptions almost cost Michigan State the game. We weren't going to give it away cheaply."

Public reaction was divided largely along partisan lines, and media people were split. Many thought Notre Dame should have made an aggressive attempt to win, as State had earlier. Someone coined the expression: "Tie one for the Gipper." It has become one of football's most repeated derisive phrases.

Sports Illustrated ran a cover banner declaring "Notre Dame Runs Out The Clock Against Michigan State." The lead in Dan Jenkins' story was "Old Notre Dame will tie over all."

Others pointed out that Notre Dame was without the services of Nick Eddy, Hanratty, and center George Goeddeke and argued that in such a situation, backed up in its own territory, conservatism was the better part of valor. Some saw the tie as a moral victory for the Irish.

The ensuing AP and UPI polls split, too. The AP version of the national standings, voted on by media people, went for Notre Dame as No. 1. The UPI, whose ratings were voted by coaches, named Michigan State. Both ballotings were very close.

But Notre Dame had one big, final clout in its battle for the national championship. It had a game remaining against Southern California at Los Angeles, while for State, the Irish contest was the finale. The Fighting Irish simply annihilated the Trojans 51-0 the following week to take over first place in both polls. State settled for second in both, a shade ahead of Alabama.

Some voices were heard in favor of declaring a tie for the national title, the most authoritative of which was the National Football Foundation and Hall of Fame. It declared the Spartans and Irish co-winners of its prestigious MacArthur Bowl.

It was a vintage year for the Spartan team and individual Spartan players. Besides the MacArthur Bowl, team laurels included a second straight Big Ten title. Six players attained All-American—Apisa, Jones, Smith, Washington, Webster, and West. An incredible 11, one-half the total listing, were named to the All-Big Ten. They were the six All-Americans plus Jess Phillips, Nick Jordan, Tony Conti, Big Dog Thornhill, and Dick Kenney.

And Duffy was coach of the East team in the East-West Shrine Game for the third time.

Difficult Days

No one could have guessed after the 1965 and 1966 seasons that Michigan State never again would have a big winner under Duffy, that the total product over the next six seasons would be 27-34-1, and that Duffy would then bow out.

Even the 3-7 results in 1967 gave no real inkling of sagging fortunes ahead. After all, an army of fine players had completed eligibility, and it would be naive to think they would not be missed. Also, Duffy had had several misfires before—3-6 in his first head coaching season of 1954, 3-5-1 in 1958 and 4-5 in 1964—and always he had bounced back strongly. Only State's 34-0 bombing of Michigan helped ease the pain of the 1967 letdown.

The 1968 Spartans came so very close to being a big winner that that season was not recognized as a trend setter. The record was 5-5, but there was a satisfying victory over Notre Dame in Spartan Stadium and four narrow defeats which, with a little luck or tighter play, could have been victories.

Storm signals went up for the first time in 1969. Duffy had been most optimistic in assessing this club's chances. At a preseason press luncheon he had expounded on the team's prospects with such "reckless abandon," to use one of his favorite phrases, that media visitors took up the call.

Dean Howe wrote in the *Flint Journal* that "The lean years are apparently over at Michigan State.

"When Duffy Daugherty, MSU's head football coach, begins comparing his 1965 and 1966 teams with the one he's grooming for Spartan fans now and when the preseason press luncheon is jammed with reporters and eavesdroppers, you know something is up."

Larry Middlemas wrote in the *Detroit News* that "Daugherty was calling his Michigan State football team just about the greatest thing since the discovery of fire.

"He might have been able to sneak up on the rest of the Big Ten, because preseason polls and a ballot of conference coaches all have Ohio State in a class by itself and MSU sharing the next step down. But not now."

And Joe Falls said in a *Detroit Free Press* column, "Duffy wrapped up the Super Bowl in his little talk with the writers and radiomen from around the state and if the Spartans don't go 10-0 this season it is going to be a very big surprise."

Duffy always was an optimist, but rarely like this. He put himself and the team on a challenging spot.

For a while it appeared the club might live up to those expectations. It beat Washington and Southern Methodist at East Lansing, then lost to Notre Dame and Ohio State on the road, and returned home to slap down Bo Schembechler's first Michigan team 23-12.

At this point, State's national ranking was nil, but it still had a shot at the conference title and Rose Bowl bid. It was 1-1 in league play and had Iowa, Indiana, Purdue, Minnesota, and Northwestern down the road. That did not appear to be too severe an obstacle course. But the big green machine developed engine trouble and sputtered through four straight losses before dumping Northwestern in the finale and winding up 4-6 overall and 2-5 in the league.

The following year brought more disappointment, a 4-6 record. It was relieved somewhat by three league victories in late season over Iowa, Indiana, and Purdue. Those conquests gave the Spartans a 3-4 Big Ten mark, good for a tie for fifth place with Wisconsin, behind Ohio State, Michigan, Northwestern, and Iowa.

The fall of 1971 turned up a 6-5 winner, thanks largely to the marvelous performance of Eric (The Flea) Allen. He set a bushel of offensive records as the Spartans beat Iowa, Purdue, Ohio State, and Minnesota back-to-back in late season for a 5-3 conference mark and a tie for third.

In 1972, Duffy's last at the Spartan helm, it was back to an even 5-5-1 and fourth place in the conference with 5-2-1. The season was spiced by successive victories once again over Purdue and Ohio State.

Eric Allen on the move.

Some of the finest players and most thrilling football in Michigan State history graced that six-year period. Attendance figures did not collapse, either. State finished among the top ten nationally in average home attendance in every one of those seasons, indicating fans were finding the kind of action which kept bringing them back. And outside of Ohio State and Michigan, no Big Ten teams did better on the won-lost ledger or in attendance.

Some of the high spots of those final Duffy years were memorable.

Even the first game in 1967, one which State lost 37-7, has a place in every Spartan fan's memory book. Former Spartan aide Bill Yeoman brought in a Houston team playing the veer offense, the basic idea for which he had picked up at Michigan State.

The following Saturday O. J. Simpson and Southern California came to town. Despite O. J.'s running for 190 yards and two touchdowns and passing for a third, the Spartans could have won on a Jimmy Raye-to-Al Brenner pass in the Trojan end zone on the end of a long third period drive. But the touchdown was called back for a vigorously debated offensive interference call well removed from the center of action. USC won

Baseball's Steve Garvey as Spartan defensive back.

21-17.

A stocky, reserved, and oh-so-polite sophomore with a large future in another sport played defensive halfback. Steve Garvey was very good, making 22 solo tackles and assisting on many others during the course of the campaign. He now, of course, is with the Los Angeles Dodgers and was the National League's most valuable player in 1974.

Frank Waters, born on the Michigan State campus when dad Frank played fullback for the Spartans, caught eight passes and scored a touchdown in a good Spartan effort against Notre Dame, which State lost 24-12. The eight receptions placed him in a tie for second in State's record book behind Gene Washington.

Sophomore Rich Saul was the defensive leader from his linebacking post with a team-leading 59 tackles, including 12 for loss.

When the 1967 season was over, an undaunted Duffy told

wintertime banquet crowds, "We won three games, lost none, and were upset in seven."

Al Brenner was the big man in 1968. He made All-American as a defensive back and pulled a unique double by being named by the UPI to first team All-Big Ten both on offense and defense. He also attained Academic All-Big Ten for the second time as well as Academic All-American. Al was given several prestigious awards for postgraduate study, topped by an NCAA scholarship and a National Football Hall of Fame fellowship.

One of his biggest days came against Baylor in Spartan Stadium. Al snared six passes for 153 yards, second best on the all-time books. One was an 83-yarder tossed by Bill Feraco.

The most gratifying team accomplishment of the season was a 21-17 upset of a Notre Dame club which contained Terry Hanratty, Jim Seymour, George Kunz, Bob Kuechenberg, and Mike McCoy. In that one, Tommy Love enjoyed perhaps his finest day as a Spartan running back. He raced for 100 yards and scored two touchdowns. Bill Triplett performed well at quarterback, and tough on defense were such as Rich Saul, Frankie Waters, Ron Curl, Charley Bailey, and Jay Breslin.

But Brenner was outstanding. He played some offense and caught a pass on the Irish one yard line to set up the winning touchdown. On defense he intercepted an Irish toss in the Notre Dame end zone. He broke up a pass, made 12 tackles, and saved the game with a final brilliant exploit.

Less than a minute remained, and it was fourth and three for a touchdown for Notre Dame. Hanratty took the ball and moved to his left on the option play. With his arm cocked to throw, he looked for split end Jim Seymour who was speeding for the corner of the end zone. Brenner was right with Seymour, but looking back toward Hanratty. Suddenly, Terry tucked in the ball and sprinted for the end zone. So did Brenner, from the opposite direction, and they collided on the two yard line. Hanratty went down, and the ball squirted free. An Irish player covered it on the five, but it went over to State, and two safe plays later the game was ended.

That was the game, too, which Duffy immortalized when he said at a pregame press dinner attended by several Irish officials, including athletic director Moose Krause, that MSU just might start the game the next day with an on-side kick. Everyone laughed. But the team did just that. Gary Boyce sliced the kick perfectly, and Ken Heft recovered for State on the Irish

42. Six plays later Tommy Love found the end zone for a touchdown.

Little Charley Wedemeyer, younger brother by 20 years of All-American Herman Wedemeyer of St. Mary's, did some remarkable blocking that fall from a flanker position. Duffy was asked about it by newsmen, and he replied that Charley was so expert that he never, never clipped.

"The reason is," Duffy explained, "that he does a 'look out' block. When he wants to block some guy and might clip him, he hollers 'look out.' Then when the guy turns to see what's up, Charley lets him have it."

New for 1969 was State's $250,000 Tartan Turf surface. One writer referred to it as "a massive crap table."

One of the most important games of the season was to be the contest with Michigan played on that surface.

In 1969 Bo Schembechler inherited a splendid collection of talent from an 8-2, 1968 Michigan team (Bump Elliott's final year as coach). Schembechler sent his team off on a winning spree right away. The only Big Ten game it lost en route to another 8-2 season, a conference co-championship with Ohio State at 6-1, and the Rose Bowl bid, was the one it dropped 23-12 in Spartan Stadium. The Spartans hit like a tidal wave from the outset, powering for 253 yards rushing in the first half and going in for the half-time breather ahead 16-3. The second half was anticlimactic.

An important element in the game was the surprise which Duffy and company had cooked up behind locked practice gates the preceding week. Plagued by multiple injuries to running backs, the team switched its offense from the veer option to the power-I. Don Highsmith was the only sound runner in the place, and run he did for 129 yards and two touchdowns. Quarterback Bill Triplett chipped in with 142 yards and another score.

The Spartan defense was outstanding, too. Linebacker Don Law and cornerback Doug Barr each made eight solo tackles, linebackers Cal Fox and Clifton Hardy broke up two passes each, tackle Ron Joseph recovered a fumble, and linebacker Rich Saul and safety Brad McLee each nailed opposing backs twice for losses.

No one will ever forget the remarkable passing performance of Dan Werner in the 1969 Purdue game at Lafayette. Dan, a lanky sophomore who had never seen a second of varsity action previously, went in for the injured Steve Piro at quarter-back and connected on 16 of 35 passes for 314 yards and one touchdown. The yardage figure was the second best in the Big Ten books at the time. (It slid to third thanks to that colossal 351-yard effort Northwestern's Mitch Anderson hurled at Michigan State in 1972.) The reason State threw so much in the Purdue game was that Purdue was flinging the ball with abandon and had piled up a 31-0 lead by the half. The final count was 41-13 in Purdue's favor, with Mike Phipps doing the heavy damage for Purdue with 292 aerial yards and two scores. Spartan end Frank Foreman raced into the record books with 155 yards gained on six pass receptions. The yardage figure is State's all-time best. State's touchdowns came on a 60-yard scamper by Eric Allen and the 47-yard Werner-to-Steve Kough pass.

To many Spartan fans it looked like a star had been born, but Werner was handicapped by the fact that he was strictly a drop back passer and could not run effectively. Spartan coaches, like their counterparts all over the land, were looking for quarterbacks who could get up and go and not just retreat and throw.

When the season ended for the Spartans, offensive guard Ron Saul and defensive tackle Ron Curl had made All-Big Ten and Saul had made several All-Americans.

Sonny Sixkiller and a slippery, waterlogged artificial turf combined to make State's 1970 opener at Seattle against Washington a soggy nightmare. It was the brilliant Indian's varsity debut, and he put on a beautiful show. He and his teammates rolled up nearly 600 total yards and 42 points, while the Spartans slid around like novices on ice skates. There was definitely something wrong, and it developed that State had improper shoes for the field.

Asked about this after the game by a newsman, Duffy shunted aside the proffered alibi with the memorable comment, "Blaming the shoes for our defeat would be like blaming the Johnstown flood on a leaky faucet in Altoona." But Washington officials said afterwards that they knew State was in trouble because they had tried and discarded the type of shoes Spartan players were using.

State beat Washington State the following week at East Lansing 28-14, and a couple of future greats hit the headlines. Eric Allen caught two touchdown passes from new quarterback Mike Rasmussen, a California junior college transfer, and a blonde sophomore from Owosso named Brad Van Pelt intercepted three passes.

Allen continued spirited work in losing causes, 156 rushing yards against Michigan and 142 in another debacle at Minnesota. He also led the offense in victories over Indiana with 103 yards and Purdue with 121 yards and two scores. He capped off the season with 108 yards and two scores in the finale at East Lansing against Northwestern, which State lost 23-20.

"The Flea" had gone over 100 yards rushing in five of the last six games and thus set the stage for his blockbuster season of 1971.

The 1971 experience exemplified well the whole frustrating final six years of Duffy's coaching tenure. The team possessed excellent defense spearheaded by such standouts as Ron Curl, Ernie Hamilton, Ron Joseph, and Doug Halliday on the front line; Gail Clark and Ken Alderson at linebacking; and Mark Niesen, Brad Van Pelt, and Paul Hayner in the secondary. Its offense was spotty—brilliant at times but butterfingered at others; it committed 46 fumbles, better than four per game. Typical Duffy comments at Monday noon press luncheons were: "If only we would stop beating ourselves" and, "I wish I knew why we fumble so much. There's no rhyme or reason to it."

Tackle Ron Curl blocks kick.

Offensive lapses were all the more mysterious in that some splendid players graced the lineup. Billy Jo DuPree, Joe DeLamielleure, Bob McClowry, Mike Hurd, Mike Holt, Henry Matthews, and Eric Allen were on State's side.

The turning point of the season was a 31-28 loss in a close game with Wisconsin at Madison. Had State won—and it had every opportunity to do so—it would have been in title contention all the way. As it turned out, State rallied with four straight Big Ten victories and a final loss to Northwestern to finish at 5-3 and in a three-way tie for third place.

State beat Illinois 10-0 in the 1971 opener at East Lansing, a game marred by 15 fumbles for the two teams and four pass interceptions. Eric Allen showed he was in good form by rushing for 104 yards.

Then came a 10-0 loss to Georgia Tech. State tried three quarterbacks in that game, in a futile effort to get some offense stirring. Next was an easy 31-14 victory over Oregon State at East Lansing, but it was followed by a 14-2 loss to Notre Dame at South Bend.

In this one the officiating was so patently one-sided for Notre Dame that Irish fans actually booed decisions which went their way. Bud Wilkinson used the word "blind" in commenting on officials' calls on the ABC-TV telecast.

State threw a surprise party for Michigan the next Saturday, injecting the wishbone offense into proceedings at East Lansing just as it had used a sudden switch to the power-I to upset the Wolverines in 1969. This time, however, Michigan combined errorless offense and brilliant defense to prevail 24-13. That State needed more work with the intricacies of the wishbone was suggested by the fact that it made just 59 yards rushing.

That loss squared MSU's Big Ten record at 1-1 and sent it off to Wisconsin, to disaster. However, "The Flea" demonstrated he was nearing his career peak by zipping all over Camp Randall for 247 yards and two touchdowns. The following week, in a 34-3 rout of Iowa in Spartan Stadium, he logged 177 yards and three touchdowns. The Spartans had shown some improvement with the wishbone but fumbled 14 times.

Not Red Grange, nor Tom Harmon, nor O. J. Simpson nor any other gridiron immortal ever had a better game than the 5-10, 170-pound senior from Georgetown, South Carolina, produced against overwhelmed Purdue the following Saturday.

By this time the Spartans had picked up some competence with the wishbone. The running lanes were opening up, and how "The Flea" flitted through them. He left Purdue tacklers flatfooted in his wake or grabbing at thin air. By half time he had rolled up 189 yards rushing and scored two touchdowns on runs of 24 and 59 yards. Both came on sweeps around right end with pitch outs from quarterback Mike Rasmussen.

Spartan sports information staffers in the Purdue press box checked the records book at half time, just in case Allen kept up his incredible pace in the second half. They spotted the NCAA and Big Ten rushing mark of 347 yards set by Michigan's Ron Johnson and figured that was still far out of reach. But when Eric added 59 more yards on a Spartan touchdown drive early in the third period, staffers became excited. They checked figures with the official statisticians and from then on kept a running total.

On State's next possession, late in the third period, Allen went up the middle for four, through the line again for 17, around right end for seven, and by the same route again for five more, before Purdue took over the ball on downs. Eric now had 282 yards with a quarter of the game left to play.

Purdue scored early in the final period and kicked off to State. Allen started going again—up the middle for four, off right tackle for 28, and around right end for 11—and ran his total to 325. Then, to the consternation of the frantically calculating Spartan sports information people, Jim Bond was substituted for Allen. "The Flea" took a seat on the bench and undoubtedly was through for the day.

Then the Spartan press box people really got to work. Official statisticians confirmed the total of 325 yards for Allen was correct. Spartan coaches working the press box phones to the bench were asked to relay the word quickly that Eric was just 23 yards short of breaking the all-time NCAA rushing record. Offensive line coach Gordie Serr took the message at the other end, nodded, and immediately said something to Duffy. Duffy turned, called Allen, threw an arm around his shoulder, and said: "They tell me in the press box you need just 23 yards to break the collegiate rushing record. You're going back and are going to carry the ball on every play until you get it."

It did not take long. Allen tried the right tackle spot first and was dumped for no gain by giant Dave Butz. On the next

Duffy calls the shot.

try he went almost the same route, found an open door, and sprinted into the end zone and the MSU, Big Ten, and NCAA records books. His clinching foray was for 25 yards.

It finally was figured out that Allen had smashed eleven Spartan, four Big Ten, and two NCAA records. Besides the new single game NCAA rushing standard of 350 yards (he did it on 29 carries), he also had caught a couple of passes for 47 yards, which gave him an all-time, all-purpose running record of 397 yards. Both marks are still tops on the NCAA books.

Writers worked on fancy leads to do justice to the phenomenal performance. Doug Mintline wrote in the *Flint Journal:*

"What a flea circus!

"Instead of tackles, Purdue University should have tried Raid!"

Ohio State did a better job on Allen the next week, holding the tiny dynamo to 79 yards rushing and two touchdowns. But Michigan State won 17-10.

At the end of the season three Spartans made All-American—Eric Allen, Ron Curl, and Brad Van Pelt. The same trio plus Joe DeLamieulleure made All-Big Ten.

The 1972 season was a repetition of the established pat-

255

Duffy and stars Billy Joe DuPree and Brad Van Pelt.

tern. There were some splendid victories, some terrific individual performances, and some wonderful thrills. But there were also some low moments of disappointment, frustration, and futility. Consistency seemed to be the missing ingredient.

State opened at Champaign and crunched Illinois 24-0. Defensive backfield star Bill Simpson scored two touchdowns, one on a pass interception and run back of 20 yards, the other on a 58-yard punt return. Billy Joe DuPree caught four passes, and quarterback George Mihaiu connected on six of eight passes. It was a promising beginning for a team which returned some 15 of 22 regulars from 1971. The arrival of a pair of hot shot junior college stars—Damond Mays and Clayton Montgomery—helped Duffy wax optimistic again. The word was, too, that there had been some potent refinements made in handling the wishbone offense.

The bubble quickly burst with four straight losses—to Georgia Tech, Southern California, Notre Dame, and Michigan. The main culprit was a hapless offense which managed 16 points against Georgia Tech (21-16), just six at Southern Cal (51-6), and was closed down completely by Notre Dame (16-0) and Michigan (10-0).

By this time some of the media people were prophesying the end of the line for Duffy, and strong currents of dissatisfaction with the football program were building within and outside the institution.

Wisconsin was blasted 31-0 to deter the dissidents momentarily. Quarterback Mark Niesen, who had been transferred from defensive back and started as signal caller for the first time in the Michigan game, ran for 114 yards. Damond Mays accounted for 125. Niesen had quarterbacked the wishbone in high school at Manistee and showed quick aptitude for the assignment. He also had worked in the position during 1972 spring drills.

The disaster of the fall, the calamity which made up Duffy's mind to call it quits at season's end, was the Iowa game the week after Wisconsin. The Hawkeyes had a poor team which wound up in eighth place in the Big Ten with a 2-6-1 mark. It certainly looked the part of a loser against State, moving the ball just 117 yards on offense, fumbling three times, and giving up two pass interceptions. But State fumbled eight times, lost the ball on five of the fumbles, and altogether committed sufficient mistakes to be tied 6-6. The gloom on the airplane carrying State back to Lansing was thick. Duffy and executive vice president Jack Breslin had a long talk in the dark outside the Lansing airport main building as the team party members dispersed for cars and busses.

The following Thursday, Tim Staudt, sports director for WJIM of Lansing, happened on a Spartan assistant football coach, in a bar, and the coach eventually let it slip that Duffy had revealed that day that he was going to resign. The announcement was to be made sometime over the upcoming Purdue game weekend.

This was a big piece of news, and Staudt sweated for 24 hours over what to do with it. Not the least of his concerns was the fact that the Staudt and Daugherty families had been neighbors and friends for years.

Tim broke the story on his Friday evening sports show, just as officials of both schools and media people were gathering at the University Club for the usual pregame reception. The word reached there quickly, and the newsmen were all set for Duffy when he arrived a few minutes later. When informed of Staudt's revelation, Duffy agreed to talk to the media and confirmed that Staudt's report was true.

There is no question that the decision was his own. Certainly he was aware of the aura of unhappiness about the football program—he was not happy with it either. But there is little doubt that he would have weathered the storm and could have remained at the football helm had he chosen to do so. Duffy had friends in powerful positions who would have stood by him.

Regrettably, the remainder of the season was almost lost in the furor over Duffy's impending resignation. The Spartans were strong in winning over Purdue (22-12) and Ohio State (19-12) back-to-back again and Northwestern (24-14) but suffering the standard defeat at Minnesota (14-10). Dirk Kryt, a colorful, free-spirited Holland native, secured himself a place in Spartan football legend with a team record four field goals against Ohio State. Niesen had a great day against Purdue, scoring touchdowns on runs of 57 and 61 yards. The team wound up with a 5-2-1 conference record, the best since 1966, and fourth place in the Big Ten.

Honors and awards were unusually heavy for a 5-5-1 team. Brad Van Pelt, Joe DeLamielleure, and Billy Joe DuPree made All-American. The same trio plus linebacker Gail Clark, defensive back Bill Simpson, and defensive tackle Gary VanElst, made All-Big Ten.

Thus ended Duffy's 19-year career as Michigan State's head coach, the longest tenure in the school's history and the sixth longest in the Big Ten. Only Amos Alonzo Stagg (41 seasons), Bob Zuppke (29), Fielding Yost (25), Woody Hayes (24), and Dr. Henry Williams (22) were around longer.

Near the end strained relations developed between Duffy and the university administration, with fans and alumni, and even with some of the media. All kinds of explanations have been advanced for the decline from the glory days of the 1950s and early 1960s, but perhaps the most valid and basic of all was the one proposed by Duffy himself in his autobiographical book entitled simply *Duffy*.

"As I look back on the coaching, I realize it's possible for a man to stay in one place too long," he commented.

A bit later he was even more explicit about it.

"I should have left Michigan State five or six years before I finally walked out," he said. "Look around at the very successful coaches and you'll find that most of them have made a couple of moves."

One prophecy may be made: when enough time has elapsed to heal all the wounds which were opened in the latter days of Duffy's Michigan State coaching career, there will come a nostalgic reappraisal of the Duffy era as the very best of times.

A widely-used tribute to Duffy after his retirement from coaching told the story well. It said, in part:

"DUFFY: A LEGEND IN HIS OWN TIME

"Legends usually are rooted in solid fact, but passage of time and tricky memory eventually make them bigger than life.

"So it surely will be with Duffy Daugherty. Ten years from now, even Duffy or wife Francie will have trouble sorting out the truth from the sentimental hyperbole about the man and his career.

"In such circumstance, the course of reason is to go back to the record. For Duffy, it speaks as loudly and eloquently as the most extravagant alumni bull session tales in 1982 possibly could do.

"Some of the diamond-hard and shining facts are these:

"...He worked his way from a Pennsylvania coal mine to the pinnacle of national fame as a coach, a wit, a beloved personality and a public relations ambassador for his school, which happily was Michigan State.

"...He suffered a broken neck playing college football at Syracuse, but came back to captain his team as a senior.

"...He went into military service in World War II as a private and came out a major.

"...He devoted eight years, one at Syracuse and seven at MSU, as a lightly regarded assistant to Head Coach Biggie Munn, despite the fact he coached some lines that became known as 'Duffy's Toughies.'

"...He took over the seemingly thankless chore of succeeding Biggie Munn as State's head coach, and not only didn't fumble the ball but carried it into new end zones.

"...He won two outright Big Ten titles and placed second four times. Seven times, his teams finished in the national top

259

10 in wire service balloting. His 1965 team was No. 1; his 1955 and 1966 teams, No. 2.

"...He developed 33 major first-team All-Americas and 51 first-team All-Big Ten players.

"...Must games for State always are those with Michigan and Notre Dame, and Duffy came out 10-7-2 (wins, losses and ties) with the Wolverines and 10-7-1 with the Irish. Notre Dame thought so much of him that he had first shot at the head coaching job there but elected to stay at State, thereby opening the door to Ara Parseghian. Along the way, there were countless other big head coaching positions tossed into his lap.

"...He battled the serious business attitude of many of the people associated with the game and sought to make football fun for players and coaches, as well as fans. As an exemplar of this philosophy, he became known for his 'Duffyisms,' spontaneous witticisms which have had the whole nation chuckling.

"...He was the first man ever to be named 'Coach of the Year' twice by the Football Writers of America. He has coached in 11 All-Star bowl games, and won a big majority of them. He wrote a column for the Associated Press for three years.

"And that's just the top of it. In Duffy's case, the legend will have a hard time outgrowing the facts."

Charley Bachman, Duffy Daugherty, and Biggie Munn—39 years of MSU coaching.

New Day With Denny

The "local boy makes good" cliche received vigorous new life with the appointment of Denny Stolz as Michigan State's 16th head football coach. Denny was born in Lansing and went to high school in nearby Mason. He played quarterback while at Alma College and then returned to the area for coaching chores at Haslett and Lansing Eastern high schools. He defected again to become head coach at Alma, but finally joined the Spartan coaching staff under Duffy in 1971.

Jack Breslin and Russ Reader were the big name stars he recalls from the first game he saw in Macklin Field as a youngster.

"The next time I saw Jack Breslin," Denny says, "he came to do his practice teaching with our high school gym class. He was really a big hero, and I couldn't wait to go to school to see him every day."

Denny had some notion of playing football at Michigan State, but, he adds, "as I got a little older, I realized I wasn't good enough." So he went to Alma and changed his dream to some day coaching at State.

Denny was selected at the end of a vigorous, broad-gauged search and selection process which saw such names as Barry Switzer, Johnny Majors, Lee Corso, Bill Mallory, and Hank Bullough mentioned as prominent candidates.

But he was the first choice, the only one to whom the job was offered.

And was he ready for the assignment! In practically no time he had a coaching staff assembled and recruiting started. Spring drills were a revelation of hard work and organization.

Stolz and first staff, left to right, kneeling, Jimmy Raye, Andy MacDonald, Charley Butler, Sherman Lewis. Standing, Ed Rutherford, Howard Weyers, Dan Underwood, Bill Davis, Ed Youngs, Denny Stolz.

Revived enthusiasm and cooperation among alumni, fans, faculty and staff people, and students developed quickly.

One of his first major actions was to scrap the wishbone offense in favor of the I-flanker attack.

Despite the late start on recruiting, the word was that the new group of 1973 freshman players was pretty good. Such fresh talent as Levi Jackson, Kim Rowekamp, Ray Spencer, Joe Hunt, John Breslin, Tony Bruggentheis, Mike Cobb, and Tom Hannon arrived on the scene by invitation. There also was an uninvited and soon welcome guest named Richie Baes to keep the rich tradition of walk-ons going at State.

But Denny, who had been defensive coordinator for his

two years on the Spartan staff, soon found out that there were some problems which he possibly did not completely comprehend in his concentration on defense.

"We don't have good depth in any area except running back," he exclaimed mournfully. "We probably lost more top football players than anybody else in the Big Ten. All the super guys—the players you need to win the Big Ten championship—are gone."

That included Billy Joe DuPree, Joe DeLamielleure, Bob McClowry, and George Mihaiu from offense and Ernie Hamilton, Brian McConnell, Gary VanElst, Gail Clark, Ken Alderson, and Brad Van Pelt from defense. But the defense was in better shape for replacements because, in Denny's words: "We have a good program developed there. There are men ready to move up. But that's not true with the offense."

His words rang with gospel truth as the 1973 season unfolded. The defense kept the campaign from sinking into disaster with grim, resolute play. It held down many opponents' scoring enough for the team to squeak through to victories. State scored only 12 touchdowns in the 11 games, one by linebacker Ray Nester on an interception return against Notre Dame, another on a 95-yard kickoff return by Mike Holt against UCLA, one on a pass, and eight by running from scrimmage. The remarkable thing was that the team still wound up with a fairly decent 5-6 record and a 4-4 conference mark—good for a fourth place tie.

State started under Denny exactly the same way the 1954 team got under way in Duffy's first year as head mentor—with a 14-10 loss to a conference team. Duffy's had been to Iowa at Iowa City. Denny's came at the hands of Northwestern at Evanston in John Pont's first game as its head coach. Quarterback Charley Baggett scored the lone touchdown for State on an eight-yard slash through the middle on the end of an 80-yard drive. Dirk Kryt made a field goal and the extra point. Six fumbles and a pass interception helped ruin the Spartans.

The Spartans gave Denny his first victory at Syracuse the following Saturday, 14-8, but it was a close call. State was down 8-7 with exactly 33 seconds left to play when the referee raised his arms to confirm that Spartan sophomore halfback Tyrone Wilson had reached the end zone on a smash from the two. Baggett had scored the first Spartan touchdown in the game on a 15-yard end sweep in the first period.

The Spartans managed 21 points against UCLA the next week but the Bruins rolled to a 34-21 victory. Kryt scored two field goals, Wilson rammed home from the one, and Mike Holt contributed his 95-yard kickoff return with seven seconds left on the clock. But the talent-loaded Californians were up 27-10 at the half and cruising.

However, Notre Dame found once again that, no matter what State had looked like previously, it had better batten down the hatches for rough weather. The low-rated Spartan team gave Ara Parseghian's men the fight of their lives the following Saturday at South Bend. The Irish, en route to an 11-0 season and the national championship, pulled ahead 14-0 by the half. It looked like a breezing victory. But State came back with a 33-yard third period field goal by Kryt and an early fourth period touchdown by linebacker Ray Nester on an intercepted pass, to pull into serious contention at 14-10. Not only that, but the audacious Spartans made a serious bid for victory shortly afterwards on two big plays. There was a 22-yard scamper by Baggett followed by a 40-yard pass play, Baggett to Dane Fortney, for a first down at the Irish 24 as State neared an upset.

It was not to be, however. Brilliant Irish defensive back Mike Townsend short-circuited the electrifying Spartan challenge with an interception on his own 16 to save the game. State's defense had been superb. Ferocious gang tackling up front and smart coverage by the secondary had kept the vaunted Irish chargers under control. But the MSU offense could not generate a single score.

The worst was yet to come. State's cherished tradition of playing well against Michigan, no matter what the odds against it, was broken on a gloomy, wet afternoon in Spartan Stadium. Streamer headlines in newspapers the next day told the sad story. "Spartans Play Giveaway in Rain" exclaimed the *Lansing State Journal.* "U-M Bludgeons Fumbling Spartans" announced the *Detroit News.*

State fumbled nine times, five in the first period, en route to a 31-0 beating. When it did hang onto the ball, the offense would not move. The defense was on the field almost all the time—and usually in bad position.

"We just lost a football game before we had a chance to win it," a disappointed Stolz said afterwards. "But we'll be back."

State was to bounce back, but not next week. In a game against Illinois in Spartan Stadium, neither team could get out of its own way when trying to move the ball, and Illinois finally prevailed 6-3 on two field goals by Danny Beaver (to one by State's Dirk Kryt). Once again, lost fumbles and interceptions (two fumbles, three interceptions), helped doom the Spartans. And again, brilliant, unrelenting defensive coups by such as linebackers Ray Nester and Terry McClowry, tackle Jim Taubert, and guard Ron Kumiega were washed down the drain. Worst of all, State's athletes and coaches were booed by their own fans—a rare, unsettling sound in Spartan Stadium.

Stolz faced the facts of the situation when he told the press afterwards: "We absolutely cannot establish a running game, and you have to do that before you can win in the Big Ten. We just don't blow people out of there."

He vigorously rose to the defense of quarterback Charley Baggett, however, who had been the target for the boos. "He has a lot of stuff," Denny declared. "They booed him pretty good and he came right back late in the game and played very well. He's still our No. 1 quarterback."

At just past the halfway mark of the season, State's record was 1-5, the offense was pitiful, and the defense was possibly tiring from overwork. Five Big Ten foes loomed ahead, including Purdue and Ohio State on the road, and Denny was showing obvious signs of worry and strain. His natural easygoing manner was lost in tension.

Just then the sun broke through. Late in the Illinois game State had put together a long sustained drive deep into enemy territory before faltering on a pass interception. It was one of the few solid forays made against an enemy all season, an omen of better things ahead. Also, a shaken but resolute Stolz had declared grimly after the Illinois futility, "I've never been associated with a fumbling team. This is going to stop."

Stop it did, at Purdue the next Saturday. State put together a 10-7 victory, and there was only one fumble and no interceptions. The offense was not spectacular but did produce a season high of 291 yards from scrimmage. Baggett began to justify Stolz's consistent confidence in him by rolling up 133 yards running, the first 100-plus performance by any back all fall. He scored the lone MSU touchdown on a 69-yard keeper around right end. The field goal by Kryt from 23 yards was set up by a pass interception and 54-yard return by Bill Simpson.

The defense, led by Simpson and tackle John Shinsky, was virtually impregnable. Shinsky was responsible for causing two Purdue fumbles. However, it was the offense which received unaccustomed acclaim.

"Our whole offense did a great job," Stolz pronounced. "The line moved out and the backs ran with authority. Baggett was superb. What more can I say?"

The happiest news other than the final score was the fact of just one fumble. Somehow the Spartans finally had found the handle on the ball. Those who had heard Denny's peremptory declaration that the fumbleitis was going to cease—and right now—had an eerie feeling that he may have brought it about by sheer will power. On the other hand, the intensive practice with balls soaked in pails of water probably had something to do with it.

The improved play continued the next week against Wisconsin in Spartan Stadium. The offense generated a respectable, season-high yardage total of 343. Again there was only one turnover, a lost fumble. All three touchdowns in the 21-0 victory were achieved on sustained drives of 68, 50, and 69 yards. Dave Brown, the husky Indiana junior, scored all of them—two on the ground and the third via a pass from Tyrone Willingham. The Badgers penetrated Spartan territory only three times, once as far as the 16 yard line, and were never a serious threat.

Brown's three scores in that game were his first of the season, and the touchdown pass was the only one State engineered all fall.

The victory against Wisconsin was a costly one. Baggett, who was developing swiftly into the kind of a game-dominating figure any team likes to have at quarterback, was knocked out of action for the rest of the fall with a knee wrecked by a Badger tackle on the end of a fine 19-yard run. It happened on the final play of the first quarter right in front of the Spartan bench. Tyrone Willingham, the tiniest Spartan of them all at 5-8 and 155, took over and worked well for the remainder of the game.

There was more bad news. First-string center Charley Ane and starting offensive tackle Phil Smolinski also suffered knee injuries, which required surgery. These two were key members of the young offensive line which was just beginning to perform with precision and authority.

While the personnel losses hurt the offense, it is doubtful

that they affected the outcome of any of the remaining three games. MSU was crushed 35-0 by Ohio State at Columbus but triumphed over Indiana 10-9 and Iowa 15-6 to close out the campaign.

The Spartans managed only four first downs and 94 total yards offense at Ohio State, but it gave few gifts, losing only one fumble and permitting no interceptions.

The convincing Buckeye victory helped get Spartan athletic director Burt Smith into a heap of trouble. He decided to vote for Woody Hayes' club to represent the conference in the Rose Bowl because of that victory and the rest of the Bucks' tremendous season. However, the Buckeyes and Michigan had fought to a 10-10 standoff at Ann Arbor in the season finale, and somehow that tie game caused Michigan coach Bo Schembechler and Wolverine fans to think they were clearly the deserving choice to spend the holidays in Pasadena. When the decision was rendered otherwise by a majority vote of the conference's athletic directors, Michigan partisans went into a towering rage rarely seen outside of a Donald Duck cartoon. Smith, a Michigan alumnus, was seen as the main villain. Things quieted down some when Ohio State scored a resounding 42-21 victory over favored Southern California in the bowl, but there were rumors that Michigan would "get even" with her disloyal sister institution.

At the 1973 season's end, linebacker Ray Nester was named most valuable player by teammates, but safety Bill Simpson achieved first string All-American and All-Big Ten. He was the only Spartan to attain either honor in this lean year.

Most Spartan followers accepted the 1973 results as a promising beginning for the Stolz regime, especially in view of the four conference victories in the final five starts. The youth of the offensive platoon and its improvement with experience was recognized. Baggett's blossoming into near stardom before his unfortunate injury had vindicated his coaches' judgment of the youngster's capabilities. The way the club overcame its propensity for errors was a hopeful sign. The hard, unceasing work and the complete dedication of Stolz and his assistants was clearly bringing results.

One question remained. Could the coaches recruit? The 1973 frosh group had been pretty good considering the late start in the pressurized competition for top high school talent, but the first real test case was the 1974 recruiting campaign.

Dr. Clifton Wharton, MSU President and ardent football fan, presents 1973 President's Award to John Shinsky, co-captain and an Academic All-American.

Denny himself had said that a couple of excellent freshman groups would be needed to give State a real chance at catching front-running Ohio State and Michigan.

In 1974 Denny and company came up with what some observers called the best class of recruits in the Big Ten. Others said the whole country. Stolz and associates urged caution with the traditional coaches' plaint that "they haven't played a game for us yet."

Five high school All-Americans and many All-Staters were lassoed and moved into the Spartan corral. Many proved their mettle in their freshman seasons; with others the word was, "Just wait. They will."

Ted Bell, Larry Bethea, Tom Birney, Bill Brown, John Daubenmeyer, Mike Dean, Jim Earley, Craig Fedore, Claude Geiger, Tom Graves, Mike Imhoff, Al Pitts, Paul Rudzinski, Tim Ruff, and Jim Thomas—these were some of the new names Spartan fans were coming to know.

What a difference one year made! State opened once again against Northwestern. In fact, it played exactly the same schedule in the same order which it had suffered through in 1973, only with game sites reversed. The Spartans made a 38-point improvement in the opener alone, all the way from a four-point defeat to a 34-point victory. And the Spartan fans saw a completely recovered, better-than-ever Charley Baggett pass for 154 yards and two touchdowns of 57 and 44 yards to Mike Jones and Mike Hurd respectively. Sophomore Richie Baes, the walk-on who worked his way from nowhere as an unknown freshman on the 1973 junior varsity team to a starting role at tailback, came through with 68 yards rushing and a touchdown. Sophomore fullback Levi Jackson pounded for 91 yards and a score. Northwestern's Mitch Anderson, the quarterback who was most responsible for the Wildcats' rating as a conference favorite, had a good day passing but could buy only one score. Linebackers Terry McClowry and Kim Rowekamp led a murderous Spartan defense.

Fifty-three Spartans played against Syracuse the next Saturday in Spartan Stadium, 27 of them freshmen and sophomores. Syracuse managed just six first downs and never came close to scoring as it lost 19-0. First year coach Frank Maloney, former defensive aide at Michigan, expressed disappointment that State did not hand over the ball more frequently. It had only two turnovers, one by fumble and the other by interception, and, said Maloney, "We expected to get more turnovers than we got. Michigan State always has been a team that has turnovers." State's scores came on a 30-yard pass play, Baggett to Mike Jones, and two short darts by Baes.

But next came the bad news part of the schedule—UCLA, Notre Dame, and Michigan in a row once again. As improved as State obviously was, it was not ready to take on this threesome.

UCLA looked like the team of the year in demolishing the Spartans by an unbelievable 56-14 count in the Los Angeles Coliseum. The UCLA team under new coach Dick Vermeil had been tied at Tennessee in its opener and then defeated by Iowa at Iowa City. This was their first home appearance, and they had a lot to prove to their fans and themselves. As for State, perhaps co-captain Jim Taubert said it best. "We underestimated UCLA, and you can't do that to any team. They beat us physically and in the whole darned game."

Bruin quarterback John Sciarra played the game of his life, directing the veer offense like a magician, connecting on nine of 11 passes for 179 yards and a score, and running like a will-o'-the-wisp.

Even in such a calamity there were redeeming features. State had moved the ball well, rolling up 338 yards rushing and recording 20 first downs. Fullback Levi Jackson produced 103 yards lugging the ball. Baggett made 98. Graves intercepted a pair of Sciarra passes.

The big question now was whether State could regroup and rebound after such a sledgehammer blow.

Had the next foe been anyone but Notre Dame, the job would have been tougher. But now the Spartans had something to prove and their beloved Irish foes to prove it on. They pulled things together again in a hurry and carried a furious fight to Ara Parseghian's men. Three mistakes betrayed them and permitted the Irish to win 19-14. Two fumbles deep in Irish territory by fullbacks Levi Jackson and Clarence Bullock and a pop-up 14-yard punt by freshman booter Tom Birney set up two Notre Dame touchdowns and a field goal. The Irish led 16-0 at the half, but the resolute Spartans battled back with scoring drives of 99 and 76 yards in the second half. It was an impressive demonstration that the MSU football team was still in business.

Four lost fumbles, two interceptions, a blown assignment on pass coverage, and assorted other miscues told the sad story of State's 21-7 loss to Michigan at Ann Arbor the following Saturday before a mighty throng of more than 104,000 people. Because of errors, the Spartans were down 21-0 at the half. Still they came back to hold the Wolverines scoreless and score once themselves in the final 30 minutes. The Spartan tally, set up by a fumble recovery by Mike Duda on the Michigan 32, was recorded on a 15-yard fourth-down pass from Baggett to Mike Cobb deep in the Wolverine end zone.

Denny took the loss—and the plague of errors—harder than anyone. Monday press luncheons and Downtown Coaches gatherings were filled with questions about Spartan fumbling. Denny skipped one session with the Downtown Coaches and sent assistant Bill Davis in his place. It was the first time in all the years the club had been in existence that the Spartan head coach was not there.

The experience at Champaign, Illinois, the following Saturday did not help the situation. It was a big day for the Illini, the 50th anniversary of its Memorial Stadium and also of Red Grange's greatest days as an all-time college star at Illinois. Red was there as the honored guest at a banquet, various parties and receptions, and the game, and helped steam up the Illini for the Spartan engagement with a pregame pep talk.

270

Illinois had been made a slight favorite due in part to these psychological factors, yet State escaped with a 21-21 tie. That could sound like a moral victory, but not to Spartan followers as they saw the various victory opportunities which were wasted through seven fumbles, of which four were lost to Illinois, and an interception. It was an exciting game, though, for someone who did not care who won. All 42 points were scored in the first half. The second half was a defensive slugging match.

Stolz had a direct hand in staving off defeat when he argued officials out of a safety call in favor of a touchback. It happened on a kickoff by Illini Danny Beaver which Tyrone Wilson fumbled at the Spartan goal line. The officials first ruled it a safety, which would have given Illinois a 23-21 lead and ultimately the game. But Stolz argued that the impetus which carried the ball into the end zone had been provided by the kick. Officials agreed and reversed the call.

"It was a tough situation," Illinois coach Bob Blackman complained later, "but two signals concurred on the safety. And then they let the MSU coaches talk them out of it."

The Spartan offense had a fine day. Baggett picked up 123 yards and one touchdown passing and two six-pointers scored personally on a keeper over tackle and a dive over center. He also combined with Richie Baes for a sensational two-point conversion to tie the game at 21-all. It was supposed to be an option run right, with Baggett either passing or running for the end zone. He found no running room nor a receiver, reversed sharply, and started for the far side of the field. There was no outlet there, so he turned once again. By this time Baes was open at about the five yard line cross field, and Baggett winged the ball to him. Baes dived into the end zone for the game-saver.

Despite Illinois' 21 points, State's defense had some big innings, too. Freshman defensive back Tom Graves intercepted two passes, Otto Smith dumped Illini backs three times for losses, and five other Spartans—Terry McClowry, Mike Duda, Greg Schaum, John Breslin, and Jim Taubert—chipped in with sacks to run the total to ten for the day.

The Illinois game was the midpoint of the season once again, and, while there had been disappointments, there was discernible improvement. At this juncture in 1973, the record had been 1-5, and then came the big rally of four victories in five games to redeem a nearly ruined season. Now the record stood at 2-3-1, and fans wondered if the turnabout would occur again.

Purdue cooperated before a homecoming throng in Spartan Stadium the following week, surrendering with a 31-7 loss. Incredibly, after several weeks of disastrous mistakes, the Spartans played an errorless ball game—no fumbles or interceptions. It netted over 400 yards offense, and bottled up the Boilermakers' offense except for one second period scoring drive. Fullback Levi Jackson, who had done penance for fumbles and poor practice work by sitting on the bench throughout the Illinois game, ploughed for 104 yards on the ground. Baes and Baggett each scored two touchdowns. State produced scoring drives of 80, 57, 74, and 58 yards, a very encouraging sign that the kind of ball control State wanted was arriving at last.

Next on the agenda was an up-and-coming Wisconsin team, which had astounded the football world earlier by defeating Nebraska 21-20 and Missouri 59-20. The Badgers were slight favorites in the Homecoming Day contest in Camp Randall at Madison. State started off to a 14-0 lead, but Wisconsin came back to tie at 14-all. Then State surged ahead at 21-14, but Wisconsin tied it again at 21-all early in the fourth. Finally Baggett engineered a 65-yard scoring drive on seven plays to put the game away 28-21. He personally carried the ball home from the five.

Richie Baes satisfied old friends from his home town of Brookfield, Wisconsin, with his first 100-yard rushing day and a touchdown.

Then came the game which football buffs say is one of the classic upsets in the history of the sport. Undefeated Ohio State, No. 1 in the nation and ballyhooed as probably Woody Hayes' greatest team and quite possibly one of the all-time gridiron powerhouses, came to town. The Buckeyes' advance toward East Lansing was spotted weeks ahead as something special. The game was a complete sellout long before the kickoff. ABC-TV moved in to beam it to some 80 percent of the nation's population as the wild card game of the week, and requests for credentials from the mass information media, a sure-fire barometer of the significance of a sporting event, were the heaviest at State since the classic Notre Dame game of 1966.

It was not that Michigan State was expected to pull off a miracle. The odds were long against it. Most prognosticators picked Ohio State by three or four touchdowns. No one was much impressed by Stolz' bravado when he said, "Don't give me any of that Big Two and Little Eight business. We're going after the Big Ten championship." This was figured as the kind of thing a coach would say to stir some flicker of enthusiasm for the ordeal.

Only Denny was not kidding. Study of Ohio State game films convinced him his team did have a chance—and a good one. Spartan strategy on offense was simply ball control—to keep the Buckeyes from getting the ball too frequently. On defense it was to keep quarterback Cornelius Greene from running wild.

Ohio State scored first with a field goal in the opening period. Two Buckeye fumbles recovered by State's Mike Dean and Mike Duda and an interception of a Cornelius Greene pass by Tom Hannon helped fend off other Buckeye offensive efforts. Duda's recovery of a Greene fumble led to a Spartan field goal on the last play from scrimmage in the half. Soccer-style kicker Hans Nielsen, a native of Denmark, popped it home from 39 yards out.

So it was 3-3 at intermission, and Spartan athletic director Burt Smith predicted on a radio appearance during the break that "we're going to win this game." The closeness of the action is indicated by statistics. Both teams had made seven first downs. Total yardage for MSU was 123, for OSU 130.

The Buckeyes took the second half kickoff, moved the ball down field 16 plays, and finally had to settle for another field goal when the Spartans held at their own three. That was all the scoring for the third period as the Bucks could not come up with a first down on two other possessions. However, MSU did not go anywhere either. The Spartans took over the ball only twice, once on its 24 and the other time on its one, and could do little except protect the ball and punt out of danger.

Early in the fourth period the Spartans' lone fumble of the day nearly proved their undoing. Baggett sprang into the open down the right side on a keeper and appeared about to break cleanly away for a long touchdown sprint when suddenly— inexplicably—he dropped the ball. Ohio State recovered at the MSU 44, and eight plays later fullback Harold Henson powered over the middle from the one for a touchdown that put the Bucks ahead 13-3. There was less than ten minutes left to play when MSU took possession on its own 20 after a kickoff clear out of the end zone by Ohio State's great Tom Skladany. There followed two short running plays, a Baggett pass to Jackson for a nice gain and a Jackson run for a first down. Nothing to get

excited about.

Suddenly, MSU struck. Baggett dropped back and waited a moment as wide receiver Mike Jones fled through the Buckeye secondary. Then he fired the bomb. Jones took it in full stride and raced into the end zone. The Spartans missed a two-point conversion try which would have put them within field goal range of victory. But now they were within one touchdown of glory.

The Spartan defense stopped Archie Griffin and company cold. Skladany boomed another magnificent punt to the Spartan ten. Tom Hannon took it, advanced two yards, and was dropped.

A veteran observer in the press box noted the ball on the 12 and remarked:

"I remember another time when the ball was on the 12 yard line in this stadium. It was State's first play from scrimmage against Notre Dame in 1951. Fullback Dick Panin went right up the middle 88 yards for a touchdown. It broke the game open, and State won 35-0. You know, it could happen

Fullback Levi Jackson goes 88 yards for winning TD against Ohio State in 1974.

again, right here and now."

Just then the Spartan huddle broke, and a moment later the ball was snapped. Fullback Levi Jackson took a handoff from quarterback Baggett and stuck his nose into the hole between right guard and tackle for what looked like a nice gain of four or five yards. But suddenly he had slid past the close-in Buckeye defensive back and was in the open. He cut to the sidelines and sped along the stripe as the Buckeye defenders fell back in their all-out effort to catch him. He went all the way untouched as sheer pandemonium enveloped the stadium.

"We call the play veer 44," Jackson said later in the locker room. "After I got through the hole, I made a shoulder fake to the outside, then went straight through the secondary until I cut for the sideline. There was no way they were going to stop me."

"He can run the 100 in 9.6, and I knew that one of these days someone had to misjudge his speed," Denny told the press afterwards. "He doesn't have just a fullback's speed."

With the point-after kick by Nielsen, MSU was ahead to

stay, at 16-13. Ohio State took the ensuing kickoff and roared back. Ten plays later, including a hotly controversial incomplete pass which looked like a clear and clean interception by MSU's Terry McClowry, the Buckeyes were on the Spartan one with the final seconds of the game ticking off. They hurried to line up for the last gasp effort. As the referee waved his arms to signal the end of the game, the ball was snapped and, after a backfield mix-up, Buckeye wingback Brian Baschnagel picked up the loose ball and ran it into the end zone. Another official signalled a touchdown. Fans by the thousands engulfed the field. The officials were never seen again. Members of both teams, first Michigan State and then Ohio State, were jumping up and down, each apparently convinced it had won. Media people in the press box were uncertain as to whether a touchdown had been scored or not. Big Ten conference commissioner Wayne Duke, a press box visitor that day, said he would find the officials and report back and that no announcement should be made until he returned.

Clearing up the issue took some doing for the officials had left the stadium. When finally located, referee Gene Calhoun confirmed that time had indeed expired, and the score was 16-13 for Michigan State. It also was learned that even had the ball been snapped before the expiration of playing time and the apparent touchdown registered by Baschnagel, it would have been disallowed and a penalty for illegal procedure would have been imposed on Ohio State. This would have meant the end of the game, and State would have won anyway. (Contrary to popular belief, a game can end on a penalty if it is against the offensive team.)

Thousands of fans waited for the answer. About 45 minutes after the game they were informed via the public address system that the 16-13 score which had remained on the scoreboard throughout was indeed official.

Press accounts were glowing, and Stolz became an instant celebrity. He was named "Coach of the Week" by the UPI. Fan mail and congratulatory phone calls were heavy, and students besieged him with game programs for his autograph.

There were some sterling performances in that game. Levi Jackson had rushed for 133 yards. Baggett ran for 65 and passed for 144. Terry McClowry led all defenders with 17 tackles, followed by defensive end Otto Smith with 15. Archie Griffin ran for 140 yards though he did not score.

There was real concern in the Spartan camp over the visit the following weekend to Indiana. On the face of the records, there should have been no reason for alarm, but now the Spartans were vulnerable to upset if they should flatten out too much from their emotional performance against Ohio State.

Indiana had the initial impetus and led 7-3 at the half. Three pass interceptions aided the Hoosiers and hobbled State's offense. But State's running game got moving in the second half and ground the Hoosiers down. For the only time in memory, three Spartan backs ran for more than 100 yards in one game. Richie Baes netted 159, Baggett came in with 151, and Levi Jackson contributed 127. Hans Nielsen kicked two field goals. Touchdowns were by Baggett and Baes on short runs after sustained drives.

So State survived 19-10, leading a relieved Stolz to comment, "Well, you have to win this kind, too."

There remained just one obstacle to a 7-3-1 record, best at Michigan State since 1966. It was Iowa's visit to East Lansing for the season finale. The Indiana shock had awakened the Spartans, and they put on a show which dazzled the fans and bedeviled the Hawkeyes. The final count was 60-21, highest score of the year in the Big Ten.

Many Spartans had a big day. Jackson ran for 156 yards. Baggett rambled for 72 yards and scored three touchdowns, one on a 47-yard scamper around right end on an option play. Mike Hurd caught touchdown passes of 33 and 38 yards, and Nielsen kicked two field goals.

Terry and Pat McClowry were outstanding on defense, as were Kim Rowekamp and Mike Dean.

But the day belonged to a freshman back who saw his first varsity action in the fourth quarter as the bench was emptied and 68 Spartans finally saw service. Slender (6-2 and 182) Claude Geiger, a high school All-American from Charleston, West Virginia, had suffered torn ligaments in his ankle earlier in the season and had fallen far behind teammates as he recuperated. But he was ready when he was waved into the Iowa game with State ahead 47-21. First off, he spearheaded a 78-yard touchdown drive by carrying the ball for 68 of them, including the final five-yard spurt off tackle into the end zone. Geiger came in again after State stopped Iowa and immediately darted for six. Then time was running out. On the final play of the contest and season, Geiger was handed the ball again by quarterback Steve

Denny at work.

Moerdyk. The lithe youngster, whose build and running style are reminiscent of Lynn Chandnois, slithered off tackle, darted through the Hawk secondary, and streaked 53 yards to a touchdown as the clock showed game's end. In his brief first season—about seven minutes—he carried the ball 127 yards on ten tries, scored two touchdowns, and firmly implanted his No. 44 in the mind of every fan as one to remember and watch.

The season was richly satisfying. State had finished at 7-3-1 in all games and 6-1-1 in the league—just one-half game behind co-champions Ohio State and Michigan.

Newspapers proclaimed that the day of the Big Two and the Little Eight was over. At the very least, it now had become the Big Three and Little Seven.

Denny was named "Coach of the Year" in the league, and five men—quarterback Charley Baggett, fullback Levi Jackson, defensive end Otto Smith, defensive tackle Jim Taubert, and linebacker Terry McClowry—made first team on one or more All-Big Ten selections. The team finished in the top 20 nationally for the first time since the great 1966 season, winding up 12th in the AP and 18th in the UPI rankings.

Recruiting again went well. In late February of 1975, Stolz announced a group of signees which leaned heavily toward big linemen. Brought aboard were such linemen as Regis McQuaide, 6-6, 255 pounds, from Pittsburgh, Pennsylvania; Ed Stanton, 6-4, 240 pounds, from Battle Creek; Ted Grabenhorst, 6-5 and 235, from Mt. Morris, Michigan; and Jim Hinesly, 6-2 and 240, from Detroit. Jim Hinesly is the son of the Jim Hinesly of the 1950s.

The best new running back appeared to be William Broadway, of Flint, who had broken several records at Flint Northern which had been set by LeRoy Bolden a generation ago.

"We needed help in a number of positions if we hoped to challenge for the Big Ten conference championship," Denny said happily, "and it is the feeling of our staff that we certainly improved the Spartans with our recent recruiting efforts."

The team was certain to be figured a Big Ten title contender—perhaps even the 1975 favorite—in view of the late 1974 successes, the return of 39 lettermen to the wars, and another bumper freshman crop. The era of Denny had come of age.

Appendix

All-Time Spartan Summary

Year	Games	Won	Lost	Tied	Pts.	Opp. Pts.	Coach	Captain (Position)
1896	4	1	2	1	26	42	No Established Coach	Wilfred R. Vanderhoef (Tackle)
1897	7	4	2	1	146	106	Henry Keep	Walton K. Brainard (Halfback)
1898	7	4	3	0	142	127	Henry Keep	J. H. Vanderstolpe (Guard)
1899	7	2	4	1	81	101	Charles O. Bemies	Ellis W. Ranney (Quarterback)
1900	4	1	3	0	51	67	Charles O. Bemies	Charles A. McCue (End)
1901	8	3	4	1	120	94	George Denman	Albert H. Case (Guard)
1902	9	4	5	0	93	206	George Denman	Arthur D. Peters (Tackle)
1903	8	6	1	1	178	24	Chester L. Brewer	Frank J. Kratz (Tackle)
1904	9	8	1	0	380	16	Chester L. Brewer	Robert F. Bell (Tackle)
1905	11	9	2	0	280	75	Chester L. Brewer	Edward B. McKenna (Halfback)
1906	11	7	2	2	195	28	Chester L. Brewer	Stephen W. Doty (Fullback)
1907	7	4	2	1	127	60	Chester L. Brewer	Walter H. Small (Quarterback)
1908	8	6	0	2	205	22	Chester L. Brewer	Bert Shedd (Tackle)
1909	9	8	1	0	233	17	Chester L. Brewer	Parnell G. McKenna (Halfback)
1910	7	6	1	0	168	8	Chester L. Brewer	Ion J. Cortright (Halfback)
1911	6	5	1	0	93	30	John F. Macklin	Fred A. Stone (End)
1912	8	7	1	0	297	98	John F. Macklin	William R. Riblett (Quarterback)
1913	7	7	0	0	180	28	John F. Macklin	Chester W. Gifford (Tackle)
1914	7	5	2	0	188	51	John F. Macklin	George E. Julian (Fullback)
1915	6	5	1	0	258	38	John F. Macklin	W. Blake Miller (Halfback)
1916	7	4	2	1	126	26	Frank Sommers	Ralph B. Henning (End)
1917	9	0	9	0	23	179	Chester L. Brewer	Sherman Coryell (Tackle)
1918	7	4	3	0	134	68	George E. Gauthier	Lawrence C. Archer (Center)
1919	9	4	4	1	132	99	Chester L. Brewer	Harry E. Franson (Tackle)
1920	10	4	6	0	270	166	George "Potsy" Clark	Harold A. Springer (Quarterback)
1921	8	3	5	0	68	126	Albert M. Barron	John Bos (Tackle)
1922	10	3	5	2	111	135	Albert M. Barron	William C. Johnson (Halfback)
1923	8	3	5	0	57	144	Ralph H. Young	Maurice R. Taylor (Guard)
1924	8	5	3	0	210	48	Ralph H. Young	Vivian J. Hultman (Guard)
1925	8	3	5	0	105	106	Ralph H. Young	Donald H. Haskins (Tackle)
1926	8	3	4	1	97	171	Ralph H. Young	Martin F. Rummel (Tackle)
1927	9	4	5	0	111	128	Ralph H. Young	Paul M. Smith (Fullback)
1928	8	3	4	1	153	66	Harry G. Kipke	Lewis A. Hornbeck (End)
1929	8	5	3	0	244	104	James H. Crowley	Fred W. Danziger (Halfback)
								Vern C. Dickeson (Halfback)
1930	8	5	1	2	151	32	James H. Crowley	Harold E. Smead (Center)
1931	9	5	3	1	291	61	James H. Crowley	Milton C. Gross (Guard)
1932	8	7	1	0	220	64	James H. Crowley	Abe Eliowitz (Fullback)
								Robert C. Monnett (Halfback)
1933	8	4	2	2	73	49	Charles W. Bachman	Bernard G. McNutt (Fullback)
1934	9	8	1	0	153	56	Charles W. Bachman	Russell H. Reynolds (Qtrback)
1935	8	6	2	0	207	57	Charles W. Bachman	Sidney P. Wagner (Guard)
1936	9	6	1	2	143	40	Charles W. Bachman	Gordon A. Dahlgren (Guard)
								Henry S. Kutchins (End)
1937	10	8	2	0	117	42	Charles W. Bachman	Harry E. Speelman (Tackle)

280

Year	Games	Won	Lost	Tied	Pts.	Opp. Pts.	Coach	Captain (Position)
1938	9	6	3	0	133	59	Charles W. Bachman	Allen O. Diebold (Quarterback)
								David D. Diehl (End)
1939	9	4	4	1	102	92	Charles W. Bachman	Michael Kinek (End)
								Lyle J. Rockenbach (Guard)
1940	8	3	4	1	108	76	Charles W. Bachman	Jack R. Amon (Fullback)
								Paul L. Griffeth (Guard)
1941	9	5	3	1	150	77	Charles W. Bachman	Wilford D. Davis (Quarterback)
								William Rupp, Jr. (Guard)
1942	9	4	3	2	120	99	Charles W. Bachman	Richard Mangrum (Tackle)
								Walter L. Pawlowski (Halfback)
1943	Football terminated (war restrictions).							
1944	7	6	1	0	167	31	Charles W. Bachman	Thomas B. Sullivan (Center)
1945	9	5	3	1	120	128	Charles W. Bachman	Jacweir Breslin (Halfback)
1946	10	5	5	0	181	202	Charles W. Bachman	Robert B. McCurry (Center)
								Kenneth E. Balge (End)
1947	9	7	2	0	167	101	Clarence L. Munn	Robert B. McCurry (Center)
1948	10	6	2	2	359	130	Clarence L. Munn	Robert B. McCurry (Center)
1949	9	6	3	0	309	107	Clarence L. Munn	Harold L. Vogler (Tackle)
1950	9	8	1	0	243	107	Clarence L. Munn	LeRoy R. Crane (Fullback)
1951	9	9	0	0	270	114	Clarence L. Munn	Robert Carey (End)
1952	9	9	0	0	312	84	Clarence L. Munn	Donald McAuliffe (Halfback)
1953	10	9	1	0	240	110	Clarence L. Munn	Donald Dohoney (End)
1954	9	3	6	0	177	149	Hugh Duffy Daugherty	LeRoy Bolden (Halfback)
								Don Kauth (End)
1955	10	9	1	0	253	83	Hugh Duffy Daugherty	Carl Nystrom (Guard)
1956	9	7	2	0	239	87	Hugh Duffy Daugherty	John Matsko (Center)
1957	9	8	1	0	264	75	Hugh Duffy Daugherty	Patrick Burke (Tackle)
1958	9	3	5	1	117	123	Hugh Duffy Daugherty	Sam Williams (End)
1959	9	5	4	0	149	118	Hugh Duffy Daugherty	Donald Wright (Guard)
1960	9	6	2	1	193	118	Hugh Duffy Daugherty	Fred Arbanas (End)
								Fred Boylen (Guard)
								Herb Adderley (Halfback)
1961	9	7	2	0	192	50	Hugh Duffy Daugherty	Ed Ryan (Halfback)
1962	9	5	4	0	189	96	Hugh Duffy Daugherty	George Saimes (Fullback)
1963	9	6	2	1	148	63	Hugh Duffy Daugherty	Dan D. Underwood (End)
								Sherman P. Lewis (Halfback)
1964	9	4	5	0	136	141	Hugh Duffy Daugherty	Chas. Migyanka, Jr. (Linebacker)
1965	11	10	1	0	263	76	Hugh Duffy Daugherty	Donald Japinga (Halfback)
								Stephen Juday (Quarterback
1966	10	9	0	1	293	99	Hugh Duffy Daugherty	Clinton Jones (Halfback)
								George Webster (Roverback)
1967	10	3	7	0	173	193	Hugh Duffy Daugherty	Anthony Conti (Tackle)
								Drake Garrett (Halfback)
1968	10	5	5	0	202	151	Hugh Duffy Daugherty	Allen Brenner (End)
1969	10	4	6	0	202	231	Hugh Duffy Daugherty	Franklin Foreman (End)
								Richard Saul (Linebacker)
1970	10	4	6	0	190	215	Hugh Duffy Daugherty	Gordon Bowdell (End)
								Michael Hogan (Linebacker)
								Wilt Martin (Tackle)
1971	11	6	5	0	225	169	Hugh Duffy Daugherty	Eric Allen (Halfback)
								Ron Curl (Tackle)
1972	11	5	5	1	158	156	Hugh Duffy Daugherty	Brad VanPelt (Safety)
								Billy Joe DuPree (Tight End)
1973	11	5	6	0	114	164	Dennis Stolz	Michael Holt (Tailback)
								John Shinsky (Tackle)
1974	11	7	3	1	270	196	Dennis Stolz	James Taubert (Tackle)
								Clarence Bullock (Fullback)

Coaches' Records

Coach	Period	Years Coached	G	W	L	T	Pct.
No established Coach	1896	(1)	4	1	2	1	.375
Henry Keep	1897–1898	(2)	14	8	5	1	.607
Charles O. Bemies (West. Theo. Sem.)	1899–1900	(2)	11	3	7	1	.318
George E. Denman (West. Theo. Sem.)	1901–1902	(2)	17	7	9	1	.441
Chester L. Brewer (Wisconsin)	1903–1910	(8)	70	54	10	6	.814
John F. Macklin (Pennsylvania)	1911–1915	(5)	34	29	5	0	.853
Frank Sommers (Pennsylvania)	1916	(1)	7	4	2	1	.642
Chester L. Brewer (Wisconsin)	1917	(1)	9	0	9	0	.000
George E. Gauthier (Mich. State)	1918	(1)	7	4	3	0	.571
Chester L. Brewer (Wisconsin)	1919	(1)	9	4	4	1	.500
Brewer Totals		(10)	88	58	23	7	.699
George "Potsy" Clark (Illinois)	1920	(1)	10	4	6	0	.400
Albert M. Barron (Penn State)	1921–1922	(2)	18	6	10	2	.389
Ralph H. Young (Chicago-W&J)	1923–1927	(5)	41	18	22	1	.451
Harry G. Kipke (Michigan)	1928	(1)	8	3	4	1	.437
James H. Crowley (Notre Dame)	1929–1932	(4)	33	22	8	3	.712
Charles W. Bachman (Notre Dame)	1933–1946	(13)	114	70	34	10	.658
Clarence Biggie Munn (Minnesota)	1947–1953	(7)	65	54	9	2	.857
Hugh D. Daugherty (Syracuse)	1954–1972	(19)	183	109	69	5	.591
Dennis E. Stolz (Alma)	1973–1974	(2)	22	12	9	1	.568
TOTALS	1896-1974	(78)	676	412	227	37	.637

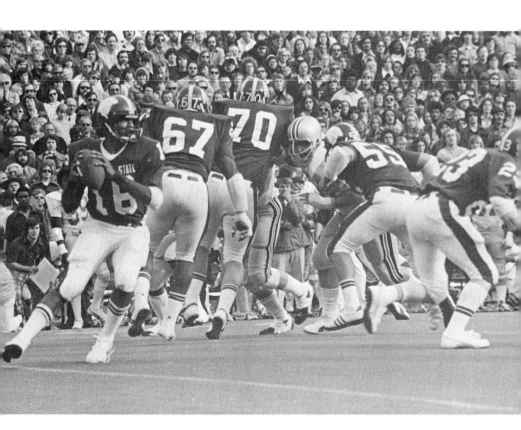

78 Years With The Spartans

1896

No Established Coach

10	Lansing High	0	(H)
0	Kalamazoo	24	(T)
0	Alma	0	(H)
16	Kalamazoo	18	(H)

Won 1, Lost 2, Tied 1

1897

HENRY KEEP
Coach

28	Lansing H.S.	0	(H)
26	Olivet	6	(H)
0	Kalamazoo	28	(H)
18	Olivet	18	(T)
30	Alma	16	(T)
38	Alma	4	(H)
6	Notre Dame	34	(T)

Won 4, Lost 2, Tied 1

1898

11	Ypsilanti	6	(T)
0	Michigan	39	(T)
0	Notre Dame	53	(T)
62	Albion	6	(H)
45	Olivet	0	(T)
24	Ypsilanti	6	(H)
0	Kalamazoo	17	(T)

Won 4, Lost 3, Tied 0

1899

CHARLES O. BEMIES
Coach

0	Notre Dame	40	(T)
6	Detroit A. C.	16	(T)
6	Kalamazoo	10	(H)
11	Alma	11	(T)
18	Ypsilanti	0	(T)
17	Olivet	18	(T)
23	DePauw	6	(H)

Won 2, Lost 4, Tied 1

1900

0	Albion	23	(H)
45	Adrian	0	(H)
6	Detroit A. C.	21	(T)
0	Alma	23	(H)

Won 1, Lost 3, Tied 0

1901

GEORGE DENMAN
Coach

5	Alma	6	(T)
22	Hillsdale	0	(H)
11	Albion	0	(T)
0	Detroit A. C.	33	(T)
42	Kalamazoo	0	(H)
17	Albion	17	(H)
5	Kalamazoo	15	(T)
18	Olivet	23	(H)

Won 3, Lost 4, Tied 1

1902

0	Notre Dame	32	(T)
11	Detroit	0	(H)
0	Michigan 119	(T)
35	Hillsdale	0	(H)
2	Michigan Fresh.	0	(H)
12	DePauw	17	(H)
6	Olivet	11	(T)
22	Albion	11	(T)
5	Alma	16	(H)

Won 4, Lost 5, Tied 0

1903

CHESTER BREWER
Coach

0	Notre Dame	12	(T)
11	Alma	0	(T)
45	Olivet	0	(H)
11	Michigan Fresh.	0	(H)
11	Kalamazoo	0	(H)
43	Hillsdale	0	(T)
51	Detroit Y.M.C.A.	6	(H)
6	Albion	6	(H)

Won 6, Lost 1, Tied 1

1904

47	Mich. Deaf Sch...	0	(H)
28	Ohio North.	6	(H)
29	P. Huron YMCA	0	(H)
0	Albion	4	(T)
104	Hillsdale	0	(H)
39	Michigan Fresh.	0	(H)
35	Olivet	6	(T)
40	Alma	0	(H)
58	Kalamazoo	0	(H)

Won 8, Lost 1, Tied 0

1905

42	Mich. Deaf Sch...	0	(H)
0	Notre Dame	28	(T)
43	P. Huron YMCA	0	(H)
24	Michigan Fresh.	0	(H)
30	Olivet	0	(H)
18	Hillsdale	0	(H)
18	Armour Inst.	0	(H)
30	Kalamazoo	0	(T)
46	Albion	10	(H)
11	Northwestern	37	(T)
18	Alma	0	(T)

Won 9, Lost 2, Tied 0

1906

23	Olivet	0	(H)
37	Albion	0	(H)
0	Alma	0	(T)
38	Kalamazoo	0	(H)
33	DePauw	0	(H)
0	Notre Dame	5	(T)
5	Albion	0	(T)
12	Alma	0	(H)
35	Hillsdale	9	(T)
6	Olivet	8	(T)
6	Detroit A. C.	6	(T)

Won 7, Lost 2, Tied 2

1907

17	Detroit	0	(H)
40	Mich. Deaf Sch...	0	(H)
0	Michigan	46	(T)
15	Wabash	6	(H)
55	Olivet	4	(H)
0	Alma	0	(T)
0	Detroit A. C.	4	(T)

Won 4, Lost 2, Tied 1

1908

0	Michigan	0	(H)
35	Kalamazoo	0	(H)
51	Mich. Deaf Sch...	0	(H)
0	DePaul	0	(T)
6	Wabash	0	(H)

46	Olivet	2	(T)
30	Saginaw Nav. Br.	6	(H)
37	Detroit A. C.	14	(T)

Won 6, Lost 0, Tied 2

1909

27	Detroit	0	(H)
34	Alma	0	(H)
28	Wabash	0	(H)
0	Notre Dame	17	(T)
29	Culver	0	(T)
51	DePaul	0	(H)
10	Marquette	0	(H)
20	Olivet	0	(H)
34	Detroit A. C.	0	(T)

Won 8, Lost 1, Tied 0

1910

35	Detroit A. C.	0	(H)
11	Alma	0	(H)
3	Michigan	6	(T)
37	Lake Forest	0	(H)
17	Notre Dame	0	(H)
3	Marquette	2	(T)
62	Olivet	0	(H)

Won 6, Lost 1, Tied 0

1911
JOHN F. MACKLIN
Coach

12	Alma	0	(H)
3	Michigan	15	(H)
29	Olivet	3	(H)
6	DePauw	0	(T)
26	Mt. Union	6	(H)
17	Wabash	6	(H)

Won 5, Lost 1, Tied 0

1912

14	Alma	3	(H)
7	Michigan	55	(T)
52	Olivet	0	(H)
58	DePauw	0	(H)
46	Ohio Wesleyan	0	(H)
61	Mt. Union	20	(H)
24	Wabash	0	(H)
35	Ohio State	20	(T)

Won 7, Lost 1, Tied 0

1913

26	Olivet	0	(H)
57	Alma	0	(H)
12	Michigan	7	(T)
12	Wisconsin	7	(T)
41	Akron	0	(H)
13	Mt. Union	7	(H)
19	South Dakota	7	(H)

Won 7, Lost 0, Tied 0

1914

26	Olivet	7	(H)
60	Alma	0	(H)
0	Michigan	3	(H)
0	Nebraska	24	(T)
75	Akron	0	(H)
21	Mt. Union	14	(H)
6	Penn State	3	(T)

Won 5, Lost 2, Tied 0

1915

34	Olivet	0	(H)
77	Alma	12	(H)
56	Carroll	0	(H)
24	Michigan	0	(H)
0	Oregon State	20	(H)
68	Marquette	6	(H)

Won 5, Lost 1, Tied 0

1916
FRANK SOMMERS
Coach

40	Olivet	0	(H)
20	Carroll	0	(H)
33	Alma	0	(H)
0	Michigan	9	(T)
30	N. Dakota State	0	(H)
3	South Dakota	3	(T)
0	Notre Dame	14	(H)

Won 4, Lost 2, Tied 1

1917
CHESTER L. BREWER
Coach

7	Alma	14	(H)
3	Kalamazoo	7	(H)
0	Michigan	27	(T)
0	Detroit	14	(H)
0	Western State	14	(H)
6	Northwestern	39	(T)
0	Notre Dame	23	(T)
7	Syracuse	21	(H)
0	Camp MacArthur	20	(H)

Won 0, Lost 9, Tied 0

1918
GEORGE E. GAUTHIER
Coach

21	Albion	6	(H)
66	Hillsdale	6	(H)
16	Western State	7	(H)
6	Purdue	14	(H)
13	Notre Dame	7	(H)
6	Michigan	21	(T)
6	Wisconsin	7	(T)

Won 4, Lost 3, Tied 0

1919
CHESTER L. BREWER
Coach

14	Albion	13	(H)
46	Alma	6	(H)
18	Western State	21	(H)
0	Michigan	26	(T)
27	DePauw	0	(H)
7	Purdue	13	(T)
13	South Dakota	0	(H)
0	Notre Dame	13	(T)
7	Wabash	7	(H)

Won 4, Lost 4, Tied 1

1920
GEO. "POTSY" CLARK
Coach

2	Kalamazoo	21	(H)
16	Abion	0	(H)
48	Alma	0	(H)
0	Wisconsin	27	(T)
0	Michigan	35	(T)
7	Marietta	23	(H)
109	Olivet	0	(H)
81	Chicago Y.M.C.A.	0	(H)
7	Nebraska	35	(T)
0	Notre Dame	25	(H)

Won 4, Lost 6, Tied 0

1921
ALBERT M. BARRON
Coach

28	Alma	0	(H)
7	Albion	24	(H)
0	Michigan	30	(T)
17	Western State	14	(H)
0	Marquette	7	(T)
14	South Dakota	0	(H)
2	Butler	3	(H)
0	Notre Dame	48	(T)

Won 3, Lost 5, Tied 0

1922

33	Alma	0	(H)
7	Albion	7	(H)
0	Wabash	26	(T)
7	South Dakota	0	(H)
6	Indiana	14	(T)
0	Michigan	63	(T)
6	Ohio Wesleyan	9	(H)
0	Creighton	9	(T)
45	Mass. State	0	(H)
7	St. Louis	7	(T)

Won 3, Lost 5, Tied 2

1923
RALPH H. YOUNG
Coach

0	Chicago	34	(T)
21	Lake Forest	6	(H)
0	Wisconsin	21	(T)
13	Albion	0	(H)
0	Michigan	37	(T)
14	Ohio Wesleyan	19	(H)
7	Creighton	27	(H)
2	Detroit	0	(T)

Won 3, Lost 5, Tied 0

1924

59	North Central	0	(H)
54	Olivet	3	(H)
0	Michigan	7	(H)
34	Chicago Y.M.C.A.	3	(H)
9	Northwestern	13	(T)
42	Lake Forest	13	(H)
3	St. Louis	9	(T)
9	S. Dakota State	0	(H)

Won 5, Lost 3, Tied 0

1925

16	Adrian	0	(H)
0	Michigan	39	(T)
0	Lake Forest	6	(H)
15	Centre	13	(H)
6	Penn State	13	(T)
0	Colgate	14	(H)
58	Toledo	0	(H)
10	Wisconsin	21	(T)

Won 3, Lost 5, Tied 0

1926

16	Adrian	0	(H)
9	Kalamazoo	0	(H)
3	Michigan	55	(T)
14	Cornell U.	24	(T)
0	Lake Forest	0	(H)
6	Colgate	38	(T)
42	Centre	14	(H)
7	Haskell Inst.	40	(H)

Won 3, Lost 4, Tied 1

1927

12	Kalamazoo	6	(H)
27	Ohio U.	0	(H)
0	Michigan	21	(T)
13	Cornell, Iowa	19	(H)
7	Detroit	24	(H)
7	Indiana	33	(T)
20	Albion	6	(H)
25	Butler	0	(H)
0	N. C. State	19	(T)

Won 4, Lost 5, Tied 0

1928
HARRY G. KIPKE,
Coach

103	Kalamazoo	0	(H)

0	Albion	2	(H)
37	Chicago Y.M.C.A.	0	(H)
0	Colgate	16	(H)
6	Mississippi St.	6	(H)
0	Detroit	39	(T)
0	Michigan	3	(T)
7	N. C. State	0	(H)

Won 3 Lost 4, Tied 1

1929
JAMES H. CROWLEY
Coach

59	Alma	6	(H)
0	Michigan	17	(T)
0	Colgate	31	(T)
74	Adrian	0	(H)
40	N. C. State	6	(H)
38	Case	0	(H)
33	Mississippi St.	19	(T)
0	Detroit	25	(H)

Won 5, Lost 3, Tied 0

1930

28	Alma	0	(H)
0	Michigan	0	(T)
32	Cincinnati	0	(H)
14	Colgate	7	(H)
45	Case	0	(H)
13	Georgetown U.	14	(T)
19	N. Dakota State	11	(H)
0	Detroit	0	(H)

Won 5, Lost 1, Tied 2

1931

74	Alma	0	(H)
47	Cornell, Iowa	0	(H)
7	Army	20	(T)
34	Ill. Wesleyan	6	(H)
6	Georgetown U.	0	(H)
10	Syracuse	15	(H)
100	Ripon	0	(H)
0	Michigan	0	(T)
13	Detroit	20	(T)

Won 5, Lost 3, Tied 1

1932

93	Alma	0	(H)
0	Michgian	26	(T)
27	Grinnell	6	(H)
27	Ill. Wesleyan	0	(H)
19	Fordham	13	(T)
27	Syracuse	13	(T)
20	South Dakota	6	(H)
7	Detroit	0	(H)

Won 7, Lost 1, Tied 0

1933
CHARLES W. BACHMAN
Coach

14	Grinnell	0	(H)
6	Michigan	20	(T)
20	Ill. Wesleyan	12	(H)
6	Marquette	0	(T)

27	Syracuse	3 (H)
0	Kansas State	0 (H)
0	Carnegie Tech	0 (H)
0	Detroit	14 (T)

Won 4, Lost 2, Tied 2

1934

33	Grinnell	20 (H)
16	Michigan	0 (T)
13	Carnegie Tech	0 (H)
39	Manhattan	0 (T)
13	Marquette	7 (H)
0	Syracuse	10 (T)
7	Detroit	6 (H)
6	Kansas	0 (T)
26	Texas A. & M.	13 (T)

Won 8, Lost 1, Tied 0

1935

41	Grinnell	0 (H)
25	Michigan	6 (T)
42	Kansas	0 (H)
6	Boston Col.	18 (T)
47	Wash. (St. L.)	13 (H)
12	Temple	7 (T)
7	Marquette	13 (H)
27	Loyola (Cal.)	0 (T)

Won 6, Lost 2, Tied 0

1936

27	Wayne State	0 (H)
21	Michigan	7 (T)
7	Carnegie Tech	0 (T)
13	Missouri	0 (H)
7	Marquette	13 (H)
13	Boston Col.	13 (T)
7	Temple	7 (T)
41	Kansas	0 (T)
7	Arizona	0 (H)

Won 6, Lost 1, Tied 2

1937

19	Wayne State	0 (H)
19	Michigan	14 (T)
0	Manhattan	3 (T)
2	Missouri	0 (T)
21	Marquette	7 (H)
16	Kansas	0 (H)
13	Temple	6 (T)
13	Carnegie Tech.	6 (H)
14	San Francisco	0 (T)

Orange Bowl

0	Auburn	6 (T)

Won 8, Lost 2, Tied 0

1938

34	Wayne State	6 (H)
0	Michigan	14 (T)
18	Ill. Wesleyan	0 (H)
26	West Virginia	0 (T)
19	Syracuse	12 (H)
6	Santa Clara	7 (H)
0	Missouri	6 (T)
20	Marquette	14 (T)
10	Temple	0 (H)

Won 6, Lost 3, Tied 0

1939

16	Wayne State	0 (H)
13	Michigan	26 (T)
14	Marquette	17 (H)
7	Purdue	20 (T)
13	Ill. Wesleyan	6 (H)
14	Syracuse	3 (T)
0	Santa Clara	6 (T)
7	Indiana	7 (H)
18	Temple	7 (H)

Won 4, Lost 4, Tied 1

1940

14	Michigan	21 (T)
20	Purdue	7 (H)
19	Temple	21 (H)
0	Santa Clara	0 (H)
32	Kansas State	0 (H)
0	Indiana	20 (T)
6	Marquette	7 (H)
17	West Virginia	0 (H)

Won 3, Lost 4, Tied 1

1941

7	Michigan	19 (T)
13	Marquette	7 (H)
0	Santa Clara	7 (T)

39	Wayne State	6 (H)
0	Missouri	19 (H)
0	Purdue	0 (T)
46	Temple	0 (H)
31	Ohio Wesleyan	7 (H)
14	West Virginia	12 (T)

Won 5, Lost 3, Tied 1

1942

0	Michigan	20 (T)
46	Wayne State	6 (H)
7	Marquette	28 (H)
14	Great Lakes	0 (H)
7	Temple	7 (T)
13	Washington St.	25 (T)
19	Purdue	6 (H)
7	West Virginia	0 (H)
7	Oregon State	7 (H)

Won 4, Lost 3, Tied 2

1943

No football due to war.

1944

40	Scranton	12 (H)
2	Kentucky	0 (T)
45	Kansas State	6 (H)
8	Maryland	0 (T)
32	Wayne State	0 (H)
7	Missouri	13 (H)
33	Maryland	0 (H)

Won 6, Lost 1, Tied 0

1945

0	Michigan	40 (T)
7	Kentucky	6 (H)
12	Pittsburgh	7 (T)
27	Wayne State	7 (H)
13	Marquette	13 (H)
14	Missouri	7 (H)
7	Great Lakes	27 (H)
33	Penn State	0 (H)
7	Miami (Fla)	21 (T)

Won 5, Lost 3, Tied 1

1946

42	Wayne State	0 (H)
20	Boston Col.	34 (H)
0	Mississippi State	6 (H)
19	Penn State	16 (T)
7	Cincinnati	18 (H)
14	Kentucky	39 (T)
7	Michigan	55 (T)
20	Marquette	0 (H)
26	Maryland	14 (H)
26	Washington St.	20 (H)

Won 5, Lost 5, Tied 0

1947

CLARENCE L. MUNN
Head Coach

0	Michigan	55 (T)
7	Mississippi State	0 (H)
21	Washington St.	7 (T)
20	Iowa State	0 (H)
6	Kentucky	7 (H)
13	Marquette	7 (H)
28	Santa Clara	0 (H)
14	Temple	6 (T)
58	Hawaii	19 (T)

Won 7, Lost 2, Tied 0

1948

7	Michigan	13 (H)
68	Hawaii	21 (H)
7	Notre Dame	26 (T)
61	Arizona	7 (H)
14	Penn State	14 (T)
46	Oregon State	21 (T)
47	Marquette	0 (H)

48 Iowa State .... 7 (T)
40 Washington
State .... 0 (H)
21 Santa Clara .... 21 (T)
Won 6, Lost 2, Tied 2

1949

3 Michigan .... 7 (T)
48 Marquette .... 7 (H)
14 Maryland .... 7 (H)
42 William & Mary 13 (H)
24 Penn State .... 0 (H)
62 Temple .... 14 (H)
21 Notre Dame ..... 34 (H)
20 Oregon State .... 25 (T)
75 Arizona .... 0 (T)
Won 6, Lost 3, Tied 0

1950

38 Oregon State .... 13 (H)
14 Michigan .... 7 (T)
7 Maryland .... 34 (H)
33 William & Mary 14 (H)
34 Marquette .... 6 (H)
36 Notre Dame ...... 33 (T)
35 Indiana .... 0 (H)
27 Minnesota .... 0 (H)
19 Pittsburgh .... 0 (T)
Won 8, Lost 1, Tied 0

1951

6 Oregon State .... 0 (H)
25 Michigan .... 0 (T)
24 Ohio State .... 20 (T)
20 Marquette .... 14 (H)
32 Penn State .... 21 (T)
53 Pittsburgh .... 26 (H)
35 Notre Dame ...... 0 (H)
30 Indiana .... 26 (T)
45 Colorado .... 7 (H)
Won 9, Lost 0, Tied 0

1952

27 Michigan .... 13 (T)
17 Oregon State .... 14 (T)
48 Texas A&M .... 6 (H)
48 Syracuse .... 7 (H)
34 Penn State .... 7 (H)
14 Purdue .... 7 (T)
41 Indiana .... 14 (T)
21 Notre Dame ...... 3 (H)
62 Marquette .... 13 (H)
Won 9, Lost 0, Tied 0

1953

21 Iowa .... 7 (T)
21 Minnesota .... 0 (T)
26 Texas Christian.. 19 (H)
47 Indiana .... 18 (H)
0 Purdue .... 6 (T)
34 Oregon State ...... 6 (H)
28 Ohio State .... 13 (T)
14 Michigan .... 6 (H)
21 Marquette .... 15 (H)

Rose Bowl

28 U.C.L.A. .... 20 (T)
Won 9, Lost 1, Tied 0

1954
HUGH D. DAUGHERTY
Head Coach

10 Iowa .... 14 (T)
0 Wisconsin .... 6 (H)
21 Indiana .... 14 (T)
19 Notre Dame ...... 20 (T)

13 Purdue .... 27 (H)
13 Minnesota .... 19 (T)
54 Washington St... 6 (H)
7 Michigan .... 33 (T)
40 Marquette .... 10 (H)
Won 3, Lost 6, Tied 0

1955

20 Indiana .... 13 (T)
7 Michigan .... 14 (T)
38 Stanford .... 14 (H)
21 Notre Dame ...... 7 (H)
21 Illinois .... 7 (H)
27 Wisconsin .... 0 (H)
27 Purdue .... 0 (T)
42 Minnesota .... 14 (H)
33 Marquette .... 0 (H)

Rose Bowl

17 UCLA .... 14 (T)
Won 9, Lost 1, Tied 0

1956

21 Stanford .... 7 (T)
9 Michigan .... 0 (T)
53 Indiana .... 6 (H)
47 Notre Dame ...... 14 (T)
13 Illinois .... 20 (T)
33 Wisconsin .... 0 (H)
12 Purdue .... 9 (H)
13 Minnesota .... 14 (T)
38 Kansas State .... 17 (H)
Won 7, Lost 2, Tied 0

1957

54 Indiana .... 0 (H)
19 California .... 0 (T)
35 Michigan .... 6 (T)
13 Purdue .... 20 (H)
19 Illinois .... 14 (H)
21 Wisconsin .... 7 (T)
34 Notre Dame ...... 6 (H)
42 Minnesota .... 13 (H)
27 Kansas State ...... 9 (H)
Won 8, Lost 1, Tied 0

1958

32 California .... 12 (H)
12 Michigan .... 12 (H)
22 Pittsburgh .... 8 (H)
6 Purdue .... 14 (T)
0 Illinois .... 16 (T)
7 Wisconsin .... 9 (H)
0 Indiana .... 6 (T)
12 Minnesota .... 39 (T)
26 Kansas State ...... 7 (H)
Won 3, Lost 5, Tied 1

1959

7 Texas A. & M..... 9 (H)
34 Michigan .... 8 (T)
8 Iowa .... 37 (T)
19 Notre Dame ...... 0 (H)
14 Indiana .... 6 (H)
24 Ohio State .... 30 (T)
15 Purdue .... 0 (H)
15 Northwestern ...... 10 (H)
13 Miami (Fla. ...... 18 (T)
Won 5, Lost 4, Tied 0

1960

7 Pittsburgh .... 7 (T)
24 Michigan .... 17 (H)
15 Iowa .... 27 (H)
21 Notre Dame ...... 0 (T)
35 Indiana .... 0 (T)
10 Ohio State .... 21 (H)
17 Purdue .... 13 (T)
21 Northwestern .... 18 (T)
43 Detroit .... 15 (H)
Won 6, Lost 2, Tied 1

1961

20 Wisconsin .... 0 (T)
31 Stanford .... 3 (H)
28 Michigan .... 0 (T)
17 Notre Dame ...... 7 (H)
35 Indiana .... 0 (H)

287

0	Minnesota	13	(T)
6	Purdue	7	(T)
21	Northwestern	13	(H)
34	Illinois	7	(H)

Won 7, Lost 2, Tied 0

1962

13	Stanford	16	(T)
38	North Carolina	6	(H)
28	Michigan	0	(H)
31	Notre Dame	7	(T)
26	Indiana	8	(T)
7	Minnesota	28	(H)
9	Purdue	17	(H)
31	Northwestern	7	(T)
6	Illinois	7	(T)

Won 5, Lost 4, Tied 0

1963

31	North Carolina	0	(H)
10	So. California	13	(T)
7	Michigan	7	(T)
20	Indiana	3	(H)
15	Northwestern	7	(T)
30	Wisconsin	13	(H)
23	Purdue	0	(T)
12	Notre Dame	7	(H)
0	Illinois	13	(H)

Won 6, Lost 2, Tied 1

1964

15	North Carolina	21	(T)
17	So. California	7	(H)
10	Michigan	17	(H)
20	Indiana	27	(T)
24	Northwestern	6	(H)
22	Wisconsin	6	(T)
21	Purdue	7	(H)
7	Notre Dame	34	(T)
0	Illinois	16	(T)

Won 4, Lost 5, Tied 0

1965

13	UCLA	3	(H)
23	Penn State	0	(T)
22	Illinois	12	(H)
24	Michigan	7	(T)
32	Ohio State	7	(H)
14	Purdue	10	(T)
49	Northwestern	7	(H)
35	Iowa	0	(T)
27	Indiana	13	(H)
12	Notre Dame	3	(T)

ROSE BOWL

12	UCLA	14	(T)

Won 10, Lost 1, Tied 0

1966

28	No. Carolina St.	10	(H)
42	Penn State	8	(H)
26	Illinois	10	(T)
20	Michigan	7	(H)
11	Ohio State	8	(T)
41	Purdue	20	(H)
22	Northwestern	0	(T)
56	Iowa	7	(H)
37	Indiana	19	(T)
10	Notre Dame	10	(H)

Won 9, Lost 0, Tied 1

1967

7	Houston	37	(H)
17	So. California	21	(H)
35	Wisconsin	7	(H)
34	Michigan	0	(T)
0	Minnesota	21	(T)
12	Notre Dame	24	(T)
7	Ohio State	21	(H)
13	Indiana	14	(H)
7	Purdue	21	(T)
41	Northwestern	27	(H)

Won 3, Lost 7, Tied 0

1968

14	Syracuse	10	(H)
28	Baylor	10	(H)
39	Wisconsin	0	(T)
14	Michigan	28	(T)
13	Minnesota	14	(H)
21	Notre Dame	17	(H)

20	Ohio State	25	(T)
22	Indiana	24	(H)
0	Purdue	9	(H)
31	Northwestern	14	(T)

Won 5, Lost 5, Tied 0

1969

27	Washington	11	(H)
23	S. Methodist	15	(H)
28	Notre Dame	42	(H)
21	Ohio State	54	(T)
23	Michigan	12	(H)
18	Iowa	19	(T)
0	Indiana	16	(H)
13	Purdue	41	(T)
10	Minnesota	14	(H)
39	Northwestern	7	(T)

Won 4, Lost 6, Tied 0

1970

16	Washington	42	(T)
28	Wash. State	14	(H)
0	Notre Dame	29	(H)
0	Ohio State	29	(H)
20	Michigan	34	(T)
37	Iowa	0	(H)
32	Indiana	7	(T)
24	Purdue	14	(H)
13	Minnesota	23	(T)
20	Northwestern	23	(H)

Won 4, Lost 6, Tied 0

1971

10	Illinois	0	(H)
0	Georgia Tech	10	(T)
31	Oregon State	14	(H)
2	Notre Dame	14	(H)
13	Michigan	24	(H)
28	Wisconsin	31	(T)
34	Iowa	3	(H)
43	Purdue	10	(T)
17	Ohio State	10	(H)
40	Minnesota	25	(H)
7	Northwestern	28	(T)

Won 6, Lost 5, Tied 0

1972

24	Illinois	0	(T)
16	Georgia Tech	21	(H)
6	So. California	51	(T)
0	Notre Dame	16	(T)
0	Michigan	10	(T)
31	Wisconsin	0	(H)
6	Iowa	6	(T)
22	Purdue	12	(H)
19	Ohio State	12	(H)
10	Minnesota	14	(T)
24	Northwestern	14	(H)

Won 5, Lost 5, Tied 1

1973

DENNIS E. STOLZ
Head Coach

10	Northwestern	14	(T)
14	Syracuse	8	(T)
21	UCLA	34	(H)
10	Notre Dame	14	(T)
0	Michigan	31	(H)
3	Illinois	6	(H)
10	Purdue	7	(T)
21	Wisconsin	0	(H)
0	Ohio State	35	(T)
10	Indiana	9	(H)
15	Iowa	6	(T)

Won 5, Lost 6, Tied 0

288

1974

41	*Northwestern	... 7
19	*Syracuse	 0
14	UCLA	 56
14	*Notre Dame	... 19
7	Michigan	 21
21	Illinois	 21
31	*Purdue	 7
28	Wisconsin	 21
16	*Ohio State	 13
19	Indiana	 10
60	*Iowa	 21

Won 7, Lost 3, Tied 1

Individual Opponent Summary

	G	W	L	T
Adrian	4	4	0	0
Akron	2	2	0	0
Albion	18	11	4	3
Alma	30	22	4	4
Arizona	3	3	0	0
Armour Inst.	1	1	0	0
Army	1	0	1	0
Auburn	1	0	1	0
Baylor	1	1	0	0
Boston College	3	0	2	1
Butler	2	1	1	0
California	2	2	0	0
Camp MacArthur	1	0	1	0
Carnegie Tech	4	3	0	1
Carroll	2	2	0	0
Case	2	2	0	0
Centre	2	2	0	0
Chicago	1	0	1	0
Chicago YMCA College	3	3	0	0
Cincinnati	2	1	1	0
Colgate	5	1	4	0
Colorado	1	1	0	0
Cornell College	2	1	1	0
Cornell U.	1	0	1	0
Creighton	2	0	2	0
Culver Military Acad.	1	1	0	0
DePaul	2	1	0	1
DePauw	6	5	1	0
Detroit Athletic Club	8	3	4	1
Detroit	14	7	6	1
Detroit YMCA	1	1	0	0
Eastern Michigan	3	3	0	0
Fordham	1	1	0	0
Georgetown	2	1	1	0
Georgia Tech	2	0	2	0
Great Lakes Naval Station	2	1	1	0
Grinnell	4	4	0	0

	G	W	L	T
Haskell Institute	1	0	1	0
Hawaii	2	2	0	0
Hillsdale	7	7	0	0
Houston	1	0	1	0
Illinois	14	7	6	1
Illinois Wesleyan	5	5	0	0
Indiana	27	18	8	1
Iowa	12	7	4	1
Iowa State	2	2	0	0
Kalamazoo	17	9	8	0
Kansas	4	4	0	0
Kansas State	6	5	0	1
Kentucky	4	2	2	0
Lake Forest	5	3	1	1
Lansing High School	2	2	0	0
Loyola (Cal.)	1	1	0	0
Manhattan	2	1	1	0
Marietta	1	0	1	0
Marquette	25	18	6	1
Maryland	5	4	1	0
Massachusetts State	1	1	0	0
Miami (Fla.)	2	0	2	0
Michigan	67	20	42	5
Michigan Frosh	4	4	0	0
Michigan School—Deaf	4	4	0	0
Minnesota	15	5	10	0
Mississippi State	4	2	1	1
Missouri	6	3	3	0
Mt. Union	4	4	0	0
Nebraska	2	0	2	0
North Carolina	3	2	1	0
North Carolina State	4	3	1	0
North Central	1	1	0	0
North Dakota State	2	2	0	0
Northwestern	19	13	6	0
Notre Dame	40	15	24	1
Ohio Northern	1	1	0	0

289

Ohio State 15	8	7	0
Ohio University 1	1	0	0
Ohio Wesleyan 4	2	2	0
Olivet 23	18	4	1
Oregon State 9	6	2	1
Penn State 10	8	1	1
Pittsburgh..............5	4	0	1
Port Huron YMCA 2	2	0	0
Purdue 29	16	12	1
Ripon 1	1	0	0
Saginaw Naval Brigade 1	1	0	0
St. Louis...............2	0	1	1
San Francisco 1	1	0	0
Santa Clara 6	1	3	2
Scranton 1	1	0	0
South Dakota 6	5	0	1
South Dakota State 1	1	0	0
Southern California 4	1	3	0
Southern Methodist 1	1	0	0
Stanford 4	3	1	0
Syracuse 11	8	3	0
Temple 10	7	1	2
Texas A. & M 3	2	1	0
Texas Christian 1	1	0	0
Toledo 1	1	0	0
UCLA 6	3	3	0
Wabash 7	5	1	1

Washington 2	1	1	0
Washington (St. Louis) 1	1	0	0
Washington State 6	5	1	0
Wayne State 9	9	0	0
Western Michigan 4	2	2	0
West Virginia 4	4	0	0
William & Mary 2	2	0	0
Wisconsin 19	12	7	0

Number of Teams Played 110
Number of Games Played 676
Number of Games Won 412
Number of Games Lost 227
Number of Games Tied 37
Percentage 637

Spartan Team Records

(Since 1944)
LONGEST PLAY

Rushing—90 yards, Lynn Chandnois vs. Arizona, 1949, TD.

Forward Pass—88 yards, Steve Juday to Sherman Lewis vs. So. California, 1963, TD.

Interception Return (Pass)—93 yards, Bob Suci vs. Michigan, 1959, TD.

Interception Return (Fumble)—90 yards, Earl Morrall vs. Purdue, 1955, TD.

Kickoff Return—98 yards, Russ Reader vs. Wayne State, 1946, TD.

Punt Return—95 yards, Allen Brenner vs. Illinois, 1966, TD.

Field Goal—54 yards, Borys Shlapak vs. Northwestern, 1970; vs. Iowa and Minnesota, 1971.

Punt—71 yards, Earl Morrall vs. Stanford, 1955; Lou Bobich vs. Purdue, 1963.

INDIVIDUAL IN GAME

Rushing Attempts—37, Don Highsmith vs. Northwestern, 1969; Eric Allen vs. Illinois, 1971.

Yards Gained Rushing—350, Eric Allen vs. Purdue, 1971.

Passes Attempted—35, Dan Werner vs. Purdue, 1969; Mike Rasmussen vs. Washington, 1970.

Passes Completed—17, Mike Rasmussen vs. Washington, 1970.

Passes Had Intercepted—4, by 5 different players.

Yards Gained Passing—314, Dan Werner vs. Purdue, 1969.

Total Yards Gained—350, Eric Allen vs. Purdue, 1971.

Touchdown Passes Thrown—4, Gene Glick vs. Iowa State, 1948; Mike Rasmussen vs. Indiana, 1970.

Passes Caught—9, Gene Washington vs. Notre Dame, 1964.

Yards Gained Passes Caught—155, Frank Foreman vs. Purdue, 1969.

Touchdown Passes Caught—3, Gene Washington vs. Indiana, 1965.

Pass Interceptions—3, Jesse Thomas vs. Michigan and Indiana, 1950; John Polonchek vs. William & Mary, 1949; Jim Ellis vs. Oregon State, 1951; Brad VanPelt vs. Washington State, 1970.

Punts—11, Bill Simpson vs. Ohio State, 1973.

Touchdowns Scored—4, Clinton Jones vs. Iowa, 1965; Bud Crane vs. Hawaii, 1947; Eric Allen vs. Purdue, Minnesota, 1971.

P.A.T. Scored—8, George Smith vs. Hawaii, 1948; vs. Temple and Arizona, 1949; Evan Slonac vs. Marquette, 1952.

Field Goals Scored—4, Dirk Kryt vs. Ohio State, 1972.

Points Scored—24, Bud Crane vs. Hawaii, 1947; Clinton Jones vs. Iowa, 1965; Eric Allen vs. Purdue, Minnesota, 1971.

TEAM OFFENSE IN GAME

Rushing Attempts—80 vs. Indiana, 1950.

Net Yards Rushing—573 vs. Purdue, 1971.

Passes Attempted—40 vs. Washington, 1970.

Passes Completed—18 vs. Washington, 1970.

Yards Gained Passing—332 vs. Marquette, 1949.

Total Yards Gained—698 vs. Purdue, 1971.

Touchdown Passes—4 vs. 5 different opponents.

Touchdowns Scored—11 vs. Arizona, 1949.

P.A.T. Scored—8 vs. 4 different opponents.

Points Scored—75 vs. Arizona, 1949.

First Downs by Rushing—25 vs. Marquette, 1952.

First Downs by Passing—12 vs. Texas A&M, 1952; vs. Purdue, 1969; vs. Michigan, 1970

Total First Downs—33 vs. Marquette, 1952.

Fumbles Lost—9 vs. Kansas State, 1956.

Yards Penalized—155 vs. Indiana, 1957.

Passes Had Intercepted—6 vs. Maryland, 1950; vs. Minnesota, 1958.

TEAM DEFENSE IN GAME

Rushing Attempts—17 by Ohio State, 1965.

Net Yards Rushing—Minus 63 by Pittsburgh, 1950.

Passes Attempted—1 by Maryland, 1944.

Passes Completed—0 by Kansas State, 1944; by Maryland, 1944; by Georgia Tech, 1971.

Yards Gained Passing—0 by Kansas State, 1944; by Maryland, 1944; by Georgia Tech, 1971.

Total Yards Gained—Minus 11 by Pittsburgh, 1950.

First Downs by Rushing—0 by Wayne State, 1945; by Wayne State, 1946; Ohio State, 1965.

First Downs by Passing—0 by 8 different opponents.

Total First Downs—1 by Maryland, 1944.

Passes Intercepted—8 vs. Washington State, 1970.

Fumbles Recovered—8 vs. Great Lakes, 1945.

Big Ten Records

LONGEST PLAY

Rushing—88 yards, Levi Jackson vs. Ohio State, TD.

Forward Pass—87 yards, Steve Juday to Sherman Lewis vs. Wisconsin, 1963, TD.

Interception Return (Pass)—93 yards, Bob Suci vs. Michigan, 1959, TD.

Interception Return (Fumble)—90 yards, Earl Morrall vs. Purdue, 1955, TD.

Kickoff Return—93 yards, Dwight Lee vs. Northwestern, 1967, TD.

Punt Return—95 yards, Allen Brenner vs. Illinois, 1966, TD.

Field Goal—54 yards, Borys Shlapak vs. Northwestern, 1970.

Punt—71 yards, Lou Bobich vs. Purdue, 1963.

INDIVIDUAL IN GAME

Rushing Attempts—37, Don Highsmith vs. Northwestern, 1969; Eric Allen vs. Illinois, 1971.

Yards Gained Rushing—350, Eric Allen vs. Purdue, 1971.

Passes Attempted—35, Dan Werner vs. Purdue, 1969.

Passes Completed—16, Steve Juday vs. Indiana, 1964; Dan Werner vs. Purdue, 1969.

Passes Had Intercepted—4, Tom Yewcic vs. Purdue, 1953; Dan Werner vs. Purdue, 1969; Mike Rasmussen vs. Minnesota, 1970.

Yards Gained Passing—314, Dan Werner vs. Purdue, 1969.

Total Yards Gained—350, Eric Allen vs. Purdue, 1971.

Touchdown Passes Thrown—4, Mike Rasmussen vs. Indiana, 1970.

Passes Caught—8, Billy Joe DuPree vs. Illinois, 1971.

Yards Gained Passes Caught—155, Frank Foreman vs. Purdue, 1969.

Touchdown Passes Caught—3, Gene Washington vs. Indiana, 1965.

Pass Interceptions–2, by 11 different players.

Punts—11, Bill Simpson vs. Ohio State, 1973.

Touchdowns Scored—4, Clinton Jones vs. Iowa, 1965; Eric Allen vs. Purdue, Minnesota, 1971.

P.A.T. Scored–6, Hans Nielsen vs. Iowa, 1974.

Field Goals Scored—4, Dirk Kryt vs. Ohio State, 1972.

Points Scored—24, Clinton Jones vs. Iowa, 1965; Eric Allen vs. Purdue, Minnesota, 1971

TEAM OFFENSE IN GAME

Rushing Attempts—73 vs. Indiana, 1957.

Net Yards Rushing—573 vs. Purdue, 1971.

Passes Attempted—39 vs. Purdue, 1969.

Passes Completed—16 vs. Indiana, 1964; vs. Purdue, 1969.

Yards Gained Passing—314 vs. Purdue, 1969.

Total Yards Gained—698 vs. Purdue, 1971.

Touchdown Passes—4 vs. Indiana, 1970.

Touchdowns Scored—8 vs. Indiana, 1956; vs. Indiana, 1957; vs. Iowa, 1966.

P.A.T. Scored–6 vs. Indiana, 1957; vs Iowa, 1974.

Points Scored –60 vs. Iowa, 1974.

First Downs by Rushing—24 vs. Indiana, 1957; vs. Purdue, 1971.

First Downs by Passing—12 vs. Purdue, 1969; vs. Michigan, 1970.

Total First Downs—32 vs. Indiana, 1957.

Fumbles Lost—5 vs. Michigan, 1962; vs. Indiana, 1962.

Yards Penalized—155 vs. Indiana, 1957.

Passes Had Intercepted—6 vs. Minnesota, 1958.

TEAM DEFENSE IN GAME

Rushing Attempts—17 by Ohio State, 1965.

Net Yards Rushing—Minus 51 by Michigan, 1965.

Passes Attempted—2 by Michigan, 1955; by Indiana, 1958.

Passes Completed—1 by Michigan, 1955; by Indiana, 1958; by Minnesota, 1972.

Yards Gained Passing—15 by Michigan, 1955.

Total Yards Gained—80 by Indiana, 1957.

First Downs by Rushing—0 by Ohio State, 1965.

First Downs by Passing—1 by 9 different opponents.

Total First Downs—4 by Indiana, 1957.

Passes Intercepted –3 vs. 20 different opponents.

Fumbles Recovered—7 vs. Purdue, 1955; vs. Illinois, 1971.

Big Names In Spartan History

1972 *Brad VanPelt, safety—AP, UPI, AFC, FWA, Time, SN, US, Walter Camp, Gridiron
*Joseph DeLamielleure, guard—SN
Billy Joe DuPree, end—Time
1973 *William T. Simpson, back—SN, US

*Major Team Selections Recognized by NCAB

Abbreviations—AFC-American Football Coaches, AP-Associated Press, B-All-American Board, CP-Central Press, CTP-Chicago Tribune Players, FN-Football News, FWA-Football Writers Association, INS-International News Service, NYN-New York News, NYS-New York Sun, PN-Paramount News, SN-Sporting News, UP-United Press, UPI-United Press International, FD-Football Digest, US-Universal Sports.

ALL-BIG TEN — First-Team Selections

1953 Don Dohoney, end	1966 Charles "Bubba" Smith, end
LeRoy Bolden, halfback	Clinton Jones, halfback
1955 Earl Morrall, quarterback	Eugene Washington, end
Norm Masters, tackle	George Webster, roverback
Carl Nystrom, guard	Robert Apisa, fullback
Gerald Planutis, fullback	Jerry West, tackle
1956 John Matsko, center	Jess Phillips, halfback
1957 Walt Kowalczyk, halfback	Nick Jordan, tackle
Dan Currie, center	Anthony Conti, guard
Jim Ninowski, quarterback	Charles Thornhill, linebacker
Pat Burke, tackle	Richard Kenney, kicker
Ellison Kelly, guard	1967 George Chatlos, guard
Sam Williams, end	1968 Allen Brenner, safety
1958 Sam Williams, end	Charles Bailey, tackle
Ellison Kelly, guard	1969 Ronald Curl, tackle
1959 Dean Look, quarterback	Ronald Saul, guard
1960 Herb Adderley, halfback	1971 Joseph DeLamielleure, guard
1961 George Saimes, fullback	Eric Allen, halfback
Dave Behrman, tackle-guard	Ronald Curl, defensive tackle
1962 George Saimes, fullback	Brad VanPelt, defensive back
Dave Behrman, center	1972 Brad VanPelt, safety
1963 Sherman Lewis, halfback	Gail Clark, linebacker
Dan Underwood, end	William Simpson, defensive back
1964 Dick Gordon, halfback	Gary VanElst, defensive tackle
Jerry Rush, tackle	Billy Joe DuPree, tight end
1965 Clinton Jones, halfback	Joe DeLamielleure, guard
Eugene Washington, end	1973 William Simpson, defensive back
George Webster, roverback	1974 Terry McClowry, linebacker
Charles Smith, end	James Taubert, defensive tackle
Stephen Juday, quarterback	Otto Smith, defensive end
Ronald Goovert, linebacker	Levi Jackson, fullback
Harold Lucas, middleguard	
Donald Japinga, defensive back	

FOOTBALL HALL OF FAME
(Coaches)
Clarence L. Munn, 1959
(Players)
John S. Pingel, 1968

CLEVELAND TOUCHDOWN CLUB PLAYER AWARD
Clinton Jones, 1966

COLUMBUS TOUCHDOWN CLUB
Brad VanPelt, 1972
(College Defensive Back of the Year)

MICHIGAN SPORTS HALL OF FAME
Clarence L. Munn, 1961
Ralph H. Young, 1962
John H. Kobs, 1968
John S. Pingel, 1973
Hugh Duffy Daugherty, 1975

UPI LINEMAN OF THE YEAR
Charles "Bubba" Smith, 1966

ROBERT W. MAXWELL AWARD
Brad VanPelt, 1972

WALTER CAMP TROPHY
Don McAuliffe, 1952

COACH OF THE YEAR
Clarence L. Munn, 1952
Hugh Duffy Daugherty, 1955, 1965

SPORTS ILLUSTRATED SILVER ANNIVERSARY ALL-AMERICAN
Clarence L. Munn, 1956
Arthur F. Brandstatter, 1961
Frank Gaines Jr., 1962

OUTLAND AWARD
Ed Bagdon, 1949

NATIONAL FOOTBALL HALL OF FAME GRADUATE FELLOWSHIP AWARD
Stephen Juday, 1965
Allen Brenner, 1968

CHICAGO TRIBUNE BIG TEN MOST VALUABLE PLAYER
Eric Allen, 1971

BIG TEN ALL-ACADEMIC
1959—Blanche Martin, halfback
1960—Ed Ryan, halfback
1964—Richard Gordon, halfback
    Eugene Washington, end
1965—James Proesbstle, end
1965—Donald Japinga, halfback
1965—Stephen Juday, quarterback
1965—Donald Bierowicz, tackle
1966—Allen Brenner, end
    Patrick Gallinagh, tackle
1968—Allen Brenner, end, safety
1969—Ronald Saul, guard
    Richard Saul, end
    Dave VanElst, tackle
1970—Joseph DeLamielleure, guard
1973—John Shinsky, tackle
    Bruce Harms, back
    Richard Pawlak, tackle
1974—Richard Baes, halfback
    Kim Rowekamp, middleguard
    Tom Cole, center

NCAA POST-GRADUATE SCHOLARSHIP
Allen Brenner, 1968
Donald Baird, 1969

DOLLY COHEN SCHOLARSHIP AWARD
Allen Brenner, 1968

COSIDA ACADEMIC ALL-AMERICAN
1952—John Wilson, back
1953—Donald Dohoney, end
1953—Carl Diener, end
1954—Donald Kauth, end
1955—Carl Nystrom, guard
1957—Robert Jewett, end
1957—Blanche Martin, back
1958—Richard Barker, end
1958—Ellison, Kelly, guard
1958—Blanche Martin, back
    (honorary)
1960—Ed Ryan, roverback
1965—Donald Japinga, halfback
1965—Donald Bierowicz, tackle
1966—Patrick Gallinagh, tackle
1968—Allen Brenner, end, safety
1969—Ronald Saul, guard
    Richard Saul, end
1973—John Shinsky, tackle

NCAA COLLEGE ATHLETICS TOP TEN
Robert McCurry, 1974

NCAA-ABC-TV PLAYER OF THE GAME CHEVROLET SCHOLARSHIP AWARD
Ron Curl, defensive winner,
    Notre Dame game, 1971, $1,000
Brad VanPelt, defensive winner
    Michigan game, 1971, $1,000
Brad VanPelt, defensive winner
    of the year, 1971, $5,000
Mark Niesen, offensive winner,
    Ohio State game, 1972, $1,000
Gail Clark, defensive winner,
    Notre Dame game, 1972, $1,000
Paul Hayner, defensive winner,
    Syracuse game, 1973, $1,000
Charles Baggett, offensive winner,
    Ohio State game, 1974, $1,000

Webster Picked Greatest Spartan

George Webster, Gene Washington, Don Coleman, Earl Morrall — these four dominate the All-Time Michigan State Football Team. Webster is the All-Time Greatest Player; Washington, the top end; Coleman, the best interior lineman; and Morrall, the supreme back.

They were the leaders on over 300 ballots which came from the 1969 homecoming game program, the Michigan State Alumni Magazine and the Michigan State News, the student newspaper.

The All-Time Spartan team, with senior seasons noted:

Ends — Gene Washington (1966) and Charles (Bubba) Smith (1966).

Lineman — Don Coleman (1951), Dan Currie (1957), Norm Masters (1955), Dave Behrman (1962) and Ed Budde (1962).

Backs — Earl Morrall (1955), Clinton Jones (1966), George Webster (1966) and Lynn Chandnois (1949).

The all-time teams were named by each of the Big Ten schools as part of the observance last year of the 75th anniversary of the league. From them an All-Time All-Big Ten Team was named.

Spartans named to the All-Time Big Ten were Washington and Webster. Cited for honorable mention were Smith and Currie.

Nearly 100 former Spartans were named on one or more ballots for all-time honors. Webster had the destinction of being named variously as a lineman, end and back.

From the ballots, an all-time two-platoon team and an Old Timers' Team (pre-1940 players only) also were assembled.

The selections:

All-Time Offensive Team: Ends — Washington and Bob Carey (1951); **Linemen** — Coleman, Masters, Jerry West (1966), Budde and Behrman; **Backs** — Morrall, Jones, John Pingel (1938) and Everett (Sonny) Grandelius (1950).

All-Time Defensive Team: Ends — Sam Williams (1958) and Smith; **Lineman** — Ed Bagdon (1949), Jerry Rush (1964) and Harold Lucas (1965); **Linebackers** — Currie and Frank Kush (1952); **Backs** — Webster, Chandnois, Herb Adderley (1960) and George Saimes (1962).

Old Timers' Team: Ends — Ed Klewicki (1934) and Blake Miller (1915); **Linemen** — Sid Wagner (1935), Hugh Blacklock (1916), Frank Butler (1934), Gideon Smith (1915) and Lyle Rockenbach (1939); **Backs** — Pingel, Bob Monnett (1932), George (Carp) Julian (1914) and Neno (Gerry) DaPrato (1915).

Other former Michigan State players who just missed making the All-Time teams on the balloting included: **Ends** — Dorne Dibble (1950), Don Dohoney (1953) and Al Brenner (1968); **Lineman** — Carl (Buck) Nystrom (1955), Don Mason (1949), Dick Tamburo (1952), Earl Lattimer (1963), and Ron Saul (1969); **Backs** — LeRoy Bolden (1954), Sherman Lewis (1963), Walt Kowalczyk (1957), Al Dorow (1951) and Bob Apisa (1967).

Spartan Awards

GOVERNOR OF MICHIGAN AWARD

This award, a gold watch, given annually since 1931 to the player who is voted the most valuable on the team by the men on the football squad. Presentation made each year by the governor of Michigan.

1931—Abe Eliowitz, fullback
1932—Robert Monnett, halfback
1933—Arthur Buss, tackle
1934—Edward Klewicki, end
1935—Sid Wagner, guard
1936—Sam Ketchman, center
1937—Harry Speelman, tackle
1938—John Pingel, halfback
1939—Lyle Rockenbach, guard
1940—Jack Amon, fullback
1941—Anthony Arena, center
1942—Richard Kieppe, halfback
1943—No award
1944—Jack Breslin, fullback
1945—Steve Contos, halfback
1946—George Guerre, halfback
1947—Warren Huey, end
1948—Lynn Chandnois, halfback
1949—Eugene Glick, quarterback
1950—Everett Grandelius, halfback
1951—Donald Coleman, tackle
1952—Richard Tamburo, linebacker

1953—LeRoy Bolden, halfback
1954—John Matsock, halfback
1955—Carl Nystrom, guard
1956—James Hinesly, end
1957—Dan Currie, center
1958—Sam Williams, end
1959—Dean Look, quarterback
1960—Thomas Wilson, quarterback
1961—George Saimes, fullback
1962—George Saimes, fullback
1963—Sherman Lewis, halfback
1964—Richard Gordon, halfback
1965—Stephen Juday, quarterback
1966—George Webster, roverback
1967—Dwight Lee, halfback
1968—Allen Brenner, end-safety
1969—Ronald Saul, guard
1970—Eric Allen, tailback
1971—Eric Allen, tailback
1972—Gail Clark, linebacker
1973—Ray Nester, linebacker
1974—Charles Baggett, quarterback

ROSS TROPHY

Given annually since 1949 to the player who has made the best contribution to the team both athletically and scholastically. Named for the late F. Ward Ross, football letterman in 1925-26-27, and contributed by his wife, Mrs. Dorothy Ross.

1949—John Polonchek, halfback
1950—John Yocca guard
1951—Frank Kapral, guard
1952—John Wilson, halfback
1953—James Neal, center
1954—Don Kauth, end
1955—Carl Nystrom, guard
1956—Pat Wilson, quarterback
1957—Don Zysk, halfback
1958—John Middleton, guard
1959—Blanche Martin, fullback
1960—Thomas Wilson, quarterback
1961—Pete Kakela, tackle

1962—George Azar, guard
1963—Ed Youngs, center
1964—Richard Flynn, tackle
1965—Stephen Juday, quarterback
1966—Patrick Gallinagh, guard
1967—Anthony Conti, guard
1968—Allen Brenner, end-safety
1969—Donald Baird, guard
1970—Victor Mittelberg, tackle
1971—Michael Rasmussen, quarterback
1972—Mark Grua, halfback-wide receiver
1973—Bruce Harms, defensive back
1974—Charles Wilson, guard

DANZIGER AWARD

Trophy given annually since 1954 to the player from the Detroit area who makes the most outstanding contribution to the team. Named for the late Frederick W. Danziger, football letterman in 1926-28-29 and team captain in 1929, and contributed by his family.

1954—Al Fracasa, quarterback
1955—Norman Masters, tackle
1956—James Hinesly, end
1957—Jim Ninowski, quarterback
1958—Cliff LaRose, tackle
1959—Blanche Martin, fullback
1960—Mickey Walker, tackle
1961—Gary Ballman, halfback
1962—Ed Budde, tackle
1963—Dewey Lincoln, halfback

1964—Jerry Rush, tackle
1965—Harold Lucas, middleguard
1966—Patrick Gallinagh, guard
1967—Ronald Ranieri, center
1968—Kenneth Heft, halfback
1969—Craig Wycinsky, tackle
1970—Gordon Bowdell, split end
1971—Ralph Wieleba, end
1972—William Simpson, halfback
1973—William Simpson, halfback
1974—Terry McClowry, linebacker

297

OIL CAN AWARD

This award is given annually to the player or manager who contributes most in a humorous way to the team.

1949—Peter Fusi, tackle
1950—Jack Morgan, tackle
1951—Douglas Weaver, center
1952—Gordon Serr, guard
1953—Larry Fowler, tackle
1954—Henry Bullough, guard
1955—Embry Robinson, guard
1956—Joseph Carruthers, tackle
1957—Robert Popp, quarterback
1958—Thomas Vernon, end
1959—Edwin McLucas, guard
1960—Ronald Ike Grimsley, guard
1961—Wayne Fontes, halfback

1962—Dewey Lincoln, halfback
1963—Earl Lattimer, guard
1964—Larry Mackey, fullback
1965—Drake Garrett, halfback
1966—Drake Garrett, halfback
1967—Drake Garrett, halfback
1968—Eddy McLoud, center
1969—Clifton Hardy, halfback
1970—Michael Tobin, linebacker
1971—Dan Kovacs, manager
1972—No award given
1973—No award given
1974 – No award given

PRESIDENT'S AWARD

This award given annually to player for perseverance shown in efforts for the football squad.

1965—James Proebstle, end
1966—Jeffrey Richardson, guard
1967—Robert Lange, linebacker
1968—Richard Berlinski, fullback
1969—Bruce Kulesza, end
1970—Gary Parmentier, guard
1971—Doug Barr, halfback
1972—Joseph DeLamielleure, tackle
1973—John Shinsky, tackle
1974 –Michael Jones, flanker

BIGGIE MUNN AWARD

This award given annually to player contributing most "extra effort" during football season.

1965—Robert Viney, end
1966—Jerry Jones, halfback
1967—Frank Waters, halfback
1968—Eddy McLoud, center
1969—Donald Highsmith, halfback
1970—Calvin Fox, end
1971—Ronald Curl, tackle
1972—Gary VanElst, tackle
1973—Paul Hayner, halfback
1974 –James Taubert, defensive tackle

LOVE AWARD

Awarded for the first time in 1971 in the memory of the late Spartan performer Tommy Love to the player who shows outstanding ability and unselfish dedication.

1971—Errol Roy, tackle
1972—Billy Joe DuPree, end

1973—Michael Holt, tailback
1974 –Michael Duda, defensive end

COWING AWARD

This award, named for Frank P. Cowing, Jr., Spartan football manager in 1938, has been presented annually since 1969 to the outgoing head manager.

1969—Robert Beery
1970—Robert Snyder
1971—Richard Drobot

1972—Richard Lilly
1973—Steve Repko
1974 – No award given

SPRING GAME OUTSTANDING PLAYER AWARD

Outstanding performers in spring football windup game have been honored since 1948.

1948—Lynn Chandnois, halfback
1949—Lynn Chandnois, halfback
1950—Everett Grandelius, halfback
1951—Wayne Benson, fullback
1952—Billy Wells, halfback
1953—James Ellis, halfback
1954—Gerald Planutis, fullback
  Howard Graves, halfback
1955—Patrick Wilson, quarterback
  James Ninowski, quarterback
1956—Clarence Peaks, halfback
1957—James Ninowski (Varsity),
  quarterback

Gerald Planutis (Old Timers),
  fullback
1958—Blanche Martin (Varsity), fullback
  Robert Jewett (Old Timers), end
1959—Thomas Wilson (Varsity),
  quarterback
  James Ninowski (Old Timers),
  quarterback
1960—Herb Adderley (Varsity), halfback
  Thomas Yewcic (Old Timers),
  quarterback
1961—Sherman Lewis (Varsity),
  halfback
  Clarence Peaks (Old Timers),
  halfback
1962—George Saimes (Varsity), fullback,

298

shared with Charles Migyanka
(Varsity), quarterback
Robert Ricucci (Old Timers),
halfback
1963—Richard Proebstle, quarterback,
outstanding back, shared with
Stephen Juday, quarterback
Matthew Snorton, end, outstanding
lineman

1964—Dave McCormick, quarterback,
Green
John Walsh, guard, White

1965—Jimmy Raye, quarterback, Green
Phil Hoag, end, White

1966—Clinton Jones, halfback, Green
Richard Berlinski, halfback, White

1967—Jimmy Raye, quarterback, Green
Gordon Bowdell, end, White

1968—Allen Brenner, end, Green, offense
Wilt Martin, end, Green, defense
Gordon Longmire, quarterback,
White, offense
Michael Hogan, linebacker, White,
defense

1969—William Triplett, back, Green
Frank Foreman, lineman, Green
Steven Piro, back, White
Frank Butler, lineman, White

1970—Henry Matthews, back, Green
Wilt Martin, lineman, Green
George Mihaiu, back, White
Gordon Bowdell, lineman, White

1971—Gail Clark, back, Green
Gary VanElst, lineman, Green
Mike Rasmussen, back, White
Frank Butler, lineman, White

1972—George Mihaiu, offense, Green
Gary VanElst, defense, Green
James Bond, offense, White
Brian McConnell, defense, White

1973—Charles Baggett, offense, Green
John Shinsky, defense, Green
David E. Brown, offense, White
Greg Schaum, defense, White

1974—No Spring Game Played

1975—No Spring Game Played

Spartan Individual Records

(CAREER/SEASON/GAME—SINCE 1945)

CAREER

Yards Gained Rushing
Eric Allen, '69, '70, '71	2,654
Lynn Chandnois, '46, '47, '48, '49	2,093
Clinton Jones, '64, '65, '66	1,921
George Guerre, '46, '47, '48	1,721
LeRoy Bolden, '51, '52, '53, '54	1,695

Rushing Attempts
Eric Allen, '69, '70, '71	521
Clinton Jones, '64, '65, '66	396
Don Highsmith, '67, '68, '69	349
Lynn Chandnois, '46, '47, '48, '49	321
LeRoy Bolden, '51, '52, '53, '54	305

Yards Gained Passing
Steve Juday, '63, '64, '65	2,576
Earl Morrall, '53, '54, '55	2,015
Mike Rasmussen, '70, '71	1,986
Al Dorow, '49, '50, '51	1,875
Gene Glick, '46, '47, '48, '49	1,748

Yards Gained Rushing-Passing
Eric Allen, '69, '70, '71	2,654
Steve Juday, '63, '64, '65	2,593
Jimmy Raye, '65, '66, '67	2,578
Charles Baggett, '73, '74	2,542
George Guerre, '46, '47, '48	2,249

Passes Attempted
Steve Juday, '63, '64, '65	384
Mike Rasmussen, '70, '71	287
Al Dorow, '49, '50, '51	259
Jimmy Raye, '65, '66, '67	232
William Triplett, '68, '69	207

Passes Completed
Steve Juday, '63, '64, '65	198
Al Dorow, '49, '50, '51	125
Mike Rasmussen, '70, '71	123
Jimmy Raye, '65, '66, '67	105
Earl Morrall, '53, '54, '55	98

Passes Caught
Gene Washington, '64, '65, '66	102
Allen Brenner, '66, '67, '68	73
Billy Joe DuPree, '70, '71, '72	69
Bob Carey, '49, '50, '51	65
Frank Foreman, '67, '68, '69,	61

Touchdown Passes Caught
Gene Washington, '64, '65, '66	16
Bob Carey, '49, '50, '51	14
Ellis Duckett, '51, '52, '53, '54	10
Sherman Lewis, '61, '62, '63	7
Ed Sobczak, '46, '48	7
Frank Foreman, '67, '68, '69	7

Yards Gained Passes Caught
Gene Washington, '64, '65, '66	1,857
Allen Brenner, '66, '67, '68	1,232
Billy Joe DuPree, '70, '71, '72	1,222
Frank Foreman, '67, '68, '69	1,128
Bob Carey, '49, '50, '51	1,074

Touchdown Passes Thrown
Steve Juday, '63, ,64, '65	21
Al Dorow, '49, '50, '51	19
Gene Glick, '46, '47, '48, '49	18
Tom Yewcic, '51, '52, '53	18
Jimmy Raye, '65, '66, '67	14

Passes Had Intercepted

Steve Juday, '63, '64, '65	24
Gene Glick, '46, '47, '48, '49	24
Al Dorow, '49, '50, '51	23
William Triplett, '68, '69	20
Jimmy Raye, '65, '66, '67	18
Mike Rasmussen, '70, '71	18
Charles Baggett, '73, '74	18

Pass Interceptions

Lynn Chandnois, '46, '47, '48, '49	20
Brad VanPelt, '70, '71, '72	14
Bill Simpson, '71, '72, '73	12
Jesse Thomas, '48, '49, '50	12
John Polonchek, '47, '48, '49	10

Touchdowns Scored

Lynn Chandnois, '46, '47, '48, '49	31
Eric Allen, '69, '70, '71	30
LeRoy Bolden, '51, '52, '53, '54	26
Clinton Jones, '64, '65, '66	23
Sherman Lewis, '61, '62, '63	23

P.A.T. Scored

George Smith, '47, '48, '49	94
Evan Slonac, '51, '52, '53	55
Dick Kenney, '65, '66	50
Bob Carey, '49, '50, '51	47
Art Brandstatter Jr., '59, '60, '61	43
Borys Shlapak, '70, '71	43

Field Goals Scored

Dick Kenney, '64, '65, '66	19
Dirk Kryt, '72, '73	15
Borys Shlapak, '70, '71	13
Art Brandstatter, Jr., '59, '60, '61	7
Dirk Kryt, '72	6
Hans Nielsen, '74	6

Points Scored

Lynn Chandnois, '46, '47, '48, '49	186
Eric Allen, '69, '70, '71	182
LeRoy Bolden, '51, '52, '53, '54	156
Sherman Lewis, '61, '62, '63	144
Bob Carey, '49, '50, '51	143

Punting Average

Bill Simpson, '71, '72, '73	39.8
Earl Morrall, '53, '54, '55	39.2
Lou Bobich, '62, '63, '64	39.0
Tom Yewcic, '51, '52, '53	38.7
Dean Look, '57, '58, '59	37.7

Yards Punt Returns

James Ellis, '51, '52, '53 (55 rets.)	619
George Guerre, '46, '47, '48 (35 rets.)	513
William Simpson, '71, '72, '73 (48 rets.)	475
Frank Waters III, '66, '67, '68 (44 rets.)	434
Jesse Thomas, '48, '49, '50 (27 rets.)	430

Yards Kickoff Returns

Eric Allen, '69, '70, '71 (62 rets.)	1,340
James Ellis, '51, '52, '53 (24 rets.)	515
Russ Reader, '45, '46 (16 rets.)	475
Frank Waters III, '66, '67, '68 (21 rets.)	414
Sherman Lewis, '61, '62, '63 (30 rets.)	380

Rasmussen   Washington   Juday

SEASON

Yards Gained Rushing

Eric Allen, '71	1,494
Everett Grandelius, '50	1,023
Levi Jackson, '74	942
Don Highsmith, '69	937
Lynn Chandnois, '49	885

Rushing Attempts

Eric Allen, '71	259
Don Highsmith, '69	209
Eric Allen, '70	186
Rich Baes, '74	181
Tommy Love, '68	177

Yards Gained Passing

Mike Rasmussen, '70	1,344
Steve Juday, '65	1,173
Jimmy Raye, '66	1,110
Charles Baggett, '74	965
Earl Morrall, '55	941
Tom Yewcic, '52	941

Yards Gained Rushing-Passing

Charles Baggett, '74	1,713
Jimmy Raye, '66	1,546
Eric Allen, '71	1,494
Mike Rasmussen, '70	1,358
Steve Juday, '65	1,306

Passes Attempted

Mike Rasmussen, '70	199
Steve Juday, '65	168
Steve Juday, '64	148
Jimmy Raye, '66	123
William Triplett, '69	117

Passes Completed

Mike Rasmussen, '70	91
Steve Juday, '65	89
Steve Juday, '64	79
Al Dorow, '51	64
Jimmy Raye, '66	62

Passes Caught

Gene Washington, '65	40
Gene Washington, '64	35
Gordon Bowdell, '70	34
Steve Contos, '45	31
Frank Foreman, '68	29

Touchdown Passes Caught

Bob Carey, '49	8
Gene Washington, '66	7
Ed Sobczak, '47	7
Gene Washington, '64	5
Sherman Lewis, '63	5
Ellis Duckett, '52	5

Yards Gained Passes Caught

Gene Washington, '66	677
Gene Washington, '65	638
Gene Washington, '64	542
Frank Foreman, '69	537
Bob Carey, '49	523

Touchdown Passes Thrown

Gene Glick, '48	11
Charles Baggett, '74	10
Jimmy Raye, '66	10
Tom Yewcic, '52	10

Passes Had Intercepted

William Triplett, 69	12
Mike Rasmussen, '70	11
Steve Juday, '64	10
Charles Baggett, '74	9
Charles Baggett, '73	9
Al Dorow, '50	9
Gene Glick, '49	9
Jimmy Raye, '67	9

Pass Interceptions

Jesse Thomas, '50	8

Eric Allen, Ohio State '69 (7 rets.) 119
John Matsock, Notre Dame '54 (4 rets.) 112
Frank Timmons, Georgia Tech '72 (3 rets.) 105

PLAY

Yards Gained Rushing

Lynn Chandnois, Arizona '49 (TD) 90
Levi Jackson, Ohio State '74 (TD) 88
Dick Panin, Notre Dame '51 (TD) 88
Sherman Lewis, Northwestern '63 (TD) 87
George Guerre, Iowa St. '47 (TD) 87

Yards Gained Passing

Steve Juday to Sherman Lewis, So. Cal. '63
(TD) 88
Steve Juday to Sherman Lewis, Wis. '63 (TD) 87
Bill Feraco to Al Brenner, Baylor '68 (TD) .. 83
Gene Glick to Lynn Chandnois,
Notre Dame '49 (TD) 83
Tom Yewcic to Ellis Duckett,
Texas A&M '52 (TD) 81

Yards Field Goals Kicked

Borys Shlapak, Northwestern '70 54
Borys Shlapak, Iowa '71 54
Borys Shlapak, Minnesota '71 54
Borys Shlapak, Purdue '71 53
Dick Kenney, So. California '64 49
Dirk Kryt, Iowa '73 49

Yards Kickoff Return

Russ Reader, Wayne State '46 (TD) 98
Mike Holt, UCLA '73 (TD) 95
Dwight Lee, Northwestern '67 (TD) 93
Jim Ellis, Michigan '51 79
Blanche Martin, Wisconsin '57 65

Yards Punt Return

Allen Brenner, Illinois '66 (TD) 95
Dean Look, Michigan '58 (TD) 92
Jesse Thomas, William & Mary '50 (TD) 90
Blanche Martin, Illinois '57 (TD) 86
Horace Smith, Santa Clara '47 (TD) 85

Yards Interception Return

Bob Suci, Michigan '59 (TD-pass) 93
Earl Morrall, Purdue '55 (TD-fumble) 90
Allen Brenner, Minnesota '68 (Pass) 84
Brad McLee, Washington '70 (pass-TD) 80
Dave Kaiser, Minnesota '57, (fumble-TD) 77

Yards Punted

Lou Bobich, Purdue '63 71
Earl Morrall, Stanford '55 71
Dean Look, Ohio State '58 68
Randy Davis, Ohio State '69 68
Earl Morrall, Illinois '55 66
Bill Simpson, Wisconsin '71 66

Spartans In All-Star Action

EAST-WEST
(San Francisco)

Munn, Clarence L.,
  Head Coach, '52, '53
Daugherty, Hugh Duffy,
  Head Coach, '58, '59, '66, '68
Adderley, Herb, B., '60
Allen, Eric, B. '71
Ane, Charles, C, '74
Arbanas, Fred, E, '60
Bagdon, Ed, G, '50
Ballman, Gary, B, '61
Bailey, Charles, T, '68
Bobbitt, James, T, '62
Bobich, Louis, B, '65
Bolden, Leroy, B, '55
Brenner, Allen, B, '68
Breslin, Jack, B, '45-'46
Brogger, Francis, E, '45
Budde, Ed, T, '62
Bullough, Henry, G, '55
Burke, Pat, T, '58
Chandnois, Lynn, B, '50
Clark, Gail, LB, '72
Coleman, Don, G, '52
Curl, Ronald, T, '71
Dekker, Paul E, '53
DeLamielleure, Joseph, T, '72
Dibble, Dorne, E, '51
Dorow, Al, B, '52
Gilbert, Don, B, '58
Gordon, Richard, B, '65
Grandelius, Everett, B, '51
Hayner, Paul, B, '73
Hughes, William, G, '52
†Jones, Clinton, B, '66
Kelly, Ellison, G, '58
Kenney, Richard, K, '66
Kowalczyk, Walt, B, '58
Lewis, Sherman, B, '63
Look, Dean, B, '59

Martin, Blanche, B, '59
Martin, Wilton, T, '71
Mason, Don, G, '50
McAuliffe, Don, B, '53
McClowry, Terry, LB, '74
O'Brien, Fran, T, '58
Pingel, John, B, '39
Pyle, Palmer, T, '59
Raye, James, QB, '67
Saimes, George, FB, '62
Saul, Ronald, G, '69
Simpson, William, B, '73
Tamburo, Dick, C, '53
Underwood, Dan, E, '63
VanPelt, Brad, B, '72
Washington, Eugene, E, '66
*Webster, George, RB, '66
Wedemeyer, Charles, F, '68
*Williams, Sam, E, '58
Wilson, Tom, B, '60
Wycinsky, Craig, T, '69

NORTH-SOUTH
(Miami)

Daugherty, Hugh Duffy,
  Head Coach, '56, '57,
  '61, '72
Azar, George, G, '62
Baker, Park, B, '59
Barker, Dick, E, '58
Behrman, Dave, C, '62
Berlinski, Richard, B, '68
Carruthers, Joe, T, '57
Creamer, Jim, C, '51
Charon, Carl, B, '61
Chatlos, George, E, '67
Conti, Anthony, T, '67
Currie, Dan, C, '57
Dawson, William, T, '71
Fontes, Wayne, B, '61
Gallinagh, Pat, T, '66

Grimsley, Ike, G., '60
Herman, Dave, T, '63
Hinesly, Jim, E, '56
Horrell, Bill, T, '51
Hudas, Larry, E, '61
*Jewett, Bob, E, '57
Johnson, Herman, B, '64
Kaiser, Dave, E, '57
Kakela, Pete, T, '61
King, Chris, LB, '72
Krzemienski, Tom, G, '64
Kuh, Dick, G, '51
Kush, Frank, G, '52
LaRose, Cliff, T, '58
Lee, Dwight, B, '67
Lincoln, Dewey, B, '63
Luke, Ed, E, '52
Macholz, Dennis, G, '72
Matsko, John, C, '56
McClowry, Robert, C, '72
McConnell, Brian, E, '72
McLoud, Eddy, C, '68
Mendyk, Dennis, B, '56
Minarik, Hank, E, '50
Mittelberg, Victor, T, '70
Nester, Ray, LB, '73
*Ninowski, Jim, B, '57
Phillips, Harold, B, '70
Richardson, Jeff, T, '66
Roberts, Marvin, T, '72
Rody, Fred, C, '54
Roy, Errol, T, '71
Rubick, Ron, B, '63
Sanders, Lonnie, E, '62
Saul, Richard, E, '69
Smith, Charles, E, '66
†Thornhill, Charles, LB, '66
Waters, Frank, B, '58
West, Jerry, T, '66
Wilson, John B, '52
Wulff, Jim, B, '58
Zagers, Bert, B, '54
Zucco, Vic, B, '56

BLUE-GRAY
(Montgomery)

Beard, Thomas, C, '70
Benson, Bill, G, '63
Benson, Wayne, B, '52
Berger, Don, C, '57
Bowdell, Gordon, E, '70
Carey, Bill, E, '51
Cundiff, Larry, T, '59
Dotsch, Roland, T, '54
DuPree, Billy Joe, E, '72
Fox, Calvin, E, '70
Garner, Dean, G, '51
Harness, Jason, E, '60
Heft, Kenneth, B, '68
Highsmith, Donald, B, '69
Hoag, Phil, E, '66
Kanicki, James, C, '62
Kapral, Frank, G, '51
Kauth, Don, E, '54
Kolodziej, Tony, '57
Lothamer, Ed, E, '63
McFadden, Marv, G, '51
Nicholson, James, G, '72
Postula, Vic, B, '54
Pruiett, Mitch, G, '67
Przybycki, Joseph, T, '67
Rochester, Paul, T, '59
Rutledge, Les, T, '57
Ryan, Ed, B, '61
Saidock, Tom, T, '56
Serr, Gordon, G, '52
Shlapak, Borys, K, '71
Smith, Pete, QB, '62
Summers, James, B, '66
Taubert, James, T, '74
Timmerman, Ed, C, '52
VanElst, Gary, T, '72
Walker, Mickey, T, '60
Wright, Don, G, '59

SENIOR BOWL
(Mobile)

Arbanas, Fred, E, '61
Bagdon, Ed, C, '50
Beard, Thomas, C, '71
Bercich, Bob, B, '60
Brandstatter, Art, E, '62
Brenner, Allen, B, '69
Budde, Ed, T, '63
Bullough, Henry, G, '55
Chandnois, Lynn, B, '50
Currie, Dan, C, '58
DeLamielleure, Joseph, T, '73
Dibble, Dorne, E, '51
Dohoney, Don, E, '54
Dorow, Al, B, '52
Garrett, Drake, B, '68
*Gordon, Richard, B, '65
Highsmith, Donald, B, '70
Kanicki, James, C, '63
Kowalczyk, Walt, B, '58
Kush, Frank, G, '53
Lowe, Gary, B, '56
Mason, Don, G, '50
McAuliffe, Don, B, '53
Neal, Jim, C, '54
Ninowski, Jim, B, '58
Nystrom, Carl, G, '56
†Przybycki, Joseph, T, '68
Rush, Jerry, T, '65
Ryan, Ed, B, '62
*Smith, Charles, E, '67
Tamburo, Dick, C, '53
VanElst, Gary, T, '73
Wells, Billy, B, '54
Zucco, Vic, B, '57

AMERICAN BOWL
(Tampa)

Daugherty, Hugh Duffy,
    Head Coach, 1970
Hardy, Clifton, B, '71

Highsmith, Donald, B, '70
Hogan, Michael, LB, '71
McConnell, Brian, E, '73
Taubert, James, T, '75
Timmons, Frank, B, '73
Wilson, Charles, G, '75

HULA BOWL
(Honolulu)

Daugherty, Hugh Duffy,
    Head Coach, '59, '68
Adderley, Herb, B, '61
Allen, Eric, B, '72
Ane, Charles, C, '75
Apisa, Robert, FB, '68
Ballman, Gary, B, '62
Behrman, Dave, C, '63
Bobich, Louis, B, '65
Bowdell, Gordon, E, '71
Brenner, Allen, B, '69
*Coleman, Don, T, '52
Curl, Ronald, T, '72
Currie, Dan, C, '58
Cundiff, Larry, T, '60
Dekker,, Paul, E, '54
DuPree, Billy Joe, E, '72
Foreman, Frank, E, '70
*Grandelius, Everett, B, '51
Jones, Clinton, B, '66
*Juday, Steve, QB, '66
Kelly, Ellison, G, '59
Lewis, Sherman, B, '64
Look, Dean, B, '60
Lopes, Roger, B, '64
Lucas, Harold, MG, '66
Masters, Norm, T, '56
Matsko, John, C, '57
McClowry, Terry, LB, '75
Nicholson, James, G, '73
Ninowski, Jim, B, '58
O'Brien, Fran, T, '59
Planutis, Gerald, B, '56
Raye, James, QB, '68
Saimes, George, FB, '63
Saul, Ronald, G, '70
Simpson, William, B, '74
VanPelt, Brad, B, '73
Webster, George, B, '66
Wedemeyer, Charles, F, '69
*Williams, Sam, E, '59
Wilson, Tom, B, '61

COACHES'
ALL-AMERICA
(Lubbock, Texas)

Daugherty, Hugh Duffy,
    Head Coach, '66
    Asst. Coach, '70

Adderley, Herb, B, '61
Arbanas, Fred, E, '61
Beard, Thomas, C, '71
Behrman, David, C, '63
Brenner, Allen, B, '69
Curl, Ronald, T, '72
Foreman, Frank, E, '70
Goovert, Ron, LB, '66
Kumiega, Tony, G, '62
Lewis, Sherman, B, '64
Lucas, Harold, MG, '66
Roberts, Marvin, T, '73
Rush, Jerry, T, '65
Ryan, Ed, B, '62
Saimes, George, B, '63
Saul, Ronald, G, '70
Viney, Robert, E, '66
Washington, Eugene, E, '67
Webster, George, LB, '67

COLLEGE ALL-STAR
GAME
(Chicago)

Adderley, Herb, B, '61
Agett, Albert, B, '37
Arbanas, Fred, E, '61
Bagdon, Ed, G, '50
Behrman, Dave, C, '63
†Budde, Ed, T, '63
Bullough, Henry, G, '55
Breslin, Jack, B, '46
Carey, Robert, E, '52
Chandnois, Lynn, B, '50
Clark, Gail, LB, '73
Coleman, Don, T, '52
Currie, Dan, C, '58
Dekker, Paul, E, '53
DeLamielleure, Joseph, T, '73
Dorow, Al, B, '52
Grandelius, Everett, B, '51
Guerre, George, B, '49
Huey, Warren, E, '49
Jewett, Robert, E, '58
Jones, Clinton, B, '67
Kanicki, James, C, C, '63
Kelly, Ellison, G, '59
Kowalczyk, Walt, B, '58
Kush, Frank, G, '53
Lothamer, Ed, E, '64
Matsko, John C, '57
McAuliffe, Don, B, '53
McCurry, Robert, C, '49
Morrall, Earl, B, '56
*Ninowski, Jim, B, '58
O'Brien, Fran, T, '59
Peaks, Clarence, B, '57
Pingel, John, B, '39
Przybycki, Joseph, T, '68
Rochester, Paul, T, '60
Rush, Jerry, T, '65
Sanders, Lonnie, E, '62
Simpson, William, B, '74
*Smith, Charles, E, '67
Snorton, Matt, E, '64
Tamburo, Dick, C, '53
VanPelt, Brad, B, '73
Washington, Eugene, E, '67
Webster, George, B, '67
Williams, Sam, E, '59

Spartan Winning Streaks

ALL GAMES

28—From fourth game of 1950 season through fourth game of 1953 season. Teams coached by Clarence (Biggie) Munn.

15—From third game of 1912 season through second game of 1914 season. Teams coached by John F. Macklin.

12—From third game of 1955 season through fourth game of 1956 season. Teams coached by Hugh Duffy Daugherty.

10—From first game through final game of regular 1965 season. Team coached by Hugh Duffy Daugherty.

BIG TEN GAMES

16—From first conference game of 1965 season through second conference game of 1967 season. Teams coached by Hugh Duffy Daugherty.

6—From third conference game of 1955 through second conference game of 1956. Teams coached by Hugh Duffy Daugherty.

5—From fifth conference game of 1960 through third conference game of 1961. Teams coached by Hugh Duffy Daugherty.

Major Letterwinners

305

Brown, Arthur L., '16
Brown, Charles E., '61, '62, '63
Brown, Charles M., '33
Brown, David E., '72, '73
Brown, Thomas B., '71, '72
Brown, William L., '74
Bruckner, Leslie C., '37, '38, '39
Bruggenthies, Anthony, '74
Buckridge, Francis P., '00
Budde, Edward L., '60, '61, '62
Budinski, John, '38
Bufe, Noel, '55, '56
Buggs, Travis, '54
Bullock, Clarence, '72, '73, '74-Co-C
Bullough, Henry, '52, '53, '54
Burge, Frederick L., Mgr., '38
Burke, Patrick F., '55, '56, '57-C
Burke, Thomas W., Mgr., '69
Burrington, Gray K., '02
Burroughs, Charles G., '05, '06, '08
Buss, Arthur, '31, '32, '33
Butler, Charles O., '15, '16
Butler, Frank J., '32, '33
Butler, Frank A., Jr., '71

"C"

Campbell, Arthur L., '06, '07, '08, '09
Campbell, James F., '08, '09, '10
Campbell, Leroy W., '11, '12
Cappaert, Carl W., '46, '47, '48, '49
Carey, Charles L., '40
Carey, Owen, '09
Carey, Robert W., '49, '50, '51-C
Carey, William R., '49, '50, '51
Carrigan, Cornelius R., '47
Carruthers, Joseph D., '55, '56, '57
Carter, Fred L., '39, '40, '41
Case, Albert H., '99, '00
Case, Athol A., '03
Case, Ralph W., '99
Caukin, Elmer A., '12
Cavender, Regis, '66, '67, '68
Chada, William H., '71
Chaddock, Frank G., '12, '14
Chamberlain, Ralph G., Mgr., '12
Chandnois, Lynn E., '46, '47,

'48, '49
Charette, Mark S., '70, '71, '72
Charon, Carl H., '59, '60, '61
Chartos, William, '39
Chastain, James W., '58, '59
Chatlos, George R., '65, '66, '67
Chesney, M. James, '60
Childs, Donald M., '02
Childs, Harold A., '02
Christensen, Koester L., '26, '27, '28
Ciolek, Eugene S., '37, '38
Ciolck, Robert, '49, '51
Clark, Ernest R., '60, '61, '62
Clark, Gail A., '70, '71, '72
Clupper, Steven R., Mgr., '68
Cobb, Leslie A., '14
Cobb, Michael, '73, '74
Colina, Richard W., '33, '34, '35
Cole, Thomas, '74
Coleman, Don E., '49, '50, '51
Colwell, Fred E., Jr., Mgr., '40
Connor, Alger V., '42, '46
Conti, Anthony N., '66, '67
Conti, Dominic F., '45
Contos, Steve G., '45
Convertini, Fred E., '65
Conway, Lynn V., '46
Coolidge, John K., '36, '37
Cordery, James W., '73
Corgiat, James G., '59, '61
Corless, Rex E., '51, '52
Cortright, Ion J., '07, '08, '09, '10-C
Cortright, Wesley H., '02
Coryell, Sherman H., '16, '17-C, '19
Costanzo, Louis, '54
Cotton, Eddie, '64, '65
Corwin, Christopher C., Mgr., '70
Cowing, Frank P., Jr., Mgr., '38
Crabill, C. Joseph, '26, '27, '28
Crall, Max B., '29
Crane, Bud C., '47, '48, '49
Crane, LeRoy R., '48, '49, '50-C
Crary, John R., Mgr., '35
Creager, Basil J., Mgr., '33
Creamer, James E., '50, '51
Crosby, Matt A., '98, '99, '00, '01
Crosthwaite, Duane T., '39
Croxton, Gregory, '73, '74
Culver, Edward G., '10, '11

Cundiff, Larry L., '57, '58, '59
Curl, Ronald C., '68, '69, '71-C
Currie, Daniel G., '55, '56, '57
Currie, Michael J., '61, '63
Curtis, Fred S., '98, '99
Cutler, Donald E., '52

"D"

Dahlgren, Gordon A., '34, '35, '36-C
Dahlke, Craig A., '72, '73
Dancui, George W., '40, '41
Danielewicz, Michael A., '72, '73
Danziger, Fred W., '26, '28, '29 Co-C
DaPrato, Neno J., '12, '14, '15
Darby, Keith A., Mgr., '53
Davis, Frank R., '11
Davis, Hugh G., '42, '43
Davis, Randolph, Jr., '70
Davis, Wilford D., '39, '40, '41-C
Davis, Wyman D., '39, '40, '41
Dawson, William, Jr., '68, '69, '71
Deacon, Fred E., '26, '27
Dean, Michael A., '74
DeBrine, Thomas R., Mgr., '63, '64
Decker, Arthur R., '00
Decker, John W., '02, '03
Deibert, Glenn E., '41, '42
Dekker, Paul N., '51, '52
DeLamielleure, Joseph M., '70, '71, '72
Delgrosso, Daniel J., '58
Demarest, Ben H., '33, '34
Demos, Constantine S., Mgr., '63, '64
Dendal, Charles T., '12
Dendrinos, Peter C., '44
Derrickson, Paul W., '38, '39
Dersnah, Bernard E., '06
Dibble, Dorne A., '49, '50
Dickeson, Verne C., '27, '28, '29
Diebold, Allen O., '36, '37, '38-C
Diehl, David D., '36, '37, '38-C
Diener, Carl A., '53, '54
Dietz, William H., '98
Dill, Reuben E., '28, '29, '31
Dimitroff, Boris N., '64, '65
Dohoney, Donald C., '51, '52
Donnahoo, Roger J., '57, '58

Dorow, Albert R., '49, '50, '51

Dotsch, Roland D., '53, '54

Doty, Stephen W., '03, '04, '05, '06-C

Drake, Gerald A., '38, '39

Drew, Franklin F., '02

Drew, Kenneth L., '25, '26, '27

Drobot, Richard T., '71-Mgr.

Duckett, Ellis, '52, '53, '54

Duda, David, '74

Duda, Michael C., '72, '73, '74

Dudley, Darwin C., '36, '37

Dukes, Harold C., '56, '57

Dunlap, Charles W., '06

Dunphy, Herbert, '18

DuPree, Billy Joe, '70, '71, '72-C

"E"

Earley, James, '74

Eaton, James P., '60

Ebey, Warren W., Mgr., '59

Eckel, Clifford B., '41

Eckerman, Harold, '22, '23, '24

Eckert, Edward C., '22, '23, '24

Eddy, Howard J., '20

Edgar, Oliver W., '00

Edmunds, Allen T., '23

Edwards, Richard A., '34, '35

Eliowitz, Abe, '30, '31, '32-Co-C

Elliott, James E., '96

Ellis, James, '51, '52, '53

Epolito, James C., '73, '74

Esbaugh, Ernest K., '45, '48, '49

Exelby, Leon C., '07, '08, '09, '10

Exo, Lester W., '29, '30

"F"

Fairbanks, Charles L., '54

Fase, Jacob P., '29, '30, '31

Faulman, Duane L., '40

Fedore, Craig A., '74

Feigelson, Arthur, Mgr., '46

Fenton, Jack W., '40, '41, '42

Feraco, William A., '67, '68

Ferrare, George D., '27, '28, '29

Ferrari, Joseph C., '32

Ferris, Dean V., '18

Ferris, Henry M., '47

Fertig, Norman, '36

Fick, Hilmar A., '15, '16

Fischer, Robert H., '46

Fisk, James E., '04, '05

Flynn, Richard O., '62, '63, '64

Flynn, Walter H., Mgr., '98

Fogg, Cecil C., '28, '29, '30

Follis, Daniel S., '58

Foltz, Dale, '54

Fomenko, Joseph, '57

Fontes, Wayne H., '60, '61

Foreman, Franklin S., '67, '68, '69-C0-C

Fornari, Peter A., '41, '42

Forman, Walter H., '65

Fortney, Dane E., '73, '74

Fouts, Leslie J., '25

Fox, Calvin J., '68, '69, '70

Fowler, Larry D., '51, '52, '53

Fracassa, Albert, '54

Fraleigh, Royden G., '41, '42

Francis, Milton J., Mgr., '25

Frank, Charles W., '51, '52, '53

Franson, Harry E., '17, '18, '19-C

Frazer, William D., '06, '07, '08

Fremont, Perry J., '24

Friedlund, Robert M., '39, '40, '41

Frimodig, Lyman L., '15, '16

Fuller, Merrill S., Mgr., '15

Fusi, Peter, '46, '47, '48, '49

"G"

Gaddini, Rudy J., '55, '56

Gaines, Frank, '35, '36, '37

Gargett, George G., '38, '39

Gallinagh, Patrick F., '65, '66

Garner, Deane H., '50, '51

Garrett, Drake F., '65, '66, '67

Garrett, James T., '65

Garver, John E., '24, '25, '26

Garvey, Steve P., '67

Gasser, Harold F., '47, '48, '49

Gauthier, George E., '12, '13

Gifford, Chester W., '11, '12, '13-C

Gilbert, Donald D., '55, '56, '57

Gilliland, William O., '33

Gilman, John L., '47, '48, '49

Gilpin, Russell L., '42, '46, '47

Gingrass, Morgan J., '41, '42

Gingrich, Wayne A., '20, '21

Glick, Gene R., '46, '47, '48, '49

Godfrey, Robert E., '44, '45

Goode, Benjamin L., '24

Goovert, Ronald E., '63, '64, '65

Gordon, Richard F., '63, '64

Gorenflo, Elmer F., '11, '12

Gortat, Thomas A., '35, '36, '37

Grandelius, Everett, '48, '49, '50

Grannell, James M., '74

Graves, Harry C., '18, '21, '22

Graves, Thomas E., '74

Griffeth, Paul L., '38, '39, '40

Grim, Bohn W., '25, '26

Grimes, Ogden E., '26, '27

Grimsley, R. Ike, '59, '60

Grondzak, Donald, '44

Gross, Milton C., '29, '30, '31-C

Grove, Roger R., '28, '29, '30

Grua, R. Mark, '72

Guerre, George T., '46, '47, '48

Gunderson, LeRoy E., '45

Guthard, Ted C., '62

"H"

Hackett, Paul M., '23, '24, '25

Haftencamp, Joseph P., Mgr., '03, '04

Hahn, Harvey D., '04

Hahn, Oscar C., '58, '59, '60

Haidys, Leo T., '55

Halbert, Charles, '36, '37

Halliday, Douglas G., '69, '70, '71

Hallmark, Ferris, '52, '53, '54

Hamilton, Ernest, '70, '71, '72

Hammes, John H., '17, '19, '20

Handloser, Robert A., '56, '58

Handy, George B., '30, '31, '32

Haney, Usif, '36, '37, '38

Hannon, Thomas, '73, '74

Harding, Lawrence F., '56, '57

Hardy, Clifton, '68, '69, '70

Harms, Bruce C., '72, '73

Harness, Jason E., '58, '59, '60

Harriatte, Cheadrick, '72

Harris, Michael H., Mgr., '62

Haskins, Donald R., '23, '24, '25-C

Hatcher, Ronald A., '59, '60, '61

Hatfield, Glen J., '44

Haun, Harold E., '29

307

311

"Z"

313